The Rapture

The Rapture

When Will It Take Place?

Which Christians Will Go?

Which Christians Will Not?

How you can be sure that <u>you</u> will

A Study on How to Prepare to be the Bride of Christ

RUDOLPH C. SCHAFER

XULON PRESS

Xulon Press
2301 Lucien Way #415
Maitland, FL 32751
407.339.4217
www.xulonpress.com

Fourth Edition

Cover photo taken by James Boyer.
Converted to computer format by Bonnie Boyer.

The Rapture

Unless otherwise indicated, all Scripture verses are from the New King James Bible. In a few cases they are from the King James Bible (KJ) or New American Standard Bible (NAS).

Brackets around words, [ ], indicates that those words have been inserted by the Author. Most attributes – bold, italics, underlining, and small caps in Prophecies and Scripture references – have been added by the Author.

In a few places "Tommy Hicks' Vision of The Rapture" underwent some minor editing changes. As a result, in some places the meaning of a word, phrase, or sentence has been enhanced and is easier to understand.

Printed in the United States of America

Paperback ISBN-13: 978-1-6628-1022-0

Three Major Revelations in This Book

(1) There is a partial Rapture, which (2) takes place right after the seven year Tribulation, (3) just before the Wrath of God is poured out on the Earth.

The evidence presented in this book – and there is an *abundance* of it – strongly supports these three revelations.

The term "partial Rapture" and who it applies to is clarified by an excerpt from the article, "Will All Christians be in The Rapture?" written by the Author. The article begins on page 45. (The excerpt is on page 47.):

"Any Christian who doesn't sell all for the cause of Christ and put Jesus first in everything in his or her life will be included in a countless number of unsuspecting Christians who – because they are lukewarm, sleeping, backslidden, or spiritually weak – will miss the Rapture."

There is *much more* evidence in the book that supports a partial Rapture. Much more than just this excerpt.

Also, there is much evidence in the book that strongly supports the three major revelations mentioned at the top of the page.

For more information on this subject read pages xxiii and xxv.

Table of Contents

Some of the Topics Covered in this Book

God's covenant. The Bride. Being perfect in Christ.Being holy. How to pray. Having dominion over sin. Our authority in Christ. Being an overcomer. Being under God's protective covering. Supernatural protection from enemies. Walking in divine health ...and more. These subjects are dealt with in the book and have an abundance of Scriptures and Prophecies associated with them.

For more information and teachings that relate to this book, read the book, "How to be Healed of Sickness and Disease" by the Author.

Parts of this book are from "How to be Healed of Sickness and Disease" and have been edited to fit the subject matter of this book.

Acknowledgments

This book contains seventy-seven prophecies, eight articles, excerpts from a David Wilkerson newsletter, three dreams, two visions, special revelations given to a Pastor, and a personal account of a Pastor who died and went to Hell.

Prophecies: Forty-five of the prophecies and one article are from the book, THE LAST CALL by R.C. Schaffter. Two prophecies are from "PROPHECIES OF THE END-TIMES" by R.C. Schaffter.

Barbara Bloedow received twenty-two of the seventy-seven prophecies in this book.

Anna Schrader received fourteen.

Nine prophecies are from Frances J. Roberts. Eight are from "Come Away My Beloved" and the ninth is from "On the High Road of Surrender." Both books were published by King's Farspan Inc.

Seven prophecies come from Kevin Barrett of "Hear His Heart Ministry." There are many others that God has given him, and they are available online. He can be contacted at: hearhisheart. wordpress.com.

Another prophecy was received by Anita Lee Riddell.

God spoke to Pastor B.H. Clendennen during an all-night prayer meeting about who would and would not be in the Rapture. Clendennen was founder of The School of Christ International and Pastor of Victory Temple Church in Beaumont, Texas. Their number is: 409-842-3954.

Six prophecies were received by Daniel Lundstrom. Two are from the book "Prophecies of the End-Times." The other four have never been published before.

Five prophecies were received by Gwen Shaw, founder of End-Time Handmaidens and Servants, located near Jasper, Arkansas.

Five prophecies were received by Vincent Xavier, Pastor of New Wine Ministries Church; 2262 Forest Hills Blvd; Bella Vista, Arkansas. His number is 858-864-8712. The website is www.NWMglobal.org

One prophecy was received by Patricia Joy Xavier, wife of Pastor Vincent Xavier, of New Wine Ministries Church; Bella Vista, Arkansas. Her number is 858-864-8714.

Website: www.NWMglobal.org.

Three prophecies were received by Glynda Lomax. One came from her book, "Wings of Prophecy – From the Beginning." The book contains more than 110 prophecies and visions, all about the End-Times and the close of this Age. Her website is www.wingsofprophecy.com. She posts a fresh Word from the Lord 2-3 times a week, 52 weeks a year, at her website.

Two prophecies are from the book, "The Word of the Lord to Stephen Hanson, Volume I." "A Compilation of prophecies from 1993-2013." Volume II was released in January of 2015. He is at www.stephenhansonprophet.com.

One prophecy was received by James P. Corbett — "Cities of Refuge." It is on page 189. He can be reached at www.fromour-fathersheart.com.

Visions and Dreams:

One vision came from Tommy Hicks and is available online.

The other vision came from Annie Schisler and is from the book "Visions of the Eternal" by Dr. R.E. Miller, editor. It is a compilation of Visions received by Annie Schisler.

Garret Crawford had one dream, "The Anointing of the First-Fruits," Eve Brast had the second, "The Latter 'Reign' Anointing," and Kevin R. had the third, "Two Witnesses Power Revival." All three came from "Unleavened Bible Study," a ministry headed up by David Eells. The ministry Web address is UBM1.org.

Articles:

One article was written by the Author.

One article is by David Wilkerson, from which several excerpts were taken. They are from a message that he preached at Times Square Church in New York City and was recorded in his newsletter of February 18, 2008.

Copies of that newsletter can be obtained by calling World Challenge in Lindale, Texas. Their number is 903-963-8626.

One article is by Ron Auch, Senior Pastor of Prayer House Assembly of God, Kenosha, Wisconsin. Their number is 262-595-0500.

One is by Thurman Scrivner, Senior Pastor of The Living Savior Ministries Church in Argyle, Texas. The number at The Living Savior Ministries is 940-242-2106.

The article about Smith Wigglesworth is an excerpt from the book, "A Man Who Walked with God" by George Stormont, published by Harrison House.

The one about Marie Woodworth-Etter is from her autobiography and was quoted in "Great Healing Evangelists – How God's Power Came" written by Andrew Strom. His website is www.revivalschool.com.

The one about "The 91st Brigade in War" appeared on a website known as Angelfire.

One is by Apostle Jonas Clark, Pastor of Spirit of Life Ministries Church, located at 27 W Hallandale Beach Blvd, Hallandale, Florida 33009. Their number is 800-943-6490.

Special thanks for help on the book go to:

Anita Lee Riddell for her insights and ideas on ways to improve the book, and for her *considerable* help in editing.

Pat Wright for her sharp eye that spotted typing and punctuation errors that I missed.

Anita Lee Riddell and Sharon Brehmer Sobcoviak for their faithful prayers and encouraging words.

Mary Lee Simpson for selecting several very special, edifying, meaningful, and hitherto unpublished prophecies to add to the book.

Darryl Wagoner for sharing what he knows about adding text to electronic photos and for helping put special files together for the covers.

Cathy Carter for solving several very difficult technical problems associated with the covers and for creating special files for them.

Sean Ehlert of Office Depot's Field Support Regional Print Center in Grand Prairie Texas for keeping the front cover, back cover, and spine in correct spatial relationship to each other.

Patricia Joy Xavier who impressed me with the need for a book like this. She recently exhorted us as God's people to constantly cover ourselves with the Blood of Jesus Christ. That instruction led the Author to write "Concluding Comments on The Blood," taken from the four prophecies in that section.

The Lord Himself, who was the major help for me in a time of need when I did not know what to write or how to write it; or what prophecies to put in the book and where to place them. And for the framework that holds the book together and for the foundation that it was built on from start to finish – the Word of God itself!

Thanks go to the following Saints who received the words from the Lord printed in this book: **Barbara Bloedow, Daniel Lundstrom, Anna Schrader, Francis J. Roberts, Gwen Shaw, Dimitru Duduman, Tommy Hicks, Kevin Barrett, James P. Corbett, Vincent Xavier, Patricia Joy Xavier, Anita Lee Riddell, Stephen Hanson, and Glynda Lomax.**

The entire experience of Pastor Daniel Ekechukwu, including his journey into Heaven and Hell, can be read in detail at www. freechristianteaching.org. (Typing in Pastor Daniel's last name after the website name can help one locate the written story about his experience.) Pastor Daniel himself can be contacted by e-mail at messagefromthedead@yahoo.com.

Forward

Seventy-seven prophecies from twelve reliable prophets of God, eight articles, quotes from a David Wilkerson newsletter, three dreams, two visions, special revelations given to a Pastor, an account of a Pastor who died and went to Hell, almost **six hundred Scripture verses**, and carefully written **Commentary** – this is not your ordinary book about the Rapture. To be sure, the timing of this spectacular event is not ignored in this book. It is important to know with a reasonable certainty when it will occur.So that issue is addressed in considerable detail; and the question "when does it happen?" is answered clearly and incontrovertibly. (As it relates to certain key events – no date-setting.)

But this book is not primarily about when the Rapture will occur, as important as that is; what's contained in it is more than that. It's about who will be in the Rapture when it does take place, and what a small number it is. But even more than that and most important of all, this book will tell us how to be in that small number; that is, how to make that seemingly exclusive group.

For most Christians, this will be both a surprise and a shock to discover the undeniable Truth of the matter, that there is an overwhelming body of evidence – in Scripture and from several reliable prophets of God – that a very small number of Believers will actually be in the Rapture. In this book much time is spent developing that subject – not only to present evidence to readers so that they will accept and believe that statement, but more important, to give them <u>the information that they need to help them grow into the one who will be in the Rapture</u> – namely, *the Bride of Jesus Christ*. And to that end, the information and instructions necessary to qualify for that Bridal group are woven deeply into the fabric of this book.

Preface

The Rapture Call[1]

"The call to come as Jesus returns and comes for His Bride will be familiar to the Bride. The call to come away is the call that the Bride has heard and responded to many times: *'Come away, My love, My fair one. Rise up, My love, and come away.* [See Song of Solomon 2:10b and 13b] *Come with Me from Lebanon, My spouse.* [4:8a] *Come, My beloved, let us go forth into the field.* [7:11a] *The Spirit and the Bride say come! Let him that is athirst come, and whosoever will, let him come and drink of the water of life freely.'"* [From Revelation 22:17]

"The Rapture call will be a clear, loud, clarion call; and the heart of the Bride will respond to it. *'Come away, My love, My dove, My undefiled one.'"* [From Song of Solomon 5:2]

Two Very Compelling Points Presented in this Book:
The Conclusions They Draw, And What Pages
They Appear On

Point #1: (a) There is a partial Rapture and most <u>genuine</u> Christians will miss it. Read Pastor B.H. Clendennen's experience – a Revelation from God. Page 47.

A teaching by **David Wilkerson** confirms Pastor Clendennen's experience. Pages 106-108.

(b) Over a dozen Prophecies <u>confirm</u> what God revealed to Pastor Clendennen and what David Wilkerson taught. Three of them are on pages 68-69, 48, and 49.

Point #2: (a) Argument #1, on pages 77-82, has many supporting Scripture verses in it. It tells us *when* the Rapture will take place with respect to the seven year Tribulation.

(b) There are two Prophecies that <u>confirm</u> Argument #1. They state that we will go through the Great Tribulation *before* the Rapture occurs. They are on pages 201-208.

These two points strongly support a partial Rapture, which will take place at the very end of the Great Tribulation, just before the Wrath of God is poured out on the Earth.

There is *much more* evidence in this book – all of which <u>when considered as a whole</u>, supports a partial Rapture (Point #1), which will take place after the Great Tribulation (Point #2), just before the Wrath of God is poured out on the Earth. There's much more evidence than what you just read on the previous page.

It should be mentioned here that perceiving or grasping the message in this book about when the Rapture occurs (Point #2) all hinges on a proper understanding of the actual meaning of just *one* verse in the Bible – **Matthew 24:31**. Argument #1 on pages 77-82 goes into considerable detail on the meaning of this verse and other verses that relate to it. It definitively answers the question: *When* does the Rapture occur?

Other topics covered in the book are: Which Christians are the Bride of Christ? Which Christians are not. How to become the Bride. How to prepare our hearts. How to pray. How to enter God's "War Room." Having dominion over sin. Being an overcomer. Being under God's protective covering. The power of the Blood of Christ. Supernatural protection from enemies. Walking in divine health. God's covenant and the blessings that go with it. And more.

"The Rapture" can be ordered online at www.Amazon.com/dp/1505575826.

If you have questions or comments, you can call the Author. The number is 479-212-2691. (Land line)

Introduction

To be the Bride of Jesus Christ, or if we're one of the few who is already the Bride and we want to make sure that we continue on that path, we're going to need a lot of help from God Almighty. And the only way we're going to get that help is (1) to search His Word and (2) draw close to the Lord in prayer. Therein lies our answer and the answer:

(1) Jesus speaking: "You search the Scriptures, for in them you think you have eternal life; and these are they which testify of Me." (**John 5:39**)

(2) "Draw near to God and He will draw near to you." (**James 4:8**) Notice who needs to move first here. It's us brother and sister, not God! So, what's next? What do we do now?

Let's walk out the two points mentioned in the first paragraph. We'll start with point (1): "search the Scriptures." We should do that, but what does it mean exactly? Is it the following statement?

Get acquainted with your Bible...
or is there more to searching the Scriptures than that?

Point (1) The foundation for getting any kind of knowledge or information from God *is* the Word of God. It is possible, however, to receive something directly from God by the Holy Spirit. As James 1:5 tells us, God will give us wisdom liberally if we ask Him; but keep in mind that whatever we receive from the Lord still has to be supported by the Word, the whole counsel of God (all of it), and must not disagree with it or clash with it in any way. If it does, it must be set aside.

(Also, what we receive must not add or subtract from the Word. If we add to it, that will put us under a curse: **Revelation 22:18-19** says: "For I testify to everyone who hears the words of the prophecy of this book: If anyone adds to these things, God will add to him the plagues [curses] that are written in this book. And if anyone takes away from the words of this prophecy, God will take away his part from the Book of Life, from the holy city, and from the things which are written in this book.")

The more time we spend in the Word of God, the more sensitive and open we will be to have something revealed to us from the Word: "For nothing is secret that will not be revealed, nor anything hidden that will not be known and come to light. Therefore, take heed how you hear." (**Luke 8:17-18a**) In other words, we need to make sure that what we're reading and hearing, what we are getting, is from the Word of God.

Therefore, our only source of information is to be the Word and is to be based solely and totally upon it. When we hear from God directly by the Holy Spirit, or "sense" that something is from God, or "know" in our heart that something is from God, it must still be based solely and totally on the Word. (Even the things that we use in the world or get from it should connect with, relate to, and be supported by the Word of God in some way.)

According to the Word, we are to depend on it for everything we need, and that would especially include information about being the Bride of Christ: "Man shall not live by bread alone, but by every word that proceeds out of the mouth of God." (**Matthew 4:4b**) But reading the Bible once a day is not sufficient. We will not receive anything from God with that approach. The following three Scriptures bear this out. They tell us simply and clearly what we need to do, and what the result for us will be:

Psalm 1:2-3: "But his delight is in the law of the Lord, and in His law he <u>meditates day and night</u>. He shall be like a tree planted by the rivers of water, that brings forth its fruit in its season, whose leaf also shall not whither; and whatever he does shall prosper."

Joshua 1:8: "This Book of the Law shall not depart from your mouth, but you shall <u>meditate in it day and night</u>, that you may observe to do according to all that is written in it. For then you will make your way prosperous, and then you will have good success."

Proverbs 4:20-23: "My son, attend to My words; incline thine ear unto My sayings. Let them <u>not depart from thine eyes</u>; keep them in the midst of thine heart. For they are life unto those that find them and health to all their flesh. Keep thy heart with all diligence, for out of it are the issues of life." (KJ)

These three references make it clear that for success in anything that we do, we as Christians need to spend time in the Word *every day*. But five to ten minutes a day are not sufficient; nor are twenty to thirty minutes. Because it's not about us being in the Word, as much as it's about the Word being in us – literally. That means reading, hearing, thinking about, meditating, and speaking the Word each day throughout the day, from the time we get up in the morning until we go to bed at night. **Deuteronomy chapter 6, verses 5-7** puts it this way: "You shall love the Lord your God with all your heart, with all your soul, and with all your might. And these words which

I command you today shall be in your heart. You shall teach them diligently to your children, and shall talk of them when you sit in your house, when you walk by the way, when you lie down, and when you rise up."

In this way the Word is absorbed and incorporated into every aspect of our life, into everything we do – at home, at work, in school, at church, in the car, shopping, running errands, etc. Eventually it becomes a permanent part of us. And since Jesus is the Word (**John 1:14**), the more time we're spending in the Word, the more time we're spending "in Him." And as we spend more time in Him, we are spending more time with Him – thereby drawing close to Him in the process.

Drawing Close to the Lord in Prayer

Drawing close to Him brings us to point (2): drawing close to the Lord in prayer. As we walk out this point, we will get all the help we need to become the Bride of Jesus Christ. And it comes about in the following fashion:

Jesus is now becoming more and more real to us, more real in us, and more real through us. And that's what being a Christian should be all about, if we are going to be effective in any way for the Lord, and if we want to become His Bride. Jesus will have to be the main interest and focus in our lives; and when He is: "We all, with unveiled face, beholding ...the glory of the Lord, are being transformed into the same image from glory to glory, just as by the Spirit of the Lord." (**2nd Corinthians 3:18**) We are becoming more and more like Him. And being more like Jesus plays a big role in our lives because then we're more willing and able to deal with sin, and thus more likely to fulfill and carry out the high calling that God has placed on us – becoming the Bride of Christ.

Philippians 3:12-13: The apostle Paul speaking: "Not that I have already attained or am already perfected; but I press on, that I may lay hold of that for which I also was laid hold of by Christ Jesus. Brethren, I do not count myself to have apprehended [yet]; but one thing I do, forgetting those things which are behind and reaching forward to those things which are ahead,"

If the apostle Paul wasn't perfect at that point in his life and was pressing on toward the goal of perfection so that one day he would be so, then let us do likewise and press on to perfection so that one day we will be so. He knew he wasn't perfect yet. We see that in verse 12, but that same verse tells us that he was pressing on so that he would be. That's what Jesus laid hold of him for in the first place. And that's what we have been apprehended for also. Therefore, con-tinuing on in **verse 14,** let's be like the apostle Paul and do what he did; that is, let's do what he's describing in that verse:

"I press toward the mark [goal] for the prize of the high calling of God in Christ Jesus." (KJ)

If this was important to the apostle Paul, then it should be important to us also.

"Therefore, leaving the discussion of the elementary principles of Christ, let us go on to perfection," (**Hebrews 6:1a**)

And when we do, then we'll be able to claim and declare the following Scripture verse:

Revelation 19:7: "Let us be glad and rejoice and give Him glory, for the marriage of the Lamb has come, and His wife [the Bride] has made herself ready."

An important part of making ourselves ready to be the wife of the Lamb, the Bride of Christ, is to have a very strong foundation of the Word of God in us – point (1) on pages xxvi-xxix. To help us lay that foundation, the next twenty-two pages are filled with Scriptures and some commentary – all having to do with basic and advanced principles of faith, plus information on how God's Covenant operates. This will help us move on to perfection in Christ at an accelerated pace. The material for it came from the book "How to be Healed of Sickness and Disease" and was edited to fit this book.

Points (1) and (2) are the two main areas we must walk out in depth to become the Bride of Jesus Christ. In the following pages we will continue to lay the foundation of the living Word in us – point (1) – and we'll pick up where we left off. Later in the book, chapters 7 and 8 on pages 35-76 will cover different aspects of drawing close to the Lord and being intimate with Him – point (2).

Chapter 1

Powerful Scriptures to Stand On

1. With God All Things are Possible

Luke 18:27: "The things which are impossible with men are possible with God."

Matthew 19:26c: "with God all things are possible."

Luke 1:37: "For with God nothing will be impossible."

Jeremiah 32:17b: "There is nothing too hard for You."

Nothing is impossible with God. But notice the authority that *we* have in the verses that follow in the next Section. And as long as we have a pure and holy walk with the Lord, this authority can be exercised by us—if we have faith, and if we know God's Word and stand on it. The possibilities for us as Believers are unlimited.

We just read that all things are possible with God. In Section 2 we'll see how all things are possible for the believing son and daughter of God. In Christ, all things are possible for us!

2. Have Faith

Knowing that "without faith it is impossible to please Him" (**Hebrews 11:6a**), and "whatever is not from faith is sin" (**Romans 14:23b**), by choice "we walk by faith, not by sight" (**2nd Corinthians 5:7**), "and call those things which do not exist [a need that we have] as though they did." (**Romans 4:17c**) That is worth repeating: Knowing that without faith it is impossible to please God and whatever is not of faith is sin, we choose to walk by faith and not by sight, calling those things which do not exist as though they did. And add to this scriptural mix the following verse: "So then faith comes by hearing and hearing by the Word of God." (**Romans 10:17**) So the more time we spend in the Word, the more faith we will have to believe Romans 4:17c for whatever need we might have in our current situation: We can then call those things which do not exist as though they did, when we speak out a particular Scripture in faith.

So we know how important <u>faith</u> is in getting answers to prayer, but notice how important faith <u>and</u> believing are. True Bible-based faith <u>believes</u> that the answer is coming; or even more than that, that by faith the answer has already arrived:

Matthew 21:21-22: "Jesus said to them, 'Assuredly, I say to you, if you have <u>faith</u> and do not doubt, you will not only do this which was done to the fig tree, but also if you say to this mountain, "Be removed and be cast into the sea," it will be done. And all things whatever you ask in prayer, <u>believing</u>, you will receive.' "

Mark 11:22-24: "[Jesus answered and said to them, 'Have <u>faith</u> in God [or have the faith of God]. For assuredly, I say to you, whoever says to this mountain, "Be removed and be cast into the sea," and does not doubt in his heart, but <u>believes</u> that

2

those things he says will come to pass, he will have whatever he says. Therefore I say to you, whatever things you ask when you pray, <u>believe</u> that you receive [have received] them, and you will have them.' "

Mark 9:23: "Jesus said to him, 'if you can believe, all things are possible to him who believes.' "

Matthew 17:20: "And Jesus said to them,'...assuredly, I say to you, if you have faith as a mustard seed, you will say to this mountain, "Move from here to there," and it will move; and <u>nothing will be impossible for you</u>.' " If you have mustard seed size faith you can move a mountain! However, as we exercise ourselves in the area of faith, our faith will grow even more, and it will then do even more for God's Kingdom:

Mark 4:31: "[The Kingdom of God] is like a mustard seed which, when it is sown on the ground, is smaller than all the seeds on earth; but when it is sown, it grows up, becomes greater than all herbs, and shoots out large branches, so that the birds of the air may nest under its shade."

Matthew 9:22b: "your faith has made you well [whole]."

Matthew 9:29b: "According to your faith let it be to you."

1st John 5:4: "Whatever is born of God overcomes the world. And this is the victory that has overcome [overcomes] the world—our faith."

"By faith Enoch was translated so that <u>he did not see death</u>, and was not found because God had translated [raptured] him, for before his translation he had this testimony, that he pleased God." (**Hebrews 11:5**)

If we have the faith for it, God can help us to grow into that Bride that He wants us to be, so that, like Enoch, we are so pleasing to God, that on the Day of the Rapture, we will be caught up – translated – to meet the Lord in the air.

3. Have Faith in God's Word

Numbers 23:19: "God is not as man, that He should lie, nor a son of man, that He should repent [change His mind]. Has He said, and will He not do it? Or has He spoken, and will He not make it good?"

2nd Corinthians 1:20: "All the promises of God in Him [in Christ] are Yes, and in Him Amen,"

Hebrews 13:8: "Jesus Christ is the same yesterday, today, and forever." Jesus is the Word. (**John 1:14**) He and the Word did not change in the past, and they will not change in the future. In fact, "Heaven and earth will pass away, but My Words will by no means pass away." (**Matthew 24:35**)

Mark 11:24: "Therefore I say to you, whatever things you ask when you pray, believe that you receive [have received] them, and you will have them."

James 1:6-7 explains it this way: "But let him ask in faith, with no doubting [nothing wavering], for he who doubts is like a wave of the sea driven and tossed by the wind. For let not that man suppose that he will receive anything from the Lord;"

1st John 5:14-15: "And this is the confidence that we have in Him, that if we ask anything according to His will, He hears us. And if we know that He hears us, whatever we ask, we know that we have the petitions that we have asked of Him." How do we know something is God's will? If it's acceptable according to His Word, it's His will.

Mark 7:27: "But Jesus said to her, 'Let the children be filled first, for it is not good to take the children's bread and throw it to the little dogs.' " Jesus referred to healing as "the children's bread." That means if we're Born-Again, we're one of His children and therefore healing belongs to us. It's as natural for us to be supplied with healing from the Lord as it is for a child to be given bread by its parents.

And that bread of healing is always there for us, because: "If we confess our sins, He is faithful and just to forgive us our sins and to cleanse us from all unrighteousness." (**1st John 1:9**) And when we confess our sins, **Psalm 103:3** describes what happens next: "Who forgives all your iniquities [sins], Who heals all your diseases," – the children's bread!

When we're healed of all of our diseases, then "Your youth is renewed like the eagle's." (**Verse 5b of Psalm 103**) If we speak this out every day, then our youth is being renewed daily. And as we do this faithfully, "His [or her] flesh shall be young like a child's; he shall return to the days of his youth." (**Job 33:25**) Praise God!

So "Let us hold fast the confession [the speaking out, the speaking forth] of our hope without wavering, for He who promised [in His Word] is faithful. Therefore, do not cast away your confidence, which has great reward. For you have need of endurance [patience], so that after you have done the will of God, you may receive the promise:" (**Hebrews 10:23 and 35-36**) And we will, because "through faith and patience [we] inherit the promises." (**Hebrews 6:12c**)

This is what is known as "standing on the Word of God" for something. If we aren't doing what is described here, then we are NOT standing on the Word for a need that we have. So we need to **read**, **believe**, and **speak out** the Promise from God's Word that we are believing for – then we are standing on the Word of God. And if we continue to stand on it without giving up, in time it will come to pass.

Ephesians 6:13c-14a: "and having done all, to stand. Stand therefore"

For more on the subject of standing on the Word, read pages 13-16.

4. No Unforgiveness

Mark 11:25-26: "And whenever you stand praying, if you have anything against anyone, forgive him, that your Father who is in Heaven may also forgive you your trespasses. **But if you do not forgive, neither will your Father who is in Heaven forgive [you] your trespasses**." And if He does not forgive us of our sins, what do you think the chances are that He will answer our prayers?

Psalm 66:18: "If I regard iniquity in my heart, the Lord will not hear [my prayer]."

In Matthew, a servant whose master forgave him of an enormous debt, did not forgive a fellow servant of a very small debt. That parable should be an example for all of us: *Since God forgave us of all of our sins when we were saved, shouldn't we forgive others when they sin against us?*

Matthew 18:32-35 gives us the answer: "Then his master, after he had called him, said to him, 'O you wicked servant! I forgave you all that debt because you begged me. Should you not also have had compassion on your fellow servant, just as I had pity on you?' And his master was angry and delivered him to the torturers until he should pay all that was due him. So My heavenly Father also will do to you, if each of you from his heart does not forgive his brother his trespasses."

Mark 11:26 agrees: "**But if you do not forgive, neither will your Father who is in Heaven forgive [you] your trespasses.**"

Since our Father forgave us of all of our sins when we were saved, if someone sins against us and we don't forgive them, what happens? Our Father <u>retracts</u> the forgiveness of sins that He extended to us when we were saved. In other words, what spiritually brought about our Salvation and caused us to be saved in the first place is gone! We are no longer Born-Again. **We have lost our Salvation!**

And to make matters worse, if that were possible, in Matthew our Father ordered the unforgiving servant to be delivered to the torturers; that is, he was turned over to <u>demon spirits</u> for his sin of unforgiveness!

Unforgiveness does sound like the number one sin to avoid, no matter what effort it requires on our part, doesn't it? If we are guilty of that sin, then we need to ask God to forgive us of it; and next, we need to repent of any unforgiveness that we have at the present time towards anyone (including ourselves), after which we need to immediately stop dwelling on it and going over it in our minds, thereby putting an end to our active involvement with that dreadful sin.

But if an unforgiving thought from the enemy of our soul comes into our mind, then we need to take authority over it and cast it down, and then cast it out in the name of Jesus! **2nd Corinthians 10:5** tells us what to do: "casting down arguments [imaginations] and every high thing that exalts itself against the knowledge of God [and His Word], bringing every thought into captivity to the obedience of Christ,"

What happens to a Christian who is angry with someone and refuses to forgive them, and they die in that condition?

That very thing happened to Pastor Daniel Ekechukwu of Onitsha, Nigeria in 2001. He and his wife argued about something, and Pastor Daniel would not forgive her, even though she forgave him. He went to bed angry and got up and left the house the next morning still angry with his wife. When driving back home later that day, the brakes in his car failed while he was driving down a long steep hill, and after picking up considerable speed, his car struck a palm tree near the side of the road. The car stopped suddenly forcing the steering wheel into his chest. He was severely injured and died shortly thereafter.

Initially he was taken to Heaven by an angel who accompanied him for a brief visit there, but in short order he found himself in Hell, surrounded by people in considerable torment. The angel told Pastor Daniel that **this was to be his abode because of his sin of not forgiving his wife – the sin of unforgiveness.**

And if some unusual events had not happened after that, he would still be there today. And it is not the sin of anger that would be keeping him there, as bad as that is. But it was his hanging on to that anger through the sin of <u>unforgiveness</u> that earned Pastor Daniel a place in Hell. But because of the prayers of his wife and mercy towards His people, God allowed the pastor to come back to tell us first-hand what sent him to Hell, so that the same thing would not happen to us. Thank You, Lord!

Note: The entire experience of Pastor Daniel Ekechukwu, including his journey into Heaven and Hell, can be read in detail at www.freechristianteaching.org. (Typing in Pastor Daniel's last name after the website name can help one locate the written story about his experience.)

Pastor Daniel himself can be contacted by e-mail at message-fromthedead@yahoo.com.

5. Ask to be Cleansed

We need to be cleansed of many of the thoughts in our hearts and many of the words of our mouths, or, God forbid, we could end up like Pastor Daniel. The following Scriptures will be of help to us:

Psalm 139:23-24: "Search me, O God, and know my heart; try me and know my anxieties [thoughts]; and see if there is any wicked way in me, and lead me in the way everlasting."

Psalm 19:12-14: "Who can understand his errors? Cleanse me from secret faults. Keep back Your servant also from presumptuous [willful] sins; let them not have dominion over me. Then I shall be blameless [perfect], and I shall be innocent of great transgression. Let the words of my mouth and the meditation of my heart be acceptable in Your sight, O Lord, my strength and my redeemer."

Psalm 39:1: "I said, 'I will guard my ways, lest I sin with my tongue.' "

James 3:2b says it this way: "If anyone does not stumble in word, he is a perfect man, able also to bridle the whole body."

If we faithfully pray and do what these verses are telling us to do, then we'll be able to say, "For with the heart [I] believe to righteousness, and with the mouth [my] confession is made to Salvation." (**Romans 10:10**)

6. Ask

As a Bride-in-the-making we will be asking the Lord for much help, advice, directions, corrections, and instructions on how to be His Bride. It is most important to know how to ask in faith, believing, so that we will receive an answer. Therefore, the following Scriptures on asking in prayer have been added to this book. This list comes from the book, "How to be Healed of Sickness and Disease," (The Scriptures for the other sections in this chapter also come from that book.)

John 14:12-14: "Most assuredly, I say to you, he who believes in Me, the works that I do he will do also; and greater works than these he will do, because I go to My Father. And whatever you ask in My Name, that I will do, that the Father may be glorified in the Son. If you ask anything in My Name, I will do it."

John 15:7: "If you abide in Me [Jesus] and My words abide in you, you shall ask what you desire, and it shall be done for you."

Matthew 21:22: "And all things, whatever you ask in prayer, believing, you will receive."

John 16:23-24: "... Most assuredly I say to you, whatever you ask the Father in My Name He will give you... Ask and you will receive, that your joy may be full."

Matthew 18:18-20: "Assuredly, I say to you, whatever you bind on earth will be bound in Heaven, and whatever you loose on earth will be loosed in Heaven. Again I say to you that if two of you agree on earth concerning <u>anything that they ask</u>, it will be done for them by My Father who is in Heaven. For where two or three are gathered together in My Name, there I am in the midst of them."

Ephesians 3:20: "Now to Him who is able to do exceedingly abundantly above all that we ask or <u>think</u>, according to the power that works in us," Even our thinking has to be right in the sight of God. And when it is, God will move "exceedingly abundantly" on our behalf.

When praying for something, how do we know that we're not on a collision course with God's Will?

1st John 5:14-15 has something to say about this: "And this is the confidence that we have in Him, that if we ask anything <u>according to His will</u>, He hears us. And if we know that He hears us, whatever we ask, we know that <u>we have the petitions that we have asked of Him</u>." How do we know something is God's will? **If it's in His Word, it's His will.**

So when we (1) pray according to God's Word, we're praying His will, and (2) He will hear us. And when He hears us, (3) He *will* answer us.

1st John 3:22 answers the question, "How do we know something is God's will?" as follows: "Whatever we ask we receive from Him [God], because we keep His commandments and do those things that are pleasing in His sight." We keep God's commandments and do those things that are pleasing in His sight by reading the Word, obeying it, and by continuously waiting on Him.

But whenever we ask, we must ask in faith and <u>thank</u> <u>God</u> for the answer: "Be anxious for nothing, but in everything by prayer and supplication,<u> with thanksgiving</u>, let your requests be made known to God; and the peace of God which surpasses all understanding will guard your hearts and minds through Christ Jesus." (**Philippians 4:6-7**) A super-natural peace will fill your heart and soul when you pray this way.

It is very important when we ask, to ask in faith, or we will receive nothing from the Lord! **James 1:5-8** explains it this way: "If any of you lacks wisdom, let him ask of God, who gives to all liberally and without reproach, and it will be given to him. But let him ask in faith, with no doubting [nothing wavering, KJ], for he who doubts is like a wave of the sea driven and tossed by the wind. For let not that man suppose that he will receive anything from the Lord; he is a double-minded man, unstable in all his ways."

7. The Greatest of All Commandments

Mark 12:30-31: "And you shall love the Lord your God with all your heart, with all your soul, with all your mind, and with all your strength. This is the first commandment. And the second, like it, is this: You shall love your neighbor as your-self. There is no other commandment greater than these."

Chapter 2

Speak It Out!

Numbers 23:19: "God is not as man, that He should lie, nor a son of man, that He should repent [change His mind]. Has He said, and will He not do it? Or has He spoken, and will He not make it good?" What God says in His Word is indeed a promise, and He will do whatever that particular Word says. Period.

2nd Corinthians 1:20 expresses the immutability of God's Word this way: "All the promises of God in Him [in Christ] are Yes, and in Him Amen, to the glory of God by us."

Abraham understood this about God's promises, and according to **Romans 4:20-21** "He did not waver at the promise of God through unbelief, but was strengthened in faith, giving glory to God, and being fully convinced that what He had promised He was also able to perform. And therefore [God saw this] and it was imputed to him [by God] for righteousness."

"For with the heart one believes to righteousness, and with the mouth confession is made to Salvation." (**Romans 10:10**) If we want results, we need to not only believe in our heart, as Abraham did, but we need to speak out what we are believing for. Then it will come to pass, depending on what we speak out and declare.

"But since we have the same spirit of faith, according to what is written, 'I believed and therefore I spoke,' we also <u>believe</u> and therefore <u>speak</u>," (**2nd Corinthians 4:13**)

Isaiah 55:11: "So shall **My Word** be that goes forth from My mouth: It shall not return to Me void, but it shall accomplish what I please, and it shall prosper in the thing for which I sent it."

When we speak out God's Word, it never returns to Him void or without purpose or results, but it always accomplishes what God pleases. And what He pleases is what that particular promise is saying. Speaking it out is what will prosper and bear fruit – if we have a pure heart and a holy walk before the Lord, obeying His Word in every area of our lives.

Romans 4:17c: "and calleth those things which be not as though they were:" (KJ) This is what God does in His Word; but it is something we can do also – *if we have faith.*

Hebrews 10:23 and 35-36: "Let us hold fast the confession [the speaking out, the speaking forth] of our hope without wavering, for He who promised [in His Word] is faithful. Therefore do not cast away your confidence, which has great reward. For you have need of endurance [patience], so that after you have done the will of God, you may receive the promise:" And we will, because according to **Hebrews 6:12c** "through faith and patience [we] inherit the promises." – the promise being what a particular Scripture (the one we are speaking out) is saying.

The main idea here is to pick a promise or promises from the Word and speak them out. They must be spoken out – several times a day and sometimes even more than that. That's the way healing (or anything else we need) will come, and usually the only way it will come. Remember, "Faith comes by hearing, and hearing by the Word of God." (**Romans 10:17**) As we speak it out, the devil is hearing that particular Word. Jesus put the devil in his place by quoting the Word [**Matthew 4:3-10**], and we can do the same thing when we speak the Word. Also, as we're speaking the Word, this builds up our faith for that Word to manifest and come to pass in our lives.

And not only are we hearing it, but God is hearing it, as we read earlier in Isaiah 55. And, according to **Psalm 103:20** His angels are hearing it also: "Bless the Lord, you His angels, who excel in strength, who do His Word, heeding the voice of His Word." God's angels consider His Word to be commandments for them to obey and instructions for them to follow. They hear the Word of God as we speak it out or pray it out, and then they do what that particular Word says to do.

Hebrews 1:14 describes what happens next: "Are they [God's angels] not all ministering spirits sent forth to minister for those who will inherit salvation?" These angels minister according to the Word that the Believer (an heir of Salvation) speaks. So we need to be careful about what we're saying and make sure it's either God's Word or lines up with God's Word. And when it does, **verse 21 in Psalm 103** describes what happens next: "Bless the Lord, all you His hosts [Armies], you ministers of His, who do His pleasure." Depending on what we have spoken out, this army of angels then moves on our behalf!

Psalm 91:2 tells us: "I will say of the Lord, 'He is my refuge and my fortress: My God; in Him I will trust.' " Speak it out!

As discussed earlier on page 6, this is what is known as "standing on the Word" for something. But if we aren't doing what is spelled out in that section and in this one, then we're NOT standing on the Word for a need that we have. We need to **read** and **believe** and **speak out** the Promise from God's Word that we are believing for – *then* we are standing on the Word.

And **if we continue to stand on it without giving up, in time it *will* come to pass**.

The Power of Your Words[2]

"Your miracle or healing is in your mouth; so start confessing God's Word to Him and see your miracle. It cannot fail because God said it can't. Praise the Lord for His Word.

"Most sickness and disease is an evil spirit from Satan. You will have to drive him out with your mouth. Jesus told us as His Church to cast out demons, and they will leave. You have to be very bold with them. They are stubborn and do not want to leave. But if you keep commanding them to leave in Jesus' name, they will have to leave. So do not give up. The Lord has promised you abundant life. Remember, your miracle is in your mouth. Praise the Lord Jesus."

The preceding two paragraphs conclude a six page collection of Scriptures entitled "I Possess What I Confess," written by Pastor Thurman Scrivner.

The words we speak can be so powerful that we are able to control the whole body! **James 3:2b** says it this way: "If anyone does not stumble in word, he is a perfect man, able also to bridle the whole body." When our speech is righteous and pure in the sight of God, we can speak to our own body, and with the authority that we have in Jesus Christ, we can command it to be healed and to stay healed!

Sickness and Disease tell us much about our walk with God. If we're on track with Him, we usually won't get sick. But if we have some sin in our life, and we're not dealing with it and getting rid of it, sickness will be the result. Obviously this is not good. But sickness and disease do serve as an indicator for us; that is, they serve as a warning for someone who is the Bride – or aspiring to be the Bride and is progressing rapidly on that path – because normally the Bride will not get sick. But if she does and immediately goes to God and finds out the reason for it (if she does not know the cause) and asks Him to forgive her, and then repents of it – when the Bride does all of that – she will be healed quickly.

(If someone is sick, and they are not getting better, this is not something to feel guilty about. That would be counter-productive. But what they need to do is follow the instructions on this page, and in time, with the Lord's help, they will improve and ultimately be healed of whatever has been afflicting them, even if it's been for a period of many years or decades.)

There is a powerful anointing on the Bride. That anointing is there because she is in covenant with God; and because of that, He is blessing her, not only with health, but also in every other way possible. And she is keeping that covenant relationship strong and healthy by not practicing sin. But if a sin does show up and she quickly turns from it and doesn't commit that sin again, this will keep her heart clean before the Lord and keep her covenant relationship solid. In this way the Bride will usually not get sick. But if she does, most of the time she will be healed quickly.

But even more important than physical health—as important as that is—she will grow rapidly in her walk with the Lord and will become the Bride that God wants her to be.

The Power of Your Prayers[3]

"Think it not strange that I have called each and every one of you. Think it not strange that you are part of the chosen. And think it not strange that your prayer last night was answered quickly. Because I'm saying today that the Lord is speaking and saying:

"When you pray, **anoint your mouth with a coal from the altar** to make sure that the words are God's Words for your prayer. Because you're going to see them starting to be answered quickly.

"So use wisdom when you pray. Use Godly wisdom when you pray. Sometimes you're going to see the answer quickly – like last night – and sometimes it's going to take a while, like Shawn. [An almost motionless young man, sitting in a wheel-chair.] But it *shall* be done because you prayed in faith, you prayed believing, and you have prayed with a sincere heart of God."

[God is inspiring the person who just gave this word from Him to continue to speak.] "And that is a beautiful, beautiful testimony that He's giving to each and every one of us: Our prayers are heard, and they are in His care because He said I will hear and answer your prayer.

"So pray with *faith;* pray *believing;* and pray that God's Will will be done in all things because He truly wants to answer each and every one of our prayers."

————

[The following two pages are comments from the Author.] *"Anoint your mouth with a coal from the altar"* in the second paragraph of this word from the Lord on this page is a reference to the cleansing of the prophet Isaiah in **Isaiah chapter 6.** This was required of him because "I [Isaiah] am a man of unclean lips, and I dwell in the midst of a people of unclean lips," (verse 5); and therefore before he could do anything for God, he needed to be cleansed. One of the seraphims that stood above the throne of the Lord, took a live coal from the altar and touched the prophet's mouth with it (verse 7), saying, "Behold, this has touched your lips; your iniquity is taken away, and your sin is purged." From that point on Isaiah was fit to be used by God and to carry out His will.

And the same is true for us, God's people today. If **we** want to be used by God to do His work and to carry out His will, then we need to be cleansed with a coal from the altar – for anything that we would do for God, but especially for the all-important ministry of prayer. That's why this particular word of the Lord came forth in a recent church service.

When we are praying out something, whether it is done privately or in a group, we need to be very careful how we pray. We need *"to make sure that the words are God's words for your prayer."* So we are to *"use wisdom when you pray. Use Godly wisdom when you pray."* Because God will take those <u>exact words</u> that we are speaking out as we're praying, and He will act on them and bring them to pass!: *"I will hear and answer your prayer."*

So we need to pray accordingly, **carefully** and **precisely**, knowing that God will move on <u>our every word</u> and bring it to pass. He is that kind of God. When we pray, He will act, because *"He truly wants to answer each and every one of our prayers."* **So we need to get our prayers right, and then we'll get the results that we're desiring, and not something that we did not mean or don't even want!**

And the prophecy also urges us to *"pray with faith; pray believing."* **Mark 11:22-24** points this out: "Jesus answered and said to them, 'Have *faith* in God [or have the faith of God]. For assuredly, I say to you, whoever says to this mountain, "Be removed and be cast into the sea," and does not doubt in his heart, but believes that those things he says will come to pass, he will have whatever he says. Therefore I say to you, whatever things you ask when you pray, *believe* that you receive [have received] them, and you will have them.' "

Matthew 21:21-22 also has something to say on the subject of praying in faith and believing:

"Jesus said to them, 'Assuredly, I say to you, if you have faith and do not doubt, you will not only do this which was done to the fig tree, but also if you say to this mountain, "Be removed and be cast into the sea," it will be done. And all things whatever you ask in prayer, *believing,* you will receive.' "

Reading, studying, thinking about, and memorizing these verses that deal with faith in Matthew and Mark will help us to build up our faith into the God kind of faith. Whatever Scripture we read, study, think over, and memorize will build us up and strengthen us according to what that particular verse is saying. We can do that with any Scripture, on any topic, and that would include those that deal with the process of how to become the Bride of Christ. Examples of that would be the following categories which are featured and discussed in this book:

> God's covenant. The Bride. Being perfect in Christ. Being holy. How to pray. Having dominion over sin. Our authority in Christ. Being an overcomer. Being under God's protective covering. Supernatural protection from enemies. Walking in divine health . . . and

more. These subjects are dealt with in the book and have an abundance of Scriptures associated with them to explain these subjects according to what's stated in God's Word.

So we need to pray. But we need to pray the way this important Word from the Lord is instructing us to. **Do it right – God's way – and He will use us to change the world!**

Chapter 3

Be Free of Sickness and Disease

Part 1

If we deal with all sins, no matter what they are, and eradicate them from our lives, then according to God's Word it is even possible to be free of sickness and disease altogether!

Exodus 15:26: "If you diligently heed the voice of the Lord your God and do what is right in His sight, give ear to His commandments and keep all His statutes, I will put none of the diseases on you which I have brought on the Egyptians [the world, the unsaved]. For I am the Lord who heals you."

We don't have to be sick or diseased in the first place, if we diligently do all that is stated here... a remarkable promise from God. But if for some reason we sin and are then afflicted with sickness and disease, if we deal with the sin, then according to the next two references, God will take the sickness away from us!

Deuteronomy 7:11 and 15: "You shall keep the commandment, the statutes, and the judgments which I command you today, to observe [do] them. And the Lord will take away from you all sickness, and will afflict you with none of the terrible diseases of Egypt which you have known, but will lay them on all those who hate you."

Exodus 23:25: "So you shall serve the Lord your God, and He will bless your bread and your water. And I will take sickness away from the midst of you." But **verse 21** warns us: "Beware of Him and obey His voice; do not provoke Him, for He will not pardon your transgressions; for My name is in Him."

It is quite clear here that if we do not obey these commandments in Exodus and Deuteronomy, God will not forgive our sins. Consequently we will suffer from sickness and disease. They will not be taken from us. There are other consequences too, and they are found in **Deuteronomy 28:15-68.** Some of them are:

Verse 58 states: "If you do not carefully observe all the words of this law that are written in this book, that you may fear this glorious and awesome name, THE LORD YOUR GOD," this falling short of observing the Law creates a generational curse, and it begins to afflict a family line. But there's more:

Verse 59: "then the LORD will bring upon you and your descendants extraordinary plagues—great and prolonged plagues—and serious and prolonged sicknesses." "Extraordinary plagues" means more than one extraordinary curse is involved. But God is not finished:

Verse 60: "Moreover He will bring back on you all the diseases of Egypt, of which you were afraid, and they shall cling to you." The curses will involve serious sicknesses of every kind, and there will be no cure for them. And finally:

Verse 61: "Also, every sickness and every plague which is not written in the book of this law will the LORD bring upon you until you are destroyed." *Death* will be the inevitable result.

However, all of this can be avoided if we simply obey the commandment stated back in **verses 1 and 2 of Deuteronomy 28**: "Now it shall come to pass, if you diligently obey the voice of the LORD your God to observe carefully all His commandments which I command you today, that the LORD your God will set you high above all the nations of the earth. And all these blessings shall come upon you and overtake you because you obey the voice of the Lord your God;"

So, we not only have the promise of good health and no sickness in Exodus 15:26, but we also have that same promise in **Deuteronomy 28:1-2**, IF we obey God's commandments in His Word. In fact, as we just read in **verse 2**, His blessings, which include divine health, will even "overtake" us!

These blessings are described in detail in **verses 3 to 13**: "Blessed shall you be in the city, and blessed shall you be in the country. Blessed shall be the fruit of your body, the produce of your ground and the increase of your herds, the increase of your cattle and the offspring of your flocks. Blessed shall be your basket and your kneading bowl. Blessed shall you be when you come in, and blessed shall you be when you go out. The Lord will cause your enemies who rise against you to be defeated before your face; they shall come out against you one way and flee before you seven ways. The Lord will command the blessing on you in your storehouses and in all to which you set your hand, and He will bless you in the land which the Lord your God is giving you. The Lord will establish you as a holy people to Himself, just as He has sworn to you, if you keep the commandments of the Lord your God and walk in His ways. Then all the peoples of the earth shall see that you are called by the name of the Lord, and they shall be afraid of you. And the Lord will grant you plenty of goods, in the fruit of your body, in the increase of your livestock, and in the produce of your ground, in the land of which the Lord swore to your fathers to give you. The Lord will open to you His good treasure, the heavens, to give the rain to your land in its season, and to bless all the work of your hand. You shall lend to many nations, but you shall not borrow. And the Lord will make you the head and not the tail; you shall be above only and not be beneath, if you heed the commandments of the Lord your God, which I command you today and are careful to observe them."

As God's children it is wonderful to be blessed like this. God does this to "establish a holy people to Himself." (verse 9) These blessings can help the Bride-to-be grow up very quickly into full bridal-hood. Then she can direct her energies into growing and maintaining an intimate walk with the Lord and doesn't have to feel pressured, anxious, or distracted by physical needs.

But there is one very important final reminder in **verse 14**: "So you shall not turn aside from any of the words which I command you this day, to the right hand or to the left, to go after other gods to serve them." "Go after other gods" means chasing after idols in our lives that take the place of God. If we do that, God will not give us any of the wonderful blessings described in verses 3 to 13. (This same warning is also given in Deuteronomy 30:17-30.) And we would not be that Bride that He intends for us to be. (This discussion is continued in Part 2.)

Part 2
God's Covenant

God is spelling out a Covenant here in **Deuteronomy 28**, as He also does in **Exodus 15:26**, **Exodus 23:25**, **Deuteronomy 7:11 and 15**, **Deuteronomy 30:15-16**, and in other places in the Bible. If we do our part and obey His commandments, then God will do His part and give us many wonderful blessings, and they include keeping us healthy. He's our Healer; He's our Deliverer. We don't even have to get sick in the first place!

Psalm 103:17-18: "But the mercy of the Lord is from everlasting to everlasting on those who fear Him, and His righteousness to children's children, to such as <u>keep His covenant</u>, and to those who remember His commandments to do them."

But if we sin and do not deal with it, whether we are aware of it or not, we have disobeyed a commandment of God; and whether we know it or not, **we are therefore no longer in covenant with Him.** We can be very sure that a sickness or an infirmity of some kind will come to our house for an unwelcome stay. And until we deal with that sin and get back into covenant with God, we will not be healed. But when we deal with it, we move back into a covenant relationship with Him, and with that back in place, we can then be healed. That's because healing and divine health are in the Covenant (along with the many other wonderful blessings just described on the previous two pages); and when we do our part, God will then do His part and bestow those blessings upon us. That's how the Covenant works.*

But if we think the Covenant with God in the Old Testament was good but passed away in the New Testament, read what **Hebrews 8:6** says about the one that we as Christians have with God now: "But now He [Jesus] has obtained a more excellent

ministry, inasmuch as He is also Mediator of a better covenant, which was [has been] established on better promises." It
doesn't get any better than that.

Here's what **2nd Corinthians 3, verses 7-9 and 11** think of
the new covenant: "But if the ministry of death ...was glorious,
so that the children of Israel could not look steadily at the face
of Moses because of the glory of his countenance, which glory
was passing away, how will the ministry of the Spirit not be
more glorious? For if the ministry of condemnation had glory,
the ministry of righteousness exceeds much more in glory. For
if what is passing away was glorious, what remains is much
more glorious."

*Footnote: One proven method of dealing with sin is according
to "The 7 Step Program" discussed in the book "How to Be
Healed of Sickness and Disease," written by the Author.

Chapter 4

Other Major Problems

Besides Sickness and Disease –
How to Defeat Them

In "How to be Healed of Sickness and Disease" the focus was on healing, but the same "7 Step Program" used in that book for healing can also be used to solve other problems in our lives caused by sins that we have not dealt with or confessed. The sins may involve something that we have done. Or it may be something that we're innocent of that someone else has done, affecting us with their sinful behavior. Or it could be both our own sins and the sins of someone else affecting us.

The problem might be depression, marital or family issues, delinquent behavior in our children, sickness in them, or sleep difficulties for us or our children. It might be fear, anxiety, stress, mental problems, or an inability to think clearly or ocus. It might be difficulty in performing normal work duties, problems with co-workers and/or people over us, difficulty in holding a job, financial and legal problems, and poverty. It might be addictions such as sexual sin, alcohol, cigarettes, food, or TV. It might be weakness, lack of coordination, chronic fatigue, premature aging.

This is only a partial list, but it shows us that un-confessed sin in our lives can cause many serious problems for us. (It can even determine and redirect our Eternal Destiny when our life on this planet comes to an end, if we refuse to deal with it. Refer to pages 6-9.)

Therefore, we need to diligently and faithfully deal with our sins, either to keep from getting sick in the first place; or we need to deal with our sins to make sure that we are cleansed of them, so that we will be in that bridal company before the Day of the Lord arrives. (The Day of the Lord is the Rapture followed by the Wrath of God.) If we follow the steps in "The 7 Step Program to Healing and Divine Health," we can be delivered from all of the problems listed on the previous page and experience complete victory over every one of them.

Chapter 5

Are You "Totally" Saved?

It is interesting that the Greek word for saved is "sozo" and for Salvation is "soteria." Both have a five-fold breakdown in their full meaning – <u>Salvation</u>, <u>healing</u>, <u>deliverance</u>, <u>preservation</u>, and <u>restoration</u>. We find "sozo" in **Romans 10:13** for example: "For whoever calls upon the Name of the Lord will be saved." But this verse and all the others like it with sozo and soteria in them really include not only (1) Salvation, but (2) healing and walking in divine health, (3) deliverance, (4) preservation and protection, and (5) restoration (making one whole) as well. That is quite an awesome package!

So, if we have been saved, we have received the most important feature of the word "sozo" – Eternal Life for God's obedient sons and daughters – but we miss out on the other four aspects of Salvation: healing and health, deliverance, preservation, and res- toration (being made whole). But when we possess all five, we not only cause our life here on Earth to be much more interesting and satisfying, but we also significantly increase the rewards that we receive at the Judgment Seat of Christ for all eternity!

So, to conclude this chapter, we can pray the following prayer:

"Jesus, I have already received you as Savior, but now I receive You as Healer. I also receive You as my Deliverer,

my Preserver and Protector, and the Restorer of all things, including my very soul."

Chapter 6

Sin Shall Not Have Dominion Over You

Hebrews 12:1-2a: "Therefore, seeing we also are surrounded by so great a cloud of witnesses, <u>let us lay aside every weight and the sin</u> which so easily ensnares us, and let us run with endurance the race that is set before us, looking to Jesus , the author and finisher of our faith,"

John 5:14b: "<u>Sin no more</u>, lest a worse thing come upon you."

Romans 6:5-6: "For if we have been united together in the likeness of His death, certainly we also shall be in the likeness of His resurrection, knowing this, that our old man was crucified with Him, that the body of sin might be done away with, that <u>we should no longer serve sin</u>."

Romans 6:7: "<u>For he who has died has been freed from sin</u>."

Romans 6:11-12: "Likewise you also reckon yourselves to be *dead* indeed *to sin,* but alive to God in Christ Jesus our Lord. Therefore <u>do not let sin reign in your mortal body, that you should obey it in its lusts</u>."

Romans 6:18: "And <u>having been set free from sin</u>, you became servants of righteousness."

Romans 6:14: "<u>For sin shall not have dominion over you</u>, for you are not under the law but under grace."

Romans 8:2: "For the law of the Spirit of life in Christ Jesus <u>has made me free from the law of sin</u> and death."

When we go through the teachings in this book and follow them as needed in our lives, then we will be able to claim and receive the following promise from God's Word: "We know that whoever is born of God does not sin [practice sin]; but he who has been born of God <u>keeps himself</u>, and the wicked one does not touch him." (**1st John 5:18**)

"The wicked one does not touch him" means that we will not be afflicted with any of the curses listed in **Deuteronomy 28:15-68.**

This verse in First John and the eight references before it should be of great encouragement to us. If we are able to "keep ourselves" from getting caught up in various sins, then the devil will not be able to "touch" us or afflict us with curses. Thus we will not be needlessly troubled with a wide variety of problems, such as the ones listed on page 28, and all the pain and suffering that goes with them; nor will we be troubled by all the demons associated with them either. For more on this subject go back to page 16 and read "The Power of Your Words." Also, read and sow into your mind and spirit **Luke 10:17-20,** and do the same thing for the following verses:

1st John 3:3 and 6a and 9: "And everyone who has this hope in Him purifies himself, just as He is pure. Whoever abides in Him does not sin. Whoever has been born of God does not practice sin, for His seed remains in him; and he cannot sin because he has been born from God."

3:3 bears repeating: "**And everyone who has this hope**

in Him purifies himself, just as He is pure."

Thank you, Lord. When I am abiding in You, I do not sin; that is, I do not practice sin. I purify myself, just as You are pure.

But if I do sin, according to **1st John 1:9**: "If I confess my sins, God is faithful and just to forgive me of my sins and to cleanse me from all unrighteousness." In this way, I can have a pure and holy walk before the Lord. In this way, I can be His Bride!

Chapter 7

Be Ye Holy
Be Ye Perfect

**Obeying these two commandments from God gives us
great power and authority and protection here on Earth**

The Scriptures on the next nine pages
will inspire us and help us to be
holy and perfect in Christ

1. Be Ye Holy

"but as He who has called you is holy, you also be holy in all
your conduct, because it is written, 'Be holy, for I am Holy.' "
(**1st Peter 1:15-16**)

After reading what the twelve references in Chapter 6 said about
overcoming sin, we don't have to think that what is stated here
in 1st Peter is unattainable. We really can be holy—in Christ—
and we can be perfect in our walk with Him. It is something
to aim for, something we can attain to in this life; and the fifty
Scripture references on the next nine pages all support this
thought. Since it only takes two or three to establish God's
Word (**2nd Corinthians 13:1**), fifty references more than firmly
establish the concept of "perfection" as something that we, in
Christ, can attain to as Believers.

2. Perfection

/Note: In the following section, the words "blameless" and "loyal" in the NKJ are translated "perfect" in the KJ./

"Therefore you shall be perfect, just as your Father in Heaven is perfect." (**Matthew 5:48**)

"And He Himself gave some to be apostles, some prophets, some evangelists, and some pastors and teachers, for the per-fecting of the Saints for the work of the ministry, for the edi-fying of the body of Christ, till we all come to the unity of the faith and the knowledge of the Son of God, to a perfect man, to the measure of the stature of the FULLNESS OF CHRIST;" (**Ephesians 4:11-13**)

Genesis 6:9b: "Noah was a just man, perfect in his generations. Noah walked with God."

Genesis 17:1: "... the Lord appeared to Abram and said to him, 'I am Almighty God; walk before Me and be blameless [perfect in the KJ].' "

Deuteronomy 18:13: "You shall be blameless [perfect KJ] before the Lord your God."

2nd Samuel 22:33: "God is my strength and power, and He makes my way perfect."

1st Kings 8:61: "Let your heart therefore be loyal [perfect KJ] to the Lord our God, to walk in His statutes and keep His com-mandments, as at this day."

1st Kings 15:5: "because David did what was right in the eyes of the Lord, and had not turned aside from anything that He commanded him all the days of his life, except in the matter of Uriah the Hittite."

1st Chronicles 28:9: "As for you, my son Solomon, know the God of your father, and serve Him with a loyal [perfect KJ] heart and with a willing mind; for the Lord searches all hearts and understands all the intent of the thoughts. If you seek Him, He will be found by you; but if you forsake Him, He will cast you off forever."

2nd Chronicles 16:9: "For the eyes of the Lord run to and fro throughout the whole earth, to show Himself strong on behalf of those whose heart is loyal [perfect towards KJ] to Him."

2nd Chronicles 19:9: "And he [King Jehoshaphat] commanded them saying, 'Thus you shall act in the fear of the Lord, faithfully and with a loyal [perfect KJ] heart:' "

Job 2:3: "Then the Lord said to Satan, 'Have you considered My servant Job, that there is none like him on the earth, a blameless [perfect KJ] and upright man, one who fears God and shuns evil? And still he holds fast to his integrity, although you incited Me against him, to destroy him without cause.' "

1st Peter 5:10: "But may the God of all grace, who has called us to His eternal glory by Christ Jesus, after you have suffered a while, perfect, establish, strengthen, and settle you."

2nd Corinthians 13:9b: "And this also we wish, even your perfection." (KJ)

Psalm 138:8a: "The Lord will perfect that which concerns me;"

Psalm 18:32: "It is God who arms me with strength, and makes my way perfect."

Psalm 19:12b-13: "Cleanse me from secret faults. Keep back Your servant also from presumptuous sins; let them not have dominion over me. Then I shall be blameless [perfect KJ], and I shall be innocent of great transgression."

Psalm 37:37: "Mark the blameless [perfect KJ] man, and observe the upright; for the future of that man is peace."

Psalm 101:2: "I will behave wisely in a perfect way. Oh, when will You come to me? I will walk within my house with a perfect heart."

Psalm 101:6: "My eyes shall be on the faithful of the land, that they may dwell with Me; he who walks in a perfect way, he shall serve Me."

Proverbs 2:21a: "For the upright will dwell in the land, and the blameless [perfect KJ] will remain in it;"

Proverbs 11:5a: "The righteousness of the blameless [perfect KJ] will direct his way aright,"

Isaiah 38:3a: "And [King Hezekiah] said, Remember now, O Lord, I beseech Thee, how I have walked before Thee in truth and with a perfect heart, and have done that which is good in Thy sight." (KJ)

Revelation 3:2: "Be watchful and strengthen the things which remain, that are ready to die, for I have not found your works perfect before God."

Matthew 19:21: "Jesus said to him [the rich young ruler], 'If you want to be perfect, go, sell what you have and give to the poor, and you will have treasure in Heaven; and come follow Me.' "

Luke 6:40b: "everyone that is perfect shall be as his master." (KJ)

John 17:23a: "I in them, and You in Me; that they may be made perfect in one,"

2nd Corinthians 13:11: "... Become complete [perfect KJ]. Be of good comfort, be of one mind, live in peace; and the God of love and peace will be with you."

Philippians 2:12c-16: (12c) "work out your own salvation with fear and trembling; (13) for it is God who works in you both to will and to do for His good pleasure. (14) Do all things without murmuring and disputing, **(15)** that you may become <u>blameless</u> and harmless, children of God, <u>without fault</u> in the midst of a crooked and perverse generation, among whom you shine as lights in the world, (16) holding fast the word of life, so that I may rejoice in the Day of Christ [the Rapture] that I have not run in vain or labored in vain." (The Day of Christ is another name for the Rapture. This is covered in the discussion that begins on page 95.)

Being blameless and without fault are conditions for being in the Rapture, as verse 15 in this passage points out. And so are the qualities mentioned in the following four references. For one to be in the Rapture, they would have to possess all of these characteristics as well. The Bride will.

1) **Philippians 1:10**: "that you may approve the things that are excellent, that you may be sincere and without offense till the Day of Christ [the Rapture]."

2) **Ephesians 5:25b-27**: "Christ also loved the church and gave Himself for it, that He might sanctify and cleanse it with the washing of water by the Word, that He might present it to

Himself a glorious church [at the Rapture], not having spot or wrinkle or any such thing, but that it should be holy and without blemish."

3) **1st Timothy 6:13 and 14**: "I urge you in the sight of God who gives life to all things ...that you keep this commandment without spot, blameless until our Lord Jesus Christ's appearing [at the Rapture],"

4) **1st Thessalonians 5:23-24: "Now may the God of peace Himself sanctify you completely; and may your whole spirit, soul, and body be preserved blameless at the coming of our Lord Jesus Christ** [for His Bride at the Rapture]. **He who calls you is faithful, who also will do it.**" A very powerful verse. It would be profitable for us in all things if we prayed this and spoke it out in faith several times a day until the Lord comes.

Hebrews 13:20a and 21: "Now may the God of peace... make you complete [perfect KJ] in every good work to do His will, working in you that which is well-pleasing in His sight, through Jesus Christ, to whom be glory forever and ever. Amen."

James 1:4: "But let patience have its perfect work, that you may be perfect and complete, lacking nothing."

1st John 4:17: "In this our love has been made perfect, that we may have boldness in the day of judgment; because as He is, so are we in this world."

Ephesians 4:11-13: "And He Himself [Jesus] gave some to be apostles, some prophets, some evangelists, and some pastors and teachers, for the perfecting of the Saints for the work of the ministry, for the edifying of the body of Christ, till we all come to the unity of the faith and the knowledge of the Son of God, to a <u>perfect</u> man, to the measure of the stature of the fullness of Christ;"

1st Corinthians 12:27 and 12: "Now you are the body of Christ and members individually. For as the body is one and has many members, and all the members of that one body, being many, are one body, so also is Christ."

Colossians 1:21c-23a and 28: "yet now has He [Jesus] has reconciled in the body of His flesh through death, to present you holy and <u>blameless</u> and irreproachable in His sight, if indeed you continue grounded and steadfast in the faith, and are not moved away from the hope of the Gospel which you have heard... Him we preach, warning every man and teaching every man in all wisdom, that we may present every man <u>perfect</u> in Christ Jesus."

Colossians 4:12: "Epaphras, who is one of you, a servant of Christ, greets you, always laboring fervently for you in prayers, that you may stand <u>perfect</u> and complete in all the will of God."

Galatians 4:19: "My little children, for whom I labor [travail KJ] in birth again until Christ is formed in you."

2nd Timothy 3:17: "that the man of God may be complete [perfect KJ], thoroughly equipped for every good work."

James 3:2b: "For we all stumble in many things. If anyone does not stumble in word, he is a perfect man, able also to bridle the whole body."

Jude 24: "Now to Him who is able to keep you from stumbling, and to present you faultless before the presence of His glory with exceeding joy,"

1st John 2:5-6: "But whoever keeps His Word, truly the love of God is perfected in him. By this we know that we are in Him. He who says he abides in Him ought himself also to walk just as He walked."

1st John 3:3 and 6a and 9: "And everyone who has this hope in Him purifies himself, just as He is pure. Whoever abides in Him does not sin. Whoever has been born of God does not practice sin, for His seed remains in him; and he cannot sin because he has been born from God."

Philippians 3:12: The apostle Paul speaking: "NOT THAT I HAVE ALREADY ATTAINED OR AM ALREADY PERFECTED; BUT I PRESS ON, THAT I MAY LAY HOLD OF THAT FOR WHICH I ALSO WAS LAID HOLD OF BY CHRIST JESUS."

Verse 14: "I press toward the mark [goal] for the prize of the high calling of God in Christ Jesus." (KJ)

If the apostle Paul wasn't perfect at this point in his life and was pressing on toward the goal of perfection so that one day he would be so, then let *us* do likewise and press on to perfection so that one day *we* will be so.

"Therefore, leaving the discussion of the elementary principles of Christ, let us go on to perfection" (**Hebrews 6:1a**) Amen!

If we want to escape the period of time known as the Wrath of God, then we must move on to being perfect in Christ, and when that work is completed in us, we will then be His Bride. Then, <u>as His Bride</u> we will go in the Rapture and in this way escape God's Wrath.

Luke 21:36 puts it this way: "Watch therefore and pray always that you may be counted worthy to escape [via the Rapture] all these things that will come to pass [the Wrath of God], and to stand before the Son of Man."

The following chapters directly address the Rapture in detail. As you are reading them, keep this in mind: "He who has begun a good work in you will complete it until [by] the Day of Jesus Christ [the Rapture]." (**Philippians 1:6**) And God will finish His work in the Bride in time for the Rapture! "He who calls you is faithful, who also will do it." (**1st Thessalonians 5:24**)

It would be very fruitful to pray the following several times a day: "Now may the God of peace Himself sanctify me completely; and may my whole spirit, soul, and body be preserved blameless at the coming of my Lord Jesus Christ." [When He returns for His Bride at the Rapture.] (**1st Thessalonians 5:23** personalized) If you do this faithfully, **God will do a deep cleansing work in you – spirit, soul, and body.**

Cherish My Words[4]

Oh My children, obey My words. Do not wander in unbelief and darkness, but let the Scripture shine as a light upon thy path. My Words shall be life unto thee, for My commandments are given for thy health and for any preservation. They will guard thee from folly, and guide thee away from danger.

Hide My commandments in thy heart, and make them the law of thy life. Cherish My words, and take not lightly the least of them. I have not given them to bind thee, but to bring thee into the life of greatest joy and truest liberty.

I have asked thee to give, in order that I may bless thee more. I have challenged thee to pray, so that I may respond and help thee. I have asked thee to rejoice, in order to keep thee from being swallowed up by anxieties. I have asked thee to be humble, to protect thee from the calamities that fall upon the proud. I have asked thee to forgive, so as to make thy heart fit to receive My forgiveness. I have asked thee not to love the world, for I would have thee loosed from unnecessary entanglements, and free to follow Me.

Sanctification is accomplished in no one by accident. Learn My rules, and put them into practice consistently, if ye desire to see progress in the growth of thy soul. Holiness is not a feeling – it is the end product of obedience. **Purity is not a gift – it is the result of repentance and a serious pursuit of God.**

After we've gone over the Scriptures, the Prophecies, and the Commentary in this book, and we ask the Lord to do something for us or to accomplish something in us, and we've done whatever it is that He requires us to do for that request to be fulfilled, we can pray something like the following, out loud and in faith:

"I thank You Father that it is done. Thank You Lord. In the mighty name of Jesus Christ, Amen."

Then praise and worship Him.

[For additional information on some of the topics in this book, read the book, "How to be Healed of Sickness and Disease" by the Author.]

Chapter 8

The Rapture

When Will It Take Place?
Which Christians Will Go?
Which Christians Will Not?
How you can be sure
that <u>you</u> will
A Study on How to Prepare to be the Bride of Christ

Will ALL Christians Be in the Rapture?[5]

We are told from the pulpit, and elsewhere, that all Christians will leave in the Rapture when Jesus returns for His own. And we are told that this applies to all Christians with no exceptions. They might be spiritually weak, lukewarm, or totally back-slidden, but when that Day comes, we are told that all will go... when, in reality, not one of these Christians will! (And that includes busy "Marthas" as well. Refer to pages 68-69.)

No thought is given to preparing for the Rapture; and preparing for it means getting ready to meet Jesus face to face! But if we're going to meet Him, we must be like Him. **If we want to meet Him up there, we must be like Him down here.** We must pick up our cross daily and follow Him.

45

But very few understand this, and almost everyone accepts the notion that when the Rapture occurs, all Christians will be in it. Consequently, practically every Believer assumes when that divine moment arrives, he or she will automatically leave this planet. Therefore very few feel any urgent need or desire to prepare their hearts, to lay hold of Christ, to go all out for Him, and thus be ready for Him when He comes for His own. And it is no wonder. **No one is equating being ready for the Rapture to selling all for the cause of Christ.**

The net result is very few Christians are seriously growing in Christ or are earnestly seeking Him or are developing a close walk and a deep relationship with Him. The rest – including the overwhelming majority of pastors and heads of many ministries – are holding back in their walk with the Lord and their relationship with Him. Thus they are lukewarm and sleeping.

So the message that all Believers will soon just fly away and meet Jesus in the air has the effect of putting almost every Christian to sleep, and the result, of course, is a sleeping Church. When one considers that this myth is preached in almost every Evangelical, Charismatic, and Pentecostal church in the country, one can see that we have a serious problem. We have a nation full of sleeping churches filled with sleeping Christians!

And a serious problem it is indeed. In this critical hour when the church in America should be spiritually strong and alert, it is for the most part slumbering, lukewarm, and weak. (And it thinks it is alert, on fire, and strong!)

This is the time to hear from all pulpits, promulgated by every shepherd, the cry to get ready, to make way for the coming of the Lord, to watch and pray because judgment is approaching; and we need to be accounted worthy to escape (via the Rapture) all these things that shall come to pass (the Wrath of God), and to stand before the Son of Man. But what is heard instead is a familiar theme, that old song, the favorite of every Laodicean church in the land: that every Christian – with no exceptions – will be in the Rapture and will escape coming judgment and the Wrath of God.

What we should be hearing at this time is: **Any Christian who doesn't sell all for the cause of Christ and put Jesus first in everything in his or her life will be included in the countless number of unsuspecting Christians who – because they are lukewarm, sleeping, backslidden, or spiritually weak – will miss the Rapture!** They will be **left behind**.

Moreover, with nothing but their shallow walk with the Lord and their somewhat shaky and casual relationship with Him, they will enter into the darkest hours that will ever descend upon this planet: The Wrath of God!

That being the case then, who <u>will</u> make the Rapture?

Who Will Be in the Rapture?[6]

God Speaks to Pastor B.H. Clendennen

[Pastor Clendennen speaking:] For many years, in the church I pastored, we had an all-night prayer meeting the last Friday night of every month. One such Friday night, out of four-hundred members, there were forty-one of us present. As I was praying, I heard this Word from the Lord: *"You are looking at the Rapture from this church."* That Word got my attention. You are preaching to four-hundred people on a Sunday. You've got forty people in a prayer meeting, and God says these forty people represent the Rapture!

47

I stopped short, and in my heart I said, "Do you mean if You came tonight, this is all that would go?" God said, *"I mean, that if I cannot call a man to a prayer meeting, I could never call him to the Rapture."* [End of Pastor Clendennen's experience.]

On the following four pages are three prophecies that support and confirm what God revealed to Pastor Clendennen.

———

Only Those Who Have Come Close to Me Will be Raptured Up[7]

Can America stand against it? saith the Lord. I'm speaking of My judgment; yea. It will *not* stand against it, saith the Lord. It is a terrible nation. It is a nation that is an abomination unto Me, saith the Lord God. There is no good in it, saith the Lord God, and I am judging it. I'm coming strong against this nation for its abominations, saith the Lord God; yea.

I am coming soon, saith the Lord God, and I'm calling My people to draw close to Me. I'm calling, but not all of them are hearing, saith the Lord God. For their ears are dull of hearing. They have yielded to the world. They are yielded to the world, and they are listening to what the world says and not to what I say, saith the Lord God.

But nevertheless, I am still calling. I'm still calling for My people to draw near. I'm still calling for My people to seek My face on a daily basis, saith the Lord God. For I am coming for My bride soon, saith the Lord God, and I am preparing her for it, saith the Lord God. **Only those who yield to Me, only**

those who have come close to Me will be raptured up, saith the Lord God; yea.

Mysteries and Treasures[8]

My children, there are mysteries and treasures hidden at the Cross for you to find and enjoy.

In the future many of you will experience the crucifixion of your fleshly desires and comforts. Do not resist when this happens; it is for your own [great] benefit. Some of the treasures of your walk can only be manifested as you gain more of Me. These are great hidden treasures I desire to give to you, though not all are willing to receive them.

Comfort on Earth is a temporary thing, and though enjoyable, it has no eternal value. My Bride must be without spot or blemish before My return. My Bride must love Me with great zeal and [have a great] passion for My return. She must be looking unto her Bridegroom with all eagerness and anticipation, watching and praying.

Instead, she is lazy, lukewarm, and preoccupied. But My True Bride shall be made ready for Me. My True Bride will submit her desires to Mine and be refined. My True Bride will not walk in compromise, but in the truth of My Holy Word.

My True Bride will walk in truth with Me, unstained by the world around her.

———

Here are some of the Scriptures associated with this prophecy, as noted by Glynda Lomax:

Watch and pray, that ye enter not into temptation: the spirit indeed is willing, but the flesh is weak. (Matthew 26:41)

Watch ye therefore, and pray always, that ye may be accounted worthy to escape all these things that shall come to pass, and to stand before the Son of man. (Luke 21:36)

And I will bring the third part through the fire, and will refine them as silver is refined, and will try them as gold is tried: they shall call on My name, and I will hear them: I will say, it is My people: and they shall say, The Lord is my God. (Zechariah 13:9)

Love not the world, neither the things that are in the world. If any man love the world, the love of the Father is not in him. For all that is in the world, the lust of the flesh, and the lust of the eyes, and the pride of life, is not of the Father, but is of the world. And the world passeth away, and the lust thereof: but he that doeth the will of God abideth for ever. (1st John 2:15-17)

And they that are Christ's have crucified the flesh with the affections and lusts. (Galatians 5:24)

That He might present it to Himself a glorious church, not having spot, or wrinkle, or any such thing; but that it should be holy and without blemish. (Ephesians 5:27)

Pure religion and undefiled before God and the Father is this ... and to keep himself unspotted from the world. (James 1:27)

My Church is Not Ready[9]

My Church is not ready for My Return. I desire to return for My Bride, but she does not ready herself for her Groom.

I will have a holy and spotless bride, shining with great radiance, excited for the Marriage Supper of the Lamb, but My

Church is sick with sin, dead in its zeal for Me, and uncaring about the dying world around it.

Those who desire Me, who desire with great zeal to join Me, to submit and do all I require, will soon be here at Home. Those who neglect the great salvation offered and those who sleep – who work not while it is day – will not.

Many of you are in church, but many in church are not in Me. Discern, My children! Do not remain where I have not placed you. Do not neglect your calling, do not neglect the pursuit of Me in your lives. Your leaders lead you to err because you discern not.

You must be without spot or blemish, and this you can only do when you abide in Me daily. Make ready for the Groom!

————

That being the case then, how can you and I make the Rapture?

What do I do? How can **I** be ready for the Rapture? How does one begin?

The next twenty-five pages will address that question. We start with two statements and a question:

> I Want to be The Bride
> I Want to be in the Rapture
> How Can I Know if **I** Qualify?

Mark 4:20: "And these are the ones sown on good ground, those who hear the Word, accept it, and bear fruit: some thirty-fold, some sixty, and some a hundred."

Romans 12:2: "And do not be conformed to this world, but be transformed by the renewing of your mind, that you may prove what is that good [sixtyfold] and acceptable [thirtyfold] and perfect will [one hundredfold] of God."

1st Corinthians 15:40-42a: "There are also celestial bodies and terrestrial bodies; but the glory of the celestial is one, and the glory of the terrestrial is another. There is one glory of the sun [one hundredfold], another glory of the moon [sixty-fold], and another glory of the stars [thirtyfold]; for one star differs from another star in glory. So also is the resurrection of the dead."

The glory of the sun describes someone who has a hundredfold walk with the Lord. That person would be the Bride of Christ; the sixty and the thirtyfold would **not** be. The Bride is totally filled with Jesus – completely dead to self and matters of the flesh; whereas the others are not.

The glory of the moon is the sixtyfold walk, and the glory of the stars, the thirtyfold walk. Even the stars differ from one another in glory. They can be anywhere from thirtyfold up to sixtyfold. It all depends on how much of Jesus they have in them and how much of their own flesh is there. If they have 30% Jesus and 70% flesh, then they are thirtyfold – star glory. But if they've been growing spiritually and they're not baby Christians anymore, they might have 60% Jesus and 40% flesh. Then they are sixtyfold – moon glory. However, if they go all the way and have 100% Jesus and 0% flesh, they are **one hundredfold** – *sun glory!* This is the Bride of Christ.

This one – the hundredfold Christian – will go in the Rapture; the thirty and sixtyfold Christian will not.

They will be **left behind**. However, the thirty and sixtyfold Christian *will* make Heaven. "Marthas" are not the Bride, but they do make Heaven. "Marys" are the Bride, and they make Heaven too, but with a hundredfold reward! And as the Bride they also make the Rapture. They are special – in the Lord. They are the Bride of Jesus Christ.

The Place of Independent Life[10]

A Vision of Those Who Miss the Hundredfold

"Today He [the Lord] spoke to me concerning those elect ones – His chosen instruments that He shall perfect and purify to bring forth the high manifestation of Himself in that great wave of glory and light that He has already spoken of.

"For many months He had poured out His grace and blessing upon certain people; but in spite of that, they still had not come to the place of independent life – the place of having life in themselves [the life of God, the strong presence of the Lord.] Because of this, they had been *rejected* from being numbered among those chosen instruments that God is preparing in this hour. He said they would not be rejected, not cut off from being His people [they would still make Heaven], and would be taken along their own plane and level of spiritual growth; but they had been rejected from being those choice and elect instruments through whom God will manifest Himself."

(From the book "Visions of the Eternal," Dr. R.E. Miller editor. A compilation of Visions received by Annie Schisler.)

The one who would become Bride of Christ (1) will prepare her heart; (2) will purify herself; and (3) will make herself perfect in Him. She will then be ready for the Rapture. Read more about these three points on this page.

1. How Do I Prepare My Heart?
2. How Do I Purify Myself?
3. How Do I Become Perfect?

(1) **1st John 1:7 and 9**: "But if we walk in the light as He is in the light, we have fellowship with one another, and the Blood of Jesus Christ His Son cleanses us from all sin." How? This way: "If we confess our sins, He is faithful and just to forgive us our sins and to cleanse us from all unrighteousness."

If we're not confessing our sins at all, or if we're only doing it occasionally, then confessing them on a regular basis will get us started on the cleansing process.

(2) **1st John 3:3**: "And everyone who has this hope in Him purifies himself, just as He is pure."

As we engage ourselves in this process of purification, we are getting closer to reaching the goal mentioned in **Philippians 3:14**: "I press toward the goal for the prize of the upward call of God in Christ Jesus."

(3) And the closer we get to the goal, then the closer we get to being counted worthy, or perfect in Christ. And when we're perfect in Christ, then we are His Bride. This in turn will allow us to stand before Jesus in the Day of the Lord. **Luke 21:36** says it this way: "Watch therefore and pray always that you may be counted worthy to escape [via the Rapture] all these things that will come to pass [the Wrath of God], and to stand before the Son of Man."

The individual who <u>seriously</u> walks out these three Steps and does whatever is necessary <u>to</u> walk them out, will be the Bride of Christ and therefore will be ready to meet the Lord in the air when the Rapture takes place.

The Words from the Lord on the following twenty one pages will help us in the preparation process.

The Last Call[11]

Soon, My beloved, the last call, the final call will be given. Only those whose hearts have been prepared will be ready to answer it. Only those who have surrendered all of their hearts to Me will be ready to enter into the Marriage Supper of the Lamb. The last call will be given: *"Behold, the Bridegroom cometh; go ye out to meet Him."* [Matthew 25:6] Only those wise virgins equipped and ready will rise up and enter. The door will then be shut. [verse 10]

The last call will come in a very dark time – a time when the love of many will be waxing cold. [24:12] The allurement and sin of the world will have enticed, ensnared, deceived, and drawn away many. Their half-hearted love for Me will be clearly evident when the last call is given. The flame of love that will be burning brightly in the vessels of the wise, will have gone out in the vessels of the foolish. [25:8] Oh, the horror of that day to realize how foolish they have been. Oh, the heart-break of lukewarm love. Oh, the despair, to be forever separated and shut out!

The hour is late, My beloved. The darkness deepens. It is an urgent hour – an hour to be awake and alert. It is the time to prepare and cast off the works of darkness and put on the armor of light. [Romans 14:12] It is the time now to zealously repent and answer My call of love to come out and separate yourselves unto Me and Me alone, to lay aside the things of the world. It is the time to cleanse and purify your heart and hands. [James 4:8]

O My children, will you not come and let Me shine the light of My Word on your heart? Will you not allow Me to search, know, and try your heart and thoughts? [Psalm 139:23] Will you not seek Me with all of your heart? [See Jeremiah 29:13] Will you not leave your other loves and come to Me with all of your heart? Oh, the hour is so late. So many of you are foolish. You are spending your oil and treasure on your other loves. You have a harlot's heart!

Return to Me. Leave your lovers and return to Me. I will gather you in My arms and love you freely. Come to Me. Come to Me with all of your heart. Answer now this call of love. It is a call to return to your first love, your bridal love – extravagant, lavish, spendthrift, doesn't-count-the-cost, intimate love. There is a price to pay for this love, and you must pay it now. It is the surrender of your whole heart to Me. Will you not answer My call now, My beloved, and come to the secret closet of love, and prepare your heart and ready yourself for the last call? The last call is **the Rapture Call. Only those whose hearts are burning with the flame of first love will be ready and pre-pared to answer that call.**

You Are Not Ready to Go[12]

How is it, My beloved Bride [called to be one], that you have not been careful to make yourself ready to meet your Beloved? You have not submitted to the heavenly "beauticians." You have rejected the myrrh of suffering which is needed in your life to crush and break your will so that you can accept My will for your life. And you have refused the anointing perfume that comes through the fragrance of a life spent in intimacy with Me, your Beloved.

I am ready to come for you and take you to Myself so that where I am, there you may be also – but you are not ready to go! Your heart is still cleaving to the things of this world. You are like Lot's wife. You still love your cities that are doomed to fiery judgment and destruction. Lot's wife lived only for herself. She was the influence for evil in the life of her husband. She loved the riches and the social life that Sodom offered her. She encouraged her daughters to marry the sons of the prosperous families of Sodom. That is why she looked back. [Genesis 19:26]

Let that which happened to her be a warning to you, My beloved. I sent My angels to bring her out. They even took her by the hand and led her out, but still her heart was attached to a doomed city. My Bride is still attached to a doomed world. The judgment has begun to fall! Flood, fire, earthquake, wars, famine, pestilence, and all the evil that has befallen you has still not been able to turn your heart back to Me. You still cleave to this doomed world! You still love the temporal more than the eternal. [See 2nd Corinthians 4:18]

My beloved, I grieve because you have lost your first love for Me. [See Revelation 2:4] I have sent out My messengers to bid you to come to My wedding feast, but you have made many excuses and have hardened your heart to My call of love. [Matthew 22:2-5] I cannot plead forever for you to come into My arms. My Father will not permit it. **Soon it will be too late, and you will have missed your last opportunity to answer My call.**

What will you do then? What will you do when those who are ready have gone into the Marriage Feast and you have been **left**

behind? [verse 8] Even those whom you despise and refuse to recognize or have fellowship with will come into the Kingdom ahead of some of you who think you are so righteous and take pride in the recognition of the religious societies of the world. You love it when other men praise you and honor you and welcome you into their midst. But what good will it do you if you are shut out of the Kingdom of God and refused entrance into the banqueting hall of the Marriage Supper of the Lamb? [verses 11-13]

These are the Last Days. The last call is going out now. Hasten to hear it and to allow My Holy Spirit to do His work in you so that you will not be **left behind** to taste the evil that will befall the earth very shortly. For know this, that the good people suffer with the evil [people] when the judgment of God falls upon a nation. Not all the people of San Francisco were wicked when the great earthquake and fire destroyed that city. [In 1906] There were also good people who suffered with the wicked. Not all the people who suffered in Hurricane Andrew were wicked. [1992] Many were My children. Nor are all the many thousands of people who are suffering in the great floods of central USA wicked. [1993] Many are good and innocent people, but they lived where the wicked lived. And **after the Rapture takes place**, those who are left, *even if they are good people,* will suffer with the wicked. [Good people don't make the Rapture; good people who are perfect in Christ do. Those Christians who are not perfect in Christ, no matter how good they appear to be, will be left behind.]

So prepare yourself <u>now</u> to be My Bride, for soon the call will go out: *"Behold, the Bridegroom cometh; go ye out to meet Him,"* and then only the wise virgins who have prepared for that event, will be taken out. [Matthew 25:4,6-10] The foolish virgins [3,11-12] will be **left behind** to taste the sorrows and sufferings that shall befall as darkness closes in upon a sin-cursed world [in that time known as the Wrath of God].

Busyness[13]

There is a busyness that pervades and prevails in and around you. Busyness leads you in your thoughts, actions, words, and deeds. As a result, you charge out ahead and enter into territory and boundaries you would not have entered, had you prayerfully and quietly and submissively listened, waited, and followed Me and My instructions, [and] My warnings and directions. Take heed: slow down, quiet yourself. Be on the alert at all times. Remove the clutter and clamor. Seek Me and My ways, and walk in them.

Slow Down[14]

I am calling you to slow down and set apart a time for Me and Me alone: A time of quietness, a time of sitting at My feet and learning, a time of cleansing, purging, and purifying. I want all filth, debris, and putrefaction removed. I want your idol of self knocked down and destroyed. I am asking for all – cleansing in every area! I want you to face yourself and see how untamed and unruly and self-willed your emotions and your affections are, how fickle your love is. It is a stench in My nostrils! There can be no sweet aroma of prayer until these things are cleansed and removed. Allow Me to do this work. Come, meet Me in the quiet place. Listen, learn, obey.

A Call to Zealous Repentance[15]

Mean business when I call you to do something for Me. It will require repentance, for your lives are filled with your own desires and comforts and healings. You try to heal yourselves; and in doing so, you pull your comforts close to your bosom and hang on tightly. Your comforts have many shapes and consistencies: They range from people, to animals, to possessions, ambitions, and even callings. YOUR thoughts, your plans, and your will – always you are focused on yourselves. You leave no room for even My suggestions. You have already determined what you can and cannot do according to what has always been in the natural for you. You leave no room for the supernatural working of My power. You leave no room for MY voice and leading to "disrupt" your normal everyday happenings. You are crippled in spirit and choose to continue on in your own way – supported and coddled and comforted by your friends and your own decisions on what, how, and where you will do your and My business.

Wake up! You are selfish and self-centered! Your world revolves around you. What about My Kingdom and My Kingdom plans? What about them? I am calling you to zealous repentance. You will do no great work for Me until you are willing to submit to My chastening and correction. Your hearts are pining away to do a "work" for Me. You are struggling and maneuvering and selecting and planning.

Stop it! Get on your faces and repent. You aren't listening and haven't seen what I've been doing all these years in preparation to bring you to this place of service. You are still in the place of control in your life, unyielding and unwilling to let go of your securities and your way of thinking and planning.

I call you to repentance and a laying down of yourself. This is not a call to rush out to do a service for Me and gratify yourself. This is a call to lay yourself down and to let go of everything of you, and let Me do the chastening, refining, purifying work I desire to do in you. I can only do it as you abandon yourself to Me and obediently submit to all that I ask of you – in every area.

Don't you see? You are too valuable to Me to not do this work. Let Me, the Potter, make you again into another vessel – molded and shaped according to My plan. Let go. Let go. Do not hold on to even a tiny shred of what you figure is okay. Give it all to Me – all areas – and let Me do a work which you could not believe even if it were told you. I desire you for Myself. I alone shall prepare you for service, but I must know you are entirely Mine – yielded, obedient, submissive.

The Way to Prepare[16]

I'm giving you time and opportunity to clean and clear and get things ready. Detach yourself from the excess things in your life; they are a burden and a hindrance. They distract you from Me, My ways and purposes. Do not be greedy. Lay not up treasure on this earth, where moth and rust doth corrupt and thieves break through and steal. [Matthew 6:19-20] Set your heart and mind on things above, where thieves cannot break through and steal. Make Me your greatest treasure! [verse 21] Seek Me as hidden treasure. There is oil and treasure in the house of the wise. [Proverbs 21:20] Lay it up, store it up, hide it.

A storm is coming, famine is coming, destruction is coming! All excess outward things will dissolve. Only that which is hidden in and with Me shall survive. Prepare, prepare! Even now the winds are beginning to blow! You need to tie things down in the Spirit, as it were. Lay them up, hide them, secure them, for the storm will be fierce! It will manifest itself in **WIND, RAIN, FLOODS, FIRE!**

Take precaution now, lay aside now, lay up treasure in Heaven now, hide in Me now, and you will stand strong on Me and in Me. The choice is yours. Yield to this cleansing, purifying, separating work that I am doing now. Let My Wind and Water and Fire cleanse you now of all that would hinder you from being My cleansed, purified vessel. Seek Me *daily* in your secret closet, and allow Me to search and know you. It **is the way you prepare.** It's the way you ready yourself.

Trouble Coming[17]

There is trouble coming into the world, My children. You see trouble around you now, but it will grow far, far worse than this as this New Age dawns. The troubles you see before you now are very minute compared to what is soon to come.

Prepare your houses! Prepare your bodies and minds for the onslaught of the enemy that is coming, My children. I desire that you would stand tall and strong for Me in this time, that your hearts would be filled with courage as you face what lies just ahead, but many of you refuse to believe anything is coming at all. Many of you believe you will never suffer in this world, and that is not true. Did My Son not suffer? Did I spare Him? No, and you are joint heirs – not only in His blessings, but in His sufferings also. [Romans 8:17]

Catastrophic events will cover the world before My Son comes back, for all nations shall be tested and shall be judged according to My Holy Word. My own children shall lose loved ones in some of these catastrophic events. As I said in My Word, there shall be famines, earthquakes, pestilences (plagues). [Matthew 24:7b]

Turmoil in many governments is coming soon, sooner than you think, and it will bring confusion to many. Governments will fight amongst themselves. Kingdom shall rise up against kingdom. [verse 7a] Sorrows will encompass you round about, but My love will encompass you even more. For those who abide in Me, it shall be a time of revealing My glory in all the earth.

IT WILL BE A TIME OF MANY MIRACLES – MIRACLES SUCH AS THIS WORLD HAS NEVER SEEN BEFORE, EVEN IN THE TIME OF MY SON!

Those who carry My glory throughout the earth will be tested and tried in every possible way. The enemy of your souls will do everything he can to stop you, to hinder your work – to delay you who are called and chosen, from stepping into your call. He will try to destroy you once you have. He will attack your family members, your friends, your ministries. He will turn friends against you.

All this and more is coming in this time of great sorrow. But those who know Me, those who abide in Me and My Word, shall know great joy in this time in spite of the sorrows surrounding them round about. They shall stand courageous, speak My Word boldly, and bring glory to My Name. They shall cause many souls to come into the Kingdom in this time.

For those who do not answer My call, be prepared to give account. Be prepared to give an account to Me for what you have done with this life I have given you.

Look up, My children, for your redemption draweth nigh, but many sorrows come ahead of it. [Matthew 24:8] Do not fear when these things begin to happen, for they must happen according to My Word before My Son returns to the earth. [verses 3-13]

Yes, My children, trouble comes into the world now, but My love will surround you. Prepare your houses, prepare your minds for what is coming, for trouble shall visit every house upon the earth in this time.

The Last Hours[18]

The last hours! And what will you do in these last hours? There is a cleaning and a purging that is going on now in the heart of the Bride. Everything must be in a state of readiness. Everything must be set in order and prepared. There is a necessary trimming down, clearing out, and eliminating that is going on. It happens as you respond to the searching light of My Spirit. It happens as you are willing to face your sin in every area of your life.

I demand truth in the inward parts. I demand purity in word, thought, deed, and action. There must be a carefulness in all that you do. You must be willing to respond to Me and others according to the purity of My Word. You must be willing to be broken and harnessed. You must be willing to be identified with Me in truth and righteousness. Mercy must be at the core of all that you do. If it is not, whatever you do will be for you and your gain, and not for Me and My Kingdom.

You are preparing to leave this world. Why do you hold so tightly to its things? Why do you continue to strive to be in control of everyone and everything? It is a prideful thing. It is not of My Kingdom.

Come, come, hold not back. The very things you fear to let go of and lay down, are the very things that will set you free – as you release them.

The thoughts of your heart must match the words of your lips, or you are a hypocrite and deceive yourself. Do not be like the Pharisees, who cleansed the outside of the cup and platter, but inside, *inside,* were ravenings and every evil work. [Luke 11:39]

I love you. I desire to do this work of purifying and preparation in you. But you must come and know that NOW is the appointed time to separate, clean, clear, and make things right in every area and relationship. Be willing to die to yourself and take up your cross and follow Me. [Luke 9:23] Come, come, I will help you and teach you and assist you. Come, come, surrender all; yield to this breaking. It is the voice of the Bridegroom who calls you. Come, that your joy may be full. Come, that you may be ready when I come [at the Rapture].

Stay Pliable in My Hand[19]

0 My child, be quick to obey. For the moving of My Spirit may at times be inconvenient to the flesh, and may at other times be diametrically opposed to reason, but obey Me regardless of the cost. Thou wilt in every case be amply repaid for any sacrifice by an abundance of blessing. The more difficult the assignment, the richer the reward.

I will not force thee to make the choice, neither make My Will inescapable. There will always be an easier way open to thee, and one seeming to thy mind more reasonable and involving less risk. In the risk involved, I have calculated to test and develop thy faith [cause it to increase], as well as thine obedience, and in the choosing process, I give thee an opportunity to prove thy love for Me.

Be sensitive to My Spirit. Be listening for My voice. I will guide thee with My hand upon thy shoulder. I do not intend to circumscribe thy way nor to handicap thy freedom, but rather to lead thee into an increasingly abundant life, and by crucifying the wills of the flesh, to liberate thy spirit.

STAY PLIABLE IN MY HAND; neither resist Me nor be unaware of My working, nor question Me as to what I am making. Trustingly give Me a free hand. It will be a surprise and a joy when the end is revealed.

Dynamos of Praise[20]

O My child, lean upon Me; for I am thy helper; I am thy shield and thy buckler. Yea, I am thy strong tower and support. No evil shall befall thee, for thou art surrounded and protected by My presence, and no evil can touch Me. Yea, let thine heart rejoice in Me, and occupy thine heart with praise. There is no need that I will not fulfill as ye praise and worship – both your needs and the needs of others.

Man has contemplated the power of faith and of *prayer,* but only rarely have I revealed to men this far greater power of *praise.* For by prayer and faith doors are opened, but **by praise and worship, great dynamos of power are set in motion,** as when a switch is thrown and an electric power plant such as Niagara is thrown into operation. Praying for specifics is like requesting light for individual houses in various scattered places, while worshipping and praise flood the whole area with available current.

I do not discount prayer (petitions). I only show you a more marvelous way – a faster means of bringing more help to more people with less elapse of time. So many need Me. So little time is available. Turn loose thy praises, and in proportion to thy liberality ye shall see My generosity expressed, and in *infinite* magnitude.

Labor not to analyze each need. Leave the diagnosis and the mechanics of it in My hands. Complexities are as nothing to Me. They exist only in thy mind, sown by the enemy, to dull thy faith. Ignore all this. Weigh nothing except the love of My heart. Ask nothing except ye inquire of thine own heart how much love for Me is there. Hold Me closely, nor let Me go. I will surely bless you, and I will make you a blessing.

I will make *you* a blessing. Think not to *take* a blessing to someone, or hope that I will *send* a blessing. Lo, I will make thee, as My ambassador, to be thyself a sweet savour of life and grace. Through thy saltiness shall others be made thirsty. Through thy joy shall others be made to long after reality.

Yea, through thy peace and confidence shall others seek for Me, and they shall themselves find Me even as ye have found Me. I will reveal Myself to them as I have revealed Myself to you. Perhaps in a different way, because each has different needs, but I will open to all who knock. I will reward those who seek. I will reward. Ye need only preserve thy soul's integrity. This is enough to fully occupy thine energies and attention. Leave the miracles to Me. You be, and I will do.

Mary or Martha[21]

Which One are You?

To the Church it seems like the "Marthas" are the ones who are doing something significant for Me and My Kingdom. There is movement and activity and outgoing personalities. There is much talk and planning and preparing. They see needs, and purpose to see them met. Immediate action is taken so many times. There is much rushing, and a flurry of activity surrounds and accompanies all that they do.

I am not in or even present in their much and endless talking and activity! They are like restless waves of the sea beating upon the shore. It is wearisome to Me. The constant pounding of the waves causes erosion. They will wear out in their own busyness, and the end-result will be death and not life.

Oh, that I could find "Marys" with a heart that will seek, crave, and desire Me and Me alone – quiet Marys, content to sit and listen to Me, apart from the busyness and demands of the so-called Church and its work. If only I could find Marys content with Me – just Me and only Me – Marys content to sit and listen and learn, Marys seeking Me with first love, and content and determined to forsake all else. They will be despised and misunderstood. Their quiet, seeking ways will be ridiculed and rejected many times. They will suffer rebuke openly and be reprimanded by the Church as it rushes on to do the "work of God."

My Marys will not be enticed or drawn away from their quiet, steady, loyal pursuit of Me. They are answering a call of love. Their heart is set. Their eyes are fixed intently on their Beloved, and they are content only to behold Him. My Marys are listening. They listen and hear My voice and Mine alone. And they are content to wait until I call them.

It is My Marys who will be an important part of the out-working of My Plan in these Last Days. It is My Marys who will hear My voice – the voice of their beloved Bridegroom calling them to Myself and the Marriage Supper of the Lamb. My Marys are even now in preparation, for *"the Bride has prepared herself."* [Revelation 19:7] For she shall be arrayed in a fine garment, clean and white. [See verse 8] She is preparing her heart. She is dying to herself and the things of this world. She is willingly laying down her life in preparation. She is becoming humble, meek, and merciful; and in doing so, her love for Me is being purified. This process is taking place in My Marys as they pull away from the din and clamor of the world, and answer My call of love to come and sit and listen and learn.

It is My Marys that I come to. It is My Marys who will be ready. They will hear My final call. They will be **raptured** from this world – **raptured** to meet their First Love, **raptured** to be with Me forever! O My Marys, My precious Marys. I can hardly wait!

I Want You as My Bride[22]

You never say "I love you" to Me. You take it for granted that I know. You assume you love Me, but you never really long to be with Me. You don't really desire My presence nor desire to be with Me. You really don't. It's all so business-like. It's not really flowing from your heart – heart-love: "mushy," over-powering, consuming heart-love. *"Greater love hath no man than this: that a man lay down his life for his friends."* [John 15:13] I did that for you. I loved you that much, and My love is still reaching out to you today.

Don't be afraid to love Me. Don't be afraid to be head-over-heals in love with Me. Think about Me constantly. Talk about Me to your friends; brag about Me. Talk to Me. Talk to Me affectionately, lovingly, often. Desire My nearness. Touch Me; embrace Me. I am real! My love is powerful, and My love is reaching out to you. I don't want to be your casual friend; I want to be your Lover! Friends are part of the wedding party but are never the Bride. [John 3:29] I want your intimate love – I want you as My Bride.

You Are Very Precious to Me[23]

Know, My child, that you are very precious to Me and that I love you with and everlasting love. [Jeremiah 31:3] It is with cords of love that I have drawn you, cords of love. [Hosea 11:4] You have never been out of My sight, for I long for you, My child, and I love you. You are very precious to Me, and I desire you. I desire to have all of your heart. And even though you feel like you have been such a failure, yet I see you today as My precious one who has returned to Me, My precious one whom I have waited for and longed for and looked for and called to these many, many months.

And you have come, My child, you have come. You have answered My call, and that's all I am asking of you at this time. For I call you to Myself, I call you to My heart, and I will give you the strength to stand against all of the attacks of the enemy. I will give you the strength. You cannot do it in yourself; you cannot even think to do it in yourself, but it is My grace and My mercy and My love, My boundless love, that will enable you to do it. It is as you come daily, My child. It is you beginning to come – even this day as you have come – not even knowing how you can do it, but you have come!

And I want you to know that it's just that way that it's going to happen – as you daily come, as you start just where you are, to read My Word and to seek My face and to come and to lift up your heart and say, "God, I want to love You with all of my heart. I don't even know how, but I know that Your Word promises that You'll help me, and that if I come, you will." And that's exactly how it will happen, My child, for I am going to put iron in your soul – iron! Your feet will be feet of iron, your shoes will be shoes of iron, and you will stomp upon the enemy!

But it's as you come, My child. It's not some magical thing or even a formula. It's not some fantasy that you hope will happen some day, but it's that coming with all of your heart. Say, "**God, I only want you. I only want to love You; I only want to serve You.**" And if I keep you enclosed, My child, for Myself for a season, do not despair. Do not think, "Oh, I want to do this or that for you, God." Do not despair. I want to bring you in to be a garden enclosed unto Myself [Song of Solomon 4:12]. I want to minister to your heart and heal all your wounds, and I want to receive your love as you come to Me, because you come in weakness. I, **I** will make you strong.

Do you see, My child, I have reserved you for Myself? I reserved you because I love you, and I see in you that which I need. I need you. I need you to bring others to Me, that they may be reconciled just as you have been. But it will only come as you daily come – just for Me, just to love Me, just to want to know Me. Then it will all flow from you. It is not a heavy thing, but it's LOVE. It all has to do with My love for you and My Son's love for you, but I will help you. I will help you. Do not be afraid. Do not dismay, for you are going to stand tall and strong, and you will do a work for Me that I have reserved for you, and you alone, to do. But I will lead you out from that garden, that garden enclosed [Ibid], where you and I will be together in deep fellowship and intimacy, for I love you, My child. I love you, and I will always love you; and I will never leave you, I will never forsake you. [Hebrews 13:5]

This is Marriage Love[24]

You are thinking of Me as being in Heaven, seated at the right hand of the Father, and you do not realize that I am with you. I *am* at the right hand of the Father, interceding for you [Romans 8:34b], but I am also *with* you as your Friend and Lover, desiring you and wanting to carry on a "torrid" love relationship with you.

I told you in My Word that I would never leave you nor forsake you, and that I'd be with you until the end of the Age. [Hebrews 13:5] I do desire you. The desire you are feeling this day, "How can I express my love to You?" is what I have been longing and waiting to hear from you. I do desire you. I do love you. I will not refuse you the kisses of My mouth – not a hen-peck kiss, but kisses of love and desire and affection. [See Song of Solomon 1:2]

Your response to My Name and the fragrance of it will grow more intense as you realize I love you. You! It's not an earthly love based on looks and education. I see your heart and your desire for Me. Don't be afraid. I won't reject you. I don't want you as My casual or even special friend; I want you as My beloved. This is marriage love: deep, intense, and single-eyed – My agape love issuing forth and pouring forth and desiring you. Come, come away, My beloved, to My chambers [Song of Solomon 1b].

You Need Love Times[25]

You need *yada** times. How do you think intimacy with Me comes? You need love times: times of gentle whispers of love, times of gentle songs and praise. These times will bring you close to Me. I will embrace you. From these times will come My burdens, My secrets. From closeness and yearning for Me and My Word will come My burdens and My thoughts.

But you must have these yada times. How else will you really get to know Me? It will be in these times that your love for Me will grow and expand. It will bring a love and a union so close that at times we will not have to say anything. <u>We will just embrace, and My love will flow to you, and your love will flow to Me</u>.

I cannot emphasize enough how important these yada times are. They will bring you into a deep, deep intimacy with Me. I need to know that you are wholly Mine, that I can trust you.

*Footnote: *Yada*: A Hebrew word meaning "to know." That is, to know intimately through close personal contact.

Listen to the Silence[26]

You are in My hands. You are not keeping yourself; I am keeping you. If I choose to hide you away, it is for a purpose. If I wish to give you a time of rest, it is for thine own good. <u>Nothing is amiss that is in My will</u>. Do not think that it will be as times in the past. I have deeper lessons to teach you. How invaluable have you found the truths to be which I have taught you in your "Arabia years." [See Galatians 1:16-17] (Arabia was not the only solitary period in the life of St. Paul. Indeed, it was rather insignificant in comparison to the later prison day experiences.)

One does not write what has already been written. One writes out of the storehouse of fresh revelation and his own personal knowledge gained through the painful experiences of growth. Ye cannot escape the growing experience without forfeiting the other. Ye shall cease writing if ye cease learning. Ye do not learn as ye write, but write as ye learn.

I would spare you if I could do so in love; but this kind of protecting love would be false and would rob you of much treasure. I only love you truly as I give you My best. My best cannot come to you without pain, even as it could not come to the Lord Jesus without pain. Pain is the result of sin, true, but sin is still an existing problem to be dealt with. It must be grappled with. Empires do not simply fall, but are taken by a stronger force. **The kingdom of Satan must likewise be opposed by a stronger force if ye hope to see it fall**.

I want to make you strong. I want you to be a <u>Devastator</u>! I have brought you to this place. Make the most of it. Drink in the silence. Seek solitude. LISTEN TO THE SILENCE. It will teach you. It will build strength. Let others share it with you. It is priceless. It is little to be found elsewhere.

Find Solitude[27]

There is no blessing I would withhold from them that walk in obedience to Me who follow when I call, and who respond when I speak unto them. They are near to My heart and precious in My sight who have eyes to discern My purpose and ears that listen to My direction

Be not intent upon great accomplishments. By what standards do ye judge the importance of a matter? It was a relatively small thing that Hannah prayed for a son [1st Samuel 1:10-11], but what great things I accomplished through Samuel! [Chapters 2-19 of 1st Samuel] It may have seemed incidental that Simeon and Anna perceived the Christ-child and prophesied over Him; but it was to Me a word worthy to be recorded in Holy Scripture and preserved forever. [Luke 2:34-35, 36-38]

Nay, ye cannot ascertain the ways of God amidst the pathways of men. Ye may feel the wind as I pass, and yet see only the swirling dust. The earthly beclouds the heavenly. The voices of men drown the voice of God. Only in much solitude can ye begin to sift away the chaff and come at last to the golden grains of truth.

The World will confuse thee. **Silence will speak more to thee in a day than the world of voices can teach thee in a lifetime.** Find it. Find solitude – and having discovered her riches, bind her to thy heart.

The Final Call[28]

As the days draw to a close and the plan of the Ages is fulfilled, I will come to My precious, purified, and spotless Bride. [Ephesians 5:27] Oh, how I long for her. Oh, how I long to have her close to My side, forever with Me, her Bridegroom and the Lover of her soul. Everything is ready; the call has gone forth: *"Come, come, all things are ready. Come to the feast. Come to the Marriage Supper of the Lamb. Do not delay!"* [see Revelation 19:7-9]

Answer the call of the Bridegroom to prepare and make yourself ready. Respond to His call of love. Respond to His wooing. Make no excuse! Set not your heart on other things. Do not be indifferent to this call. Come, come to the secret place and prepare your heart to be My Bride. Cut all ties to earthly desires and loves so that you will be ready when you hear My final call to come – to come up and be with Me forever.

The wedding day draws near. Final preparations are being made. There is much excitement in Heaven! Oh, My love, My dove, hasten to the place of love and intimacy. *Daily* answer My call of love to <u>prepare your heart</u>. Listen, watch, and wait for the final call to arise, My love, My fair one; and come away. [Song of Solomon 2:10]

Chapter 9

Now we are ready to address *timing* of the Rapture. After that, we will consider *who* goes, in greater detail.

When Will The Rapture Take Place?

Argument #1: What Does Scripture Say?

Matthew 24:29-31: (**29**) "Immediately after the Tribulation of those days the sun will be darkened and the moon will not give its light; the stars will fall from heaven, and the powers of the heavens will be shaken. (**30**) And then the sign of the Son of Man will appear in heaven, and then all the tribes of the earth will mourn, and they will see the Son of Man coming on the clouds of heaven with power and great glory. (**31**) And He will send His angels with a great sound of a trumpet, and they will gather together His elect from the four winds, from one end of heaven to the other."

Mark 13:27 describes the event in Matthew 24, verse 31 this way: "And then He will send His angels and gather together His elect from the four winds, from the farthest part of earth to the farthest part of heaven."

[Note: "Tribulation" and "Tribulation period" are used inter-changeably in this book. They both refer to the same thing – the seven year period of time known as Daniel's 70th week from Daniel chapter 9. That seven year period is comprised of two parts: It starts first with a 3½ year period known as "the Time of Sorrows" and concludes with a second 3½ year period, "the Great Tribulation." These two periods together total seven years. So when this book uses the words "Tribulation" or "Tribulation Period," it is referring to the Time of Sorrows and the Great Tribulation together – a <u>seven year</u> period of time, not counting the time that God cuts the Great Tribulation short. (See Matthew 24:22)]

What is being described here in these two references? Many Bible experts and prophecy teachers say that the Rapture is not mentioned in Matthew 24. They insist that verses 29-31 are talking about Jesus returning at the end of the seven year Tribulation to judge the earth, and that this is not the Rapture. They say the Rapture will take place first, before the seven year Tribulation begins – the Pre-Tribulation position. This is not true, and there is no basis for it in Scripture, as we shall find out in the following *four* Arguments.

(Hear what Scripture says about people who believe in a Pre-Tribulation Rapture and tell it to others: "All the sinners of My people shall die by the sword, who say, 'The calamity shall not overtake us nor confront us.' " (**Amos 9:10**) This verse declares that Believers who spread this view ... they themselves could go into the Tribulation and die a violent death. Or they might make it through that period of judgment, only to perish later when God's Wrath is poured out. We need to watch very carefully what we believe and who we listen to. It is vitally important for us to diligently study the Word or a book that is rightly dividing the Word and seek the Lord regarding the Truth of a matter. It can mean life or death – **yours!**)

Bible scholars and teachers who hold to a Pre-Trib Rapture doctrine read Matthew 24:29-31 and insist that it is referring to God's Wrath. They will also say that it's the same as Revelation 19:11-21, for example. These eleven verses do clearly describe one aspect of what happens during the Wrath of God at the End of the Age. No one is debating that. But when you read it, ask yourself if this is what Matthew 24:29-31 is talking about:

Revelation 19:11-21: "And I saw Heaven opened and behold, a white horse. And He who sat on him was called Faithful and True, and with righteousness He judges and makes war. His eyes were like a flame of fire, and on His head were many crowns. And He had a name that no one knew except Himself. And He was clothed with a robe dipped in blood, and His name is called The Word of God. And the armies in Heaven, clothed in fine linen, white and clean, followed Him on white horses. And out of His mouth goes a sharp sword, that He should strike the nations. He Himself treads the winepress of the fierceness and Wrath of Almighty God. And He has on His robe and on His thigh a name written: KING OF KINGS AND LORD OF LORDS. And I saw an angel standing in the sun; and he cried with a loud voice, saying to all the birds that fly in the midst of heaven, 'Come and gather together for the supper of the great God, that you may eat the flesh of kings, the flesh of captains, the flesh of mighty men, the flesh of horses and of those who sit on them, and the flesh of all people, free and slave, both small and great.' And I saw the beast, the kings of the earth and their armies, gathered together to make war against Him who sat on the horse and against His army. And the beast was taken and with him the false prophet, who worked signs in his presence, by which he deceived those who had received the mark of the beast and those who worshipped his image. These two were cast alive into the lake of fire burning with brimstone. And the rest were killed with the sword which proceeded out of the mouth of Him who sat on the horse. And all the birds were filled with their flesh."

After reading this passage from **Revelation 19** and comparing it to the passage in **Matthew 24** on page 77, I believe anyone can see the difference. Matthew is talking about the Son of Man returning for His own, His elect, His beloved – He's coming in love, not anger. He's coming in love to gather them together. Revelation 19, however, is describing the fierceness of His Wrath upon the rebellious, wicked children of the devil who refuse to repent, and the resulting bloody judgments that follow. The two passages are polar opposites. They are talking about two totally different events. Therefore it is clear that Matthew 24:29-31 is referring to the Rapture of the elect – the Bride of Christ – and not to the Wrath of God.

This is further supported by the following classic Rapture passage of the Bible that almost no Christian denies or debates the meaning of: **1st Thessalonians 4:15-17**: "For this we say to you by the word of the Lord, that we who are alive and remain until the coming of the Lord will by no means precede those who are asleep. For the Lord Himself will descend from Heaven with a shout, with the voice of an archangel, and with the trumpet of God. And the dead in Christ will rise first. Then we who are alive and remain shall be caught up together with them in the clouds to meet the Lord in the air. And thus we shall always be with the Lord."

Notice the language and how it parallels that of **Matthew 24:29-31. Verse 29**: "Immediately after the Tribulation of those days the sun will be darkened and the moon will not give its light; the stars will fall from heaven, and the powers of the heavens will be shaken. **30:** And then the sign of the Son of Man will appear in heaven, and then all the tribes of the earth will mourn, and they will see the Son of Man coming on the clouds of heaven with power and great glory. **31:** And He will send His angels with a great sound of a trumpet, and they will gather together His elect from the four winds, from one end of heaven to the other."

(1) A <u>trumpet</u> is mentioned in both passages, (2) as are <u>clouds</u>. (3) In both a <u>gathering</u> is taking place, not some huge wipe-out. (4) In the **Thessalonians** passage the Lord is <u>in the air</u> to gather His people who are caught up to meet Him. In Matthew 24:30 Jesus is seen in "heaven," and in verse 31 He sends out His angels to gather together His elect from one end of heaven – <u>the air</u> – to the other. (5) Even <u>angels</u> are mentioned in Matthew, and an archangel is mentioned in 1st Thessalonians; and where there is an archangel, there are more than likely other angels with him. That's a total of five strong parallels between the two passages. **Therefore, Matthew 24:29-31 is referring to the Rapture and not to the Wrath of God.**

And verse 29 says it will be "immediately after the Tribulation of those days." "Tribulation of those days" in this verse is referring to something that has already been said, and we need to find out where that reference is and what was *actually* said. Starting with verse 29, we work our way back verse by verse, and it doesn't take long before we come to verse 21: "For then there will be **Great Tribulation** such as has not been since the beginning of the world to this time, no, nor ever shall be." We don't have to go any further. The subject of verse 21 is "Great Tribulation," and this is what verse 29 is referring to. "Those days" in 29 is referring to "Great Tribulation" in 21. And since it will be "Great Tribulation such as has not been since the beginning of the world to this time, no, nor ever shall be," we know verse 21 is talking about The **Great** Tribulation, and not some other time of stress, death, and turmoil like a World War.

Now, returning to verse 29, where we started our search from, it says that: "immediately after the Tribulation of those days" – which we now know is The Great Tribulation – *something* is going to happen, some event. Verse 30 continues: "And then the sign of the Son of Man will appear in heaven, and then all the tribes of the earth will mourn, and they will see the Son of Man coming on the clouds of heaven with power and great glory. 31: And He will send His angels with a great sound of a trumpet, and they will gather together His elect from the four winds, from one end of heaven to the other."

That "something" (from the first sentence of the preceding paragraph) is analyzed and discussed on the previous page, with additional information about it on the page before that (80). And it *is* an event – **the Rapture**! So that means that **the Rapture will take place when the Great Tribulation ends**. In fact, God will *use* the Rapture to end the Great Tribulation. Why He does that is explained on page 89.

But it will still be before **verses 37-39**, which refer to the **Wrath of God**: "But as the days of Noah were, so also will the coming of the Son of Man be. For as in the days before the flood, they were eating and drinking, marrying and giving in marriage, until the day that Noah entered the Ark, and [the people] did not know until the flood came and took them all away, so also will the coming of the Son of Man be."

Since the Rapture is before all of this, it is Pre-Wrath. But, as just discussed, it's at the end of the Great Tribulation; so it's also Post-Great Trib. Or, putting it all together:

THE RAPTURE IS POST-GREAT TRIB but PRE-WRATH. Not something else.

When Will The Rapture Take Place?
"The Lord Could Come at Any Moment"

Argument #2: What Does Scripture Say?

In Argument #1, we looked at **Matthew 24:29-31** and used it and **1st Thessalonians 4:15-17** to make the argument that the Rapture will take place after the Great Tribulation. But can we build on what we learned in #1 – can we learn more that would be helpful to us as Brides-in-the-making? For that we will examine 2nd Thessalonians and see if it has anything of interest to tell us about the Rapture.

2nd Thessalonians 1:10-11a: "when He [Jesus] comes in that Day to be glorified in His Saints [at the Rapture] and to be admired among [in] all those who believe, because our testimony among you was believed. Therefore we also pray always for you that our God would count you worthy of this calling," This moment in time when Jesus "comes to be glorified in His Saints" is the Rapture, and this is what verse 10 is talking about here. It refers to it as "that Day." **Second Thessalonians chapter 2, verse 2** calls this special moment in time, that special day, "the day of Christ." We need to keep that in mind when we read verses 1 and 2 of Chapter 2:

2nd Thessalonians 2:1-2: (1) "Now we ask you, brethren, by the coming of our Lord Jesus Christ and our gathering together to Him [the Rapture], (2) not to be soon shaken in mind or troubled, neither by spirit nor by word nor by letter, as if from us, as though the day of Christ [still the Rapture] had come."

"The coming of the Lord Jesus Christ and our gathering together to Him" in verse 1 obviously refers to the Rapture; so the subject has not changed from the three verses before it in Chapter 1 – verses 10-12. Paul continues in verse 2 of Chapter 2 by telling the Believers in that day not to think that the "day of Christ" had taken place – that is, the Rapture had not taken place yet. So the Rapture is still the subject. Nothing has changed. The Rapture was the main subject in **1st Thessalonians chapters 4 and 5**. The Rapture is the subject **in 2nd Thessalonians chapter 1, verses 10-12.** And it's the subject in **2nd Thessalonians chapter 2, verses 1-2.** All of these verses are consistent and logical and make complete sense in the overall context of what is being stated and declared here.

And that subject flow continues into **verse 3:** "Let no one deceive you by any means; for <u>that Day</u> [the Rapture] will not come unless [or until] the falling away comes first, and the man of sin is revealed, the son of perdition." "**<u>that Day</u>**" in verse 3 refers back to "the day of Christ" in verse 2. In verse 2 "the day of Christ," as we know now, is directly connected to verse 1 which clearly describes the Rapture. Therefore, "that Day" in verse 3 also means the Rapture.

We can now summarize: The subject of verse 1 is the Rapture; the subject of verse 2 is the Rapture; and the subject of verse 3 is also the Rapture. So nothing has changed here. All three verses are talking about **<u>the Rapture</u>!**

Is that any surprise? Yet, as we saw in Argument #1, there are people who read Matthew 24:31 and think it is referring to the Wrath of God! Read what **Revelation chapter 16, verses 1-21** says. This passage describes the actual pouring out of the Wrath of God—the Seven Bowl Judgments of God (also known as the Seven Vials). In Argument #1, the Revelation 19:11-21 passage on pages 79 and 80 was describing events that will take place during the Wrath of God. The following passage, **Revelation 16:1-21**, describes the actual pouring out of each of the Seven Bowl Judgments of God's Wrath and what happens as a result. We begin with verses 1-15:

These Bowls or Vials are used by angels of the Lord to pour out God's Wrath upon the earth: "And I heard a loud voice out of the temple saying to the seven angels, 'Go and pour out the bowls of the Wrath of God on the earth.' And the first one went and poured out his bowl on the earth, and a foul and loathsome sore came on the men who had the mark of the beast and on those who worshipped his image. And the second angel poured out his bowl on the sea, and it became like the blood of a dead man; and every living creature in the sea died. And the third angel poured out his bowl on the rivers and springs of water, and they became blood. And I heard the angel of the waters saying, 'You are righteous, O Lord, the One who is and who was and who is to come, because You have judged these things. For they have shed the blood of Saints and prophets, and You have given them blood to drink. For they are worthy of it.' And I heard another out of the altar saying, 'Even so, Lord God Almighty, true and righteous are Your judgments.' And the fourth angel poured out his bowl on the sun, and power was given to him to scorch men with fire. And men were scorched with great heat, and they blasphemed the name of God who has power over these plagues; and they did not repent to give Him glory. And the fifth angel poured out his bowl on the throne of the beast, and his kingdom became full of darkness; and they gnawed their tongues because of the pain. And they blasphemed the God of Heaven because of their pains and their sores, and did not repent of their deeds. And the sixth angel poured out his bowl on the great river Euphrates, and its water was dried up, so that the way of the kings from the east might be prepared. And I saw three unclean spirits like frogs coming out of the mouth of the dragon, out of the mouth of the beast, and out of the mouth of the false prophet. For they are spirits of demons, working signs which go out to the kings of the earth and to the whole world, to gather them to the battle of the great day of God Almighty. (**15**) 'Behold, I am coming as a thief. Blessed is he who watches and keeps his garments, lest he walk naked and they see his shame.'" **(Revelation 16:1-15)**

This is a reminder that God is able to take us out of all of these judgments, even before they begin, if we "watch and keep our garments" (verse 15); that is, if we keep them clean. But if we don't keep them clean, we won't be ready, and the Lord will come as a thief. But if we do, then we'll be ready, and He won't come as a thief.

And as a result, at the Rapture Jesus will come for us and take us to Heaven and thereby keep us from all of the terrible judgments mentioned in this passage. He will do that for us, but *only* if we're His Bride. So, to escape the Wrath of God one must be the prepared Bride of Jesus Christ; that is, the one who watches and keeps his garments clean.

We conclude the passage from Revelation with verses 16-21:

"And they gathered them together to the place called in Hebrew 'Armageddon.' And the seventh angel poured out his bowl into the air, and a loud voice came out of the temple of Heaven, from the throne, saying, 'It is done!' And there were noises, thunderings, and lightnings; and there was a great earthquake, such as had not been since men were on the earth. And the great city was divided into three parts, and the cities of the nations fell. And great Babylon was remembered before God, to give her the cup of the wine of the fierceness of His Wrath. And every island fled away, and the mountains were not found. And great hail out of heaven fell on men, every stone about the weight of a talent. [75 lbs.] And men blasphemed God because of the plague of the hail, since that plague was exceedingly great." **(Revelation 16:16-21)**

Does this passage sound like the Rapture? Is the Rapture hidden somewhere in one of these verses? Hardly. (Other than, as pointed out earlier on the bottom of the previous page and the top of this page, the clear and open warning in verse 15 that we can escape these judgments if we're prepared – if we "watch and keep our garments clean." Then we're ready for the Rapture.)

As we learned on page 83, the subject of the first three verses in Second Thessalonians chapter 2 does NOT change. It is the Rapture in all three verses. So, to repeat, "that Day" in **verse 3** of chapter 2 of Second Thessalonians <u>refers to the Rapture,</u> NOT to the Seven Bowl Judgments of the Wrath of God, which Revelation 16:1-21 describes so graphically.

With that understanding firmly established, now read **Verse 3** again: **"Let no one deceive you by any means; for '<u>that Day</u>'** [THE RAPTURE] <u>**will not come**</u> **unless** [or until] **[1] the falling away comes <u>first</u>, and [2] the man of sin is revealed, the son of perdition."** (2nd Thessalonians chapter 2, verse 3)

What this is saying is that two events – **the falling away and the revelation of the son of perdition, as just mentioned in verse 3 of chapter 2 in Second Thessalonians, must take place FIRST –** <u>before</u> **the Rapture can occur.** Well, neither event has happened, so the Rapture cannot take place at this time. So much for the Doctrine of Imminency which says that Jesus can return at any moment. **Second Thessalonians 2:3** emphatically states otherwise, because it says **there are TWO THINGS that must happen FIRST before the Lord can return in the air for His own:** (1) the falling away and (2) the arrival of the son of perdition on the scene:

"Let no one deceive you by any means; for that Day [the Rapture] will not come unless [or until] [1] <u>the falling away</u>

comes first, and [2] <u>the man of sin is revealed</u>, the son of perdition." (2nd Thessalonians 2:3)

So **two events** have to happen first BEFORE the Rapture can take place. These two events have not happened yet, so the Rapture cannot take place at this time.

It is important that we truly understand what is being said here.

When Will The Rapture Take Place?

Argument #3: What Does Scripture Say?

The Antichrist is revealed openly to the world in **Revelation 13. Verse 5** says that he will be given authority for forty-two months, or 3 1/2 years, to wage war on the Saints. **Chapter 11, verse 2** states that the Gentiles will tread the outer court of the temple of God for forty-two months – the same words that were used in Chapter 13, verse 5. *(See Footnote #1 on page 91.)

This open revealing of the Antichrist takes place at the middle of the seven year tribulation. We know this from **Daniel 9:27a**: "Then he [the Antichrist operating as a diplomatic peacemaker] shall confirm a covenant with many for one week [one week of years, or seven years]; but in **the middle of the week** he shall bring an end to sacrifice and offering." Here, for the first time he openly shows us what he's really like, and in the process, who he really is: "And forces shall be mustered by him, and they shall defile the sanctuary fortress; then they shall take away the daily sacrifices, and place there the abomination of desolation." (**Daniel 11:31**) This is the Antichrist in action.

We know that the Rapture occurs **after** the son of perdition, this Antichrist, is revealed. Therefore the Rapture occurs sometime

after the mid-point of the seven year Tribulation. To explore this further we go to **Matthew Chapter 24,** starting with **verse 21:** "For then there will be Great Tribulation, such has not been since the beginning of the world to this time, no, nor ever shall be."

Verse 24:29: "**Immediately after the Tribulation of those days** the sun will be darkened and the moon will not give its light; the stars will fall from heaven, and the powers of the heavens will be shaken.

Verse 21 mentions "Great Tribulation." That's what **verse 29** is referring to it when it says, "immediately after the Tribulation of those days." It's referring to "Great Tribulation" mentioned in verse 21 – "such has not been since the beginning of the world to this time, no, nor ever shall be." Obviously this is referring not just to "Great Tribulation," but to The Great Tribulation of the Last Days.

And something is going to take place right after the Great Tribulation of verse 29. That something is identified in **verse 31:** "And He [Jesus] will send His angels with a great sound of a trumpet, and they will gather together His elect from the four winds, from one end of heaven to the other." This, of course, is the Rapture. **Therefore, the Rapture clearly occurs after the Great Tribulation, not before or during.**

Those Days Will be Shortened

At this point, however, we learn something unusual. Verse 22 tells us that: "And unless those days were shortened, no flesh would be saved; but for the elect's sake those days will be short-ened." (**Matthew 23:22**)

That means that the Great Tribulation ("those days") will not be a full forty-two months, or 3 ½ years in length, because God will cut it short with the Rapture. How much or how little we are not told.

In the meantime, God has plenty for us to do <u>right now</u> – like preparing to be His Bride, the Bride of Christ.

———

At this point we should be starting to understand that the Rapture occurs when the Great Tribulation is cut short by God. And since the Tribulation is seven years long, that means:

The Rapture will take place seven years AFTER the Tribulation starts (minus whatever amount of time God cuts the Great Tribulation short).

Or: **3 ½ years after the Antichrist confirms a covenant of peace with many** (minus whatever amount of time God cuts the Great Tribulation short).

But keep this in mind. No matter how much the Great Tribulation is cut short, "He who has begun a good work in you will complete it until [by] the Day of Jesus Christ [the Rapture]." (**Philippians 1:6**) God will finish His work in the Bride in time for the Rapture!

———

Major Note: Whenever you see the words "Post-Great-Trib," — which means that something will occur after the Great Tribulation — understand that this means <u>immediately</u>. So when God cuts the Great Tribulation short with the Rapture,

He will immediately beg_n to pour out His Wrath. There won't be any delay between the Rapture and the Wrath of God.

*Footnote #1: In Chapter 12 of Revelation the devil is cast down to the earth, "having great wrath" in verse 12, and in verse 17 he makes war with those who have the testimony of Jesus Christ. In **verse 11a:** "they [the Saints] overcame him by the Blood of the Lamb and by the word of their testimony," Halleluiah! In other words, we will still be here at that time. We'll be engaging the enemy in battle. (More about this in Chapters 16 and 17.)

When Will The Rapture Take Place?

Argument #4: What Does Scripture Say?

Argument #1 concluded that the Rapture is Post Great-Trib but Pre-Wrath. Can we confirm that in this Argument?

The most obvious and the best evidence for the timing of the Rapture is found in the following passage:

Matthew 24:29-31: **(29)** "Immediately after the Tribulation of those days [the Great Tribulation] the sun will be darkened and the moon will not give its light; the stars will fall from heaven, and the powers of the heavens will be shaken. **(30)** And then the sign of the Son of Man will appear in heaven, and then all the tribes of the earth will mourn, and they will see the Son of Man coming on the clouds of heaven with power and great glory. **(31)** And He will send His angels with a great sound of a trumpet, and they will gather together [Rapture] His elect [the Bride] from the four winds, from one end of heaven to the other."

(If you want to understand the following paragraph, read it slowly and carefully.) **Verse 29** tells us that the Rapture will

take place "**immediately <u>after</u> the Tribulation of those days**."
And, as we already know from the Verse 29 discussions on
pages 80-81 of Argument #1, "Tribulation of <u>those</u> days" refers
back to verse 21 which calls it "Great Tribulation." And, as that
discussion concluded, "Great Tribulation" turns out to mean
"<u>The</u> Great Tribulation." (As it does on page 89 also.) Therefore,
verse 29 is saying that the Rapture will take place immediately
after <u>the Great Tribulation</u>. **But** since the Great Tribulation
is the second half of the seven year Tribulation and since the
Rapture is at the end of the Great Tribulation, this means that
the Rapture will occur at the *end* of that seven year Tribulation
period – minus whatever time God cuts the Great Tribulation
short with the Rapture and takes the Bride out (as we learned
in Argument #3).

Also, we know from the following verse in **First Thessalonians**
(and other Scriptures) that raptured Believers will not go
through the Wrath of God:

Verse 9 of Chapter 5: "**For God has not appointed us to
wrath, but to obtain salvation** [deliverance] **by our Lord
Jesus Christ**." They were already saved. (That's why we see
the word "brethren" mentioned eight times in Chapters 4 and 5.
They were Christians of that Era.) This verse is referring to the
fact that the Rapture *will deliver* Believers from the Wrath of
God. That's because deliverance is one of the five-fold aspects,
or benefits, of Salvation, of being saved. (For more on this subject read page 30.) In that day some of them knew all about
Salvation, about its five-fold aspect.

And so should we by now, especially when we have an *abundance* of Scriptures and prophecies on the subject, and they're
both saying the same thing – we're appointed to obtain deliverance from God's Wrath! Some will take advantage of that
provision and will not have to go into that period known as the

Wrath of God. But many other Believers will not take advantage of that provision, and they will have to go into that period. The Bride won't have to.

In the following passage from Scripture notice that the Rapture and the Wrath of God are referred to:

Luke 21:34-36: **(34)** "But take heed to yourselves, lest your hearts be weighed down with carousing, drunkenness [on the things of the world], and the cares of this life, and that Day [the Rapture followed by the Wrath of God] come upon you unexpectedly. **(35)** For it will come as a snare on all those who dwell on the face of the whole earth. **(36)** Watch therefore and pray always, that you may be counted worthy to escape [via the Rapture] all these things that will come to pass [the Wrath of God], and to stand before the Son of Man."

The Rapture occurs first, then the Wrath of God. Notice that if we are accounted worthy (in Christ) to stand before the Lord, we will escape the Wrath of God. That alone should give us a fairly strong desire to be the Bride of Christ. There are other reasons of course and better ones for getting ready to be sure, but wanting to escape God's Wrath is a start.

So to summarize: This Argument is saying that if we're accounted worthy, we will escape the Wrath of God via the Rapture; and this escape will take place at the end of the 3 1/2 year Great Tribulation – minus whatever length of time God cuts it short (for the elect's sake). (See Matthew 24:22) In other words, the Rapture is Pre-Wrath and immediately Post-Great Tribulation. That is,

The Rapture is Post-Great Trib but Pre-Wrath.

Or, to phrase it another way:

<u>Post Most-of-the-Seven-Year Trib</u> but <u>Pre-Wrath</u>.

This, then, confirms Argument #1.

When Will The Rapture Take Place?
What Do the Scriptures Say?

Argument #5:
The Genesis Account of the Flood

Genesis chapter 7, verse 1: "Then the Lord said to Noah, 'Come into the ark, you and all your household, because I have seen that you are righteous before Me in this generation. (2) You shall take with you seven each of every clean animal, a male and his female; two each of the animals that are unclean, a male and his female; (3) also seven each of the birds of the air, male and female, to keep the species alive on the face of all the earth. (4) For after seven more days I will cause it to rain on the earth forty days and forty nights, and I will destroy from the face of the earth all living things that I have made.' "

(10) "And it came to pass after seven days that the waters of the flood were on the earth. (11b) on that day all the fountains of the great deep were broken up, and the windows of heaven were opened. (12) And the rain was on the earth forty days and forty nights."

(13) "<u>On the very same day</u> [that the Flood began] Noah and Noah's sons, Shem, Ham, Japheth, and Noah's wife and the three wives of his sons with them <u>entered the ark</u> – (14) They and every beast after its kind, all cattle after their kind, every creeping thing that creeps on the earth after its kind, and every bird after its kind, every bird of every sort. (15) And they went into the ark to Noah, two by two, of all flesh in which is the breath of life. (16b) and the Lord shut him in. (17) Now the

flood was on the earth forty days. The waters increased and lifted up the ark, and it rose high above the earth."

In verse 1 God tells Noah to come into the ark and to bring family with him; and to take with him all of the animals and birds referred to in verses 2 and 3 – all the species on the face of the earth! God then tells Noah in verse 4 that "after seven more days" judgment would begin, meaning the Wrath of God.

When God told Noah after seven more days, He meant that Noah had seven days to load up all the animals – seven pairs and two pairs, and seven pairs of all the birds – all the animals that existed on the face of the earth! Two by two they went into the ark! That took time. It could not be done in one day. And that's why God gave him seven days to complete the task; then the heavy rains began.

Verses 13 and 16b are the key that puts all of this into perspective: **(13)** "**On the very same day** [that the flood began] Noah and Noah's sons, Shem, Ham, Japheth, and Noah's wife and the three wives of his sons with them entered the ark —**"** Then **(16b)** "**the Lord shut him in.**" And the rains began immediately: **(17)** "**Now the flood was on the earth forty days. The waters increased and lifted up the ark, and it rose high above the earth. (18a): The waters prevailed and greatly increased on the earth,**" (The next five verses, 19-23, describe the flood and the effect it had on the earth.)

It is very clear here. Noah entered the ark, and "the Lord shut him in" first. The "Rapture" of Noah and his family was getting underway. (We have lift-off!) Then immediately the massive world-wide flooding erupted – the beginning of the Wrath of God!

Note #1: Together these two Mega-Events, the Rapture followed immediately by the Wrath of God, are called "The Day of the Lord" in Scripture.

Rapture here, in the case of Noah, serves as a type. (See page 187.) Again, Scripture shows us, even way back in Genesis, that God spared His very small righteous remnant and delivered them from His Wrath, poured out in verses 17-23, which followed right on the heels of Noah's "Rapture" (verses 16b, 17b, and 23c). **"Only Noah and those who were with him in the Ark remained alive." (23c)**

The Ark is a type of Christ; and that Ark will save, protect, and deliver the Bride from all danger, including the Wrath of God, just as it saved Noah and his family.

Note #2: Saving, protection, and deliverance are three of the five aspects of Salvation. See page 30 for a discussion of all five.

The Wrath of God

As mentioned above in the first Note, the Rapture followed by the Wrath of God is called "The Day of the Lord." There are two ways of looking at this: The Day of the Lord is (1) the Rapture followed immediately by the very first Judgment of the Wrath of God – right at that moment in time. Or (2) the Day of the Lord is the Rapture followed by all seven Judgments of the Wrath of God, beginning with the first Vial and continuing until the last one is poured out. Either view is correct.

The Wrath of God can also be viewed in two ways: (1) the initial pouring out of the first Vial (Bowl) Judgment with the focus being on just that Vial. Or (2) the total out-pouring of all seven Vial (Bowl) Judgments one right after the other with the focus being on all seven Vials. Either view is correct. But no matter how you look at it, the Wrath of God is still one huge Mega-Event at the very end of the Age.

The seven Vial Judgments will begin this way: The first Vial will be poured out and its effects will be felt. But starting with the second Vial the effects of these Judgments will accumulate; that is, when the second one is poured out, its effects will be added to and felt along with the first Vial. The third Vial will be poured out and its effects will be felt along with the first two, etc.

When the last one is poured out, there will be an earthquake that is so violent that every island and mountain in the world will disappear! It will be the greatest quake ever in the history of mankind. And those left alive will feel the unceasing, unrelenting, accumulating effects of seven Vial Judgments—all being poured out on the earth *at the same time!*

For those who played church and were never truly saved, and for those who were saved but for some reason lost their Salvation, it will be an extremely painful time when they realize that they could have been spared from these Judgments. There will be much sorrow and agony on their part.

However, many true Christians for a wide variety of reasons will miss the Rapture. They will still make Heaven, but will not make the Bride. When the Wrath of God gets underway, they'll be faced with just trying to survive and endure as long as they can while God is pouring out His Wrath on the world.

This is not a period of time that anyone would want to be here for. In fact, some will not be. <u>The Bride will be raptured out of here</u>, and the pouring out of God's Wrath will then begin. The further unleashing of His Wrath and the escalation of it will take place after she is raptured. God knows how to take care of His Bride.

When Will The Rapture Take Place?

Argument #6: A Vision

Tommy Hicks' Vision of the Rapture[29]

Introduction

The following is a startling vision which was given to American preacher Tommy Hicks. He had been a major figure in the powerful Argentina Revival of 1954. This message begins July 25, 1961 about 2:30 in the morning:

I had hardly fallen asleep when the vision and the revelation that God gave me came before me. The vision came three times, exactly the same [in considerable detail]. I was so stirred and so moved by the revelation that it has completely changed my outlook on the body of Christ and on End-Time ministries.

The Vision

As the vision appeared to me after I was asleep, I suddenly found myself at a great high distance. Where I was, I do not know. But I was looking down upon the earth. Suddenly the whole earth came into my view. Every nation, every kindred, every tongue came before my sight, from the east and west, the north and south. I recognized every country and many cities that I had been in, and I was almost in fear and trembling as I beheld the great sight before me; and at that moment when the world came into view, it began to lightning and thunder.

As the lightning flashed over the face of the earth, my eyes went downward, and I was facing the north. Suddenly I beheld what looked like a great giant, and as I stared and looked at it, I was almost bewildered by the sight. It was so gigantic and so great. His feet seemed to reach to the North Pole and his head to the South [Pole]. Its arms were stretched from sea to sea. I could not even begin to understand whether this be a mountain or this be a giant, but as I watched, I suddenly beheld a great giant. I could see his head was struggling for life. He wanted to live, but his body was covered with debris from head to foot, and at times this great giant would move his body and act as though it would even raise up at times. And when it did, thousands of little creatures seemed to run away. Hideous creatures would run away from this giant, and when he became very calm, they would come back.

All of a sudden this great giant lifted his hand toward heaven, and then it lifted its other hand; and when it did these creatures seemed to flee away from this giant by the thousands and go into the darkness of the night.

Slowly this great giant began to rise and as he did, his head and hands went into the clouds. As he rose to his feet he seemed to have cleansed himself from the debris and filth that was on him, and he began to raise his hands into the heavens as though praising the Lord, and as he raised his hands, they went even unto the clouds.

Suddenly, every cloud became silver, the most beautiful silver I have ever seen. As I watched this phenomenon, it was so great I could not even begin to understand what it all meant. I was so stirred as I watched it, and I cried unto the Lord and said, "Oh Lord, what is the meaning of this?" And I felt as if I was actually in the Spirit, and I could feel the presence of the Lord even when I was asleep.

And from those clouds suddenly there came great drops of liquid light raining down upon this mighty giant, and slowly, slowly this giant began to melt, began to sink in the very earth itself, and as he melted, his whole form seemed to melt upon the face of the earth, and a great rain began to come down. *Liquid drops of light* began to flood the very earth itself, and as I watched this giant that seemed to melt, suddenly it became millions of people over the face of the earth. As I beheld the sight before me, people stood up all over the world! They were lifting their hands, and they were praising the Lord.

At that very moment there came a great thunder that seemed to roar from the heavens. I turned my eyes toward the heavens, and suddenly I saw a figure in white, in glistening white—the most glorious thing that I have ever seen in my entire life. I did not see the face, but somehow I knew it was the Lord Jesus Christ, and He stretched forth His hand, and as He did, He would stretch it forth to one and to another and to another. And as He stretched forth His hand upon the nations and the people of the world – men and women – as He pointed toward them, this *liquid light* seemed to flow from His hands into them, and a mighty anointing of God came upon them, and these people began to go forth in the name of the Lord.

I do not know how long I watched it. It seemed like it went into days and weeks and months. And I beheld this Christ as He continued to stretch forth His hand; but there was a tragedy. As He stretched forth His hand, there were many people who refused the anointing of God and the call of God. I saw men and women that I knew – people that I felt would certainly receive the call of God. But as He stretched forth His hand toward this one or that one, they simply bowed their heads and began to back away. And each of those that seemed to bow down and back away, seemed to go into darkness. Blackness seemed to swallow them up everywhere.

I was bewildered as I watched it, but those people that He had anointed [and did not back away], hundreds of thousands all over the world – in Africa, England, Russia, China, America, all over the world – the anointing of God was upon them as they went forward in the Name of the Lord. I saw these men and women as they went forth. They were ditch diggers, they were washerwomen, they were rich men, they were poor men. I saw people who were bound with paralysis and sickness and blindness and deafness. As the Lord stretched forth [His hand] to give them this anointing, they became well, they became healed, and they went forth!

And this is the miracle of it, this is the glorious miracle of it. Those people would stretch forth their hands exactly as the Lord did, and it seemed as if there was the same liquid fire in their hands. As they stretched forth their hands they said, "According to my word, be thou made whole."

As these people continued in this mighty End-Time ministry, I did not fully realize what it was, and I looked to the Lord and said, "What is the meaning of this?" And He said, *"This is that which I will do in the Last Days. I will restore all that the cankerworm, the palmerworm, the caterpillar – I will restore all that they have destroyed.* [Joel 2:25] *They, My people in the End-Times, will go forth.* **As a mighty army they shall sweep over the face of the earth!"**

As I was at this great height, I could behold the whole world. I watched these people as they were going to and fro over the face of the earth. Suddenly there was a man in Africa, and in a moment he was transported by the Spirit of God; and perhaps he was transported to Russia, or China, or America, or some other place; and vice-versa. All over the world these people were sent, and they came through fire and through pestilence and through famine. Neither fire nor persecution – nothing seemed to stop them.

Angry mobs came to them with swords and guns. But like Jesus, they passed through the multitudes, and they could not find them; but they went forth in the name of the Lord, and **everywhere they stretched forth their hands the sick were healed, the blind eyes were opened**. There was not a long prayer, and after I had reviewed the vision many times in my mind, and I thought about it many times, I realized that I never saw a church, and I never saw or heard of any denomination, but these people were going in the Name of the Lord of Hosts. Hallelujah!

As they marched forth, in everything they did as the ministry of Christ in the End-Times, these people were ministering to multitudes over the face of the earth. Tens of thousands, even **millions**, came to the Lord Jesus Christ as these people stood forth and gave the message of the Kingdom, of the coming Kingdom, in this last hour. It was so glorious, but it seems as though there were those that rebelled, and they would become angry, and they tried to attack those workers who were giving the message.

In this last hour God is going to give the world a demonstration that the world has never known. These men and women are of all walks of life; degrees will mean nothing to them. I saw these workers as they were going over the face of the earth. When one would stumble and fall, another would come and pick him up. There was no "big I" and "little you," but every mountain was brought low and every valley was exalted; and they seemed to have one thing in common – there was a divine love, a divine love that seemed to flow forth from these people as they worked together and as they lived together. It was the most glorious sight that I have ever known. Jesus Christ was the theme of their life. They continued, and it seemed that days went by as I stood and beheld this sight. I could only cry, and sometimes I laughed. It was so wonderful as these people went throughout the face of the whole earth, bringing forth in this last day.

As I watched from heaven itself, I could see there were times when *great deluges of this liquid light* seemed to fall upon great congregations and that congregation would lift up their hands and praise God for seemingly **hours and even days** as the Spirit of God came upon them. God said, *"I will pour out My Spirit upon all flesh,"* [Acts 2:17a] and that is exactly what happened. And to every man and every woman who received this power and the anointing of God and the miracles of God, there was no end to it.

We have talked about miracles. We have talked about signs and wonders, but I could not help but weep as I read again at 4 o'clock this morning a letter from our native workers. This is evidence for the beginning of one man, a "do-nothing, unheard of" man, who would go and stretch forth his hand and say, "In the name of the Lord Jesus Christ I command life to flow into your body." I dropped to my knees and began to pray again, and I said, "Lord, I know that this time is coming soon!"

And then again, as these people were going about the face of the earth, a great persecution seemed to come from every angle.

The Tommy Hicks' Vision Continues:

(1) **The Rapture of The Bride**

(a) The Dead in Christ Rise First

Suddenly there was another great clap of thunder, that seemed to resound around the world, and I heard again the voice, the voice that seemed to speak, *"Now these are MY people. **This is My beloved Bride**."* And when the voice spoke, I looked upon the earth, and I could see the lakes and the mountains. The graves were opened, and people from all over the world, the Saints of all ages, seemed to be rising. And as **they rose from their graves,** suddenly all these people came from every direction—from the east and the west, from the north and the south—and they seemed to be forming this gigantic body. As the dead in Christ seemed to be rising first, I could hardly comprehend it. It was so marvelous. It was so far beyond anything that I could ever dream or think of.

(b) Those Who are Alive and Remain Rise Next

But as this body began to form and take shape, it took shape again in the form of a mighty giant, but this time it was different. It was arrayed in the most beautiful, gorgeous white. Its garments were without spot or wrinkle as its body began to form; and **the people of all ages seemed to be gathered into this body** [from all over the world]; and slowly, slowly, as it began to form up into the very heavens, suddenly from the heavens above, the Lord Jesus came and became the head; and I heard another clap of thunder that said, *"This is **My beloved Bride** for whom I have waited. She will come forth even tried by fire. This is she whom I have loved from the beginning of time."* [1st Peter 1:7]

Then again I turned my eyes to this glorious sight, this body arrayed in beautiful white, shining garments. Slowly, slowly, it began to lift from the earth, and as it did, I awoke. What a sight I had beheld! I had seen the End-Time ministries, the last hour.

(2) **The Wrath of God**

As I watched, my eyes suddenly turned to the far north, and I saw seemingly destruction: men and women in anguish and crying out and buildings being destroyed. Then I heard again the fourth voice that said, *"Now is My Wrath being poured out upon the face of the earth."* From the ends of the whole world, the Wrath of God seemed to be poured out, and it seemed that there were great Vials of God's Wrath being poured out on the face of the earth. I can remember it as though it happened a moment ago. I shook and trembled as I beheld the awful sight of seeing cities and whole nations going down into destruction.

I could hear the weeping and wailing. I could hear people crying. They seemed to cry as they went into caves, but the caves in the mountains opened up. People leaped into the water, but the water would not drown them. There was nothing that could destroy them. They were wanting to take their lives, but they could not. [Read Revelation 9:6]

Again on July 27th at 2:30 in the morning [which is the same time as the earlier vision], **the same revelation – the <u>same vision</u> – appeared again, <u>exactly as it did before</u>!**

So, according to this Vision,
**The Rapture is Pre-Wrath,
And only the Bride goes.
All other Christians will be LEFT BEHIND.**

———

For a condensed summary of the preceding six Arguments, go to page 139.

Getting Ready
for the Coming of the Lord[30]

(Excerpts from a message that was preached at Times Square Church in New York City by David Wilkerson in 2008. It was recorded in his February 18th newsletter. The complete message is available and can be obtained from World Challenge.)

From the third page, first column, bottom paragraph:

"In Matthew, Jesus speaks of the elect being taken up by God: 'He shall send his angels with a great sound of a trumpet, and they shall gather together his elect from the four winds, from one end of heaven to the other.' (Matthew 24:31 KJ)"

In verse 31, which Pastor Wilkerson quotes in his message and in his newsletter, the gathering together of the elect for the Rapture is described. Pastor Wilkerson believes that verse 31 is talking about the Rapture. This is confirmed by what follows in his newsletter further on:

"Paul makes this clear, stating: 'The Lord himself shall descend from heaven with a shout, with the voice of the archangel, and with the trump of God: and the dead in Christ shall rise first: and then we which are alive and remain shall be caught up together with them in the clouds, to meet the Lord in the air: and so shall we ever be with the Lord. Wherefore comfort one another with these words.' (1st Thessalonians 4:16-18)"

Two paragraphs later in his newsletter Pastor Wilkerson states: "It will be a day like any other. All of humankind will be unaware, but then, in a single moment, **Christ will gather his bride**." [Bold emphasis by the Author] So Pastor Wilkerson quotes the most famous Rapture passage in the Bible and uses it to confirm the fact that the gathering together of God's elect in Matthew 24:31 is referring to the Rapture!

———

So, according to a message that was preached at Times Square Church by David Wilkerson and recorded in his newsletter of February 18, 2008, **Only the Bride of Jesus Christ will go in the Rapture. All other Christians will be left behind.**

David Wilkerson continues in his message as recorded in his newsletter in the third column on the last page:

"Let me ask you again: Are you ready? Have you begun to love the thought of Christ's appearing? Paul says: 'Henceforth there is laid up for me a crown of righteousness, which the Lord, the righteous judge, shall give me at that day: and not to me only, *but unto all them also that love his appearing.*' (2nd Timothy 4:8, my italics.) "James urges us likewise: 'Be ye also patient; establish your hearts: for the coming of the Lord draweth nigh.' (James 5:8) 'Unto them that look for him shall he appear the second time without sin unto salvation.' (Hebrews 9:28)" "Finally, Paul writes, 'For the grace of God that bringeth salvation hath appeared to all men, teaching us that, denying ungodliness and worldly lusts, we should live soberly, righteously, and godly, in this present world; looking for that blessed hope and the glorious appearing of the great God and our Saviour Jesus Christ; who gave himself for us, that he might redeem us from all iniquity and purify unto himself a peculiar people, zealous of good works. These things speak, and exhort, and rebuke with all authority.' (Titus 2:11-15)"

Pastor Wilkerson continues in the closing words of his message: "I've got a crown waiting for me, because I love his appearing. [Do you?] I am ready. Come, Lord Jesus."

———

So, to repeat, according to a message that was preached at Times Square Church by David Wilkerson and recorded in his newsletter of February 18, 2008, **Only the Bride of Jesus Christ will go in the Rapture. All other Christians will be left behind.**

Chapter 10

A Warning to Those Not Ready for the Rapture[31]

Now is the time to tell My people to prepare to escape this thing [the Wrath of God]. Did I not say to My children **"to pray always that you may be counted worthy to escape** [via the Rapture] **all these things** [the Wrath of God] **and to stand before the Son of Man?"** [Luke 21:36]

O fear not to declare it. Yea, by all My ministries declare that My coming is at hand and that the five foolish virgins will not go into the Marriage Supper. But there will be weeping and wailing and outer darkness and gnashing of teeth [Matthew 25:30; 24:51] when the Great Wedding is on, when it is spread out, when it is in full sway. Then shall the King see that a guest has come that has not on the wedding garment. This is the parable that I spoke through My servant Matthew [Chapter 22:11-14] and others about this great consternation, that some will come right up to the hour of the Rapture and right up to the hour of being caught away, and because they have indulged in foolishness, and in jesting and joking, and television filth – yea, **television** scenes corrupted by Hollywood and satanic forces – even these will NOT go with Me [in the Rapture].* And I have foretold it.

Yea, I have prepared this escape, and that is by the great moving of the Rapture, and that will come suddenly [to those who are not prepared]. No man knoweth the day nor the hour.

*Note: This Word from the Lord was given over 40 years ago when television was somewhat innocent and had fairly high standards. Swearing was not even permitted. Imagine what God thinks of TV today!

Many Have Missed This Calling[32]

Send out this truth, that I am the Word that was in the beginning with God and became flesh. Yea, I became flesh, and now I am glorified, that <u>My people shall go through the same process I went through</u>, figuratively; and they shall come into My presence as they follow Me to the cross and they are identified with Me in My crucifixion, in My burial, and in My resurrection, of the means of baptism [Romans 6:4-6a] and the glorious outpouring of the Spirit.

I will know you after the flesh; for that is why I came in the flesh – to know you after the flesh. I took not on the nature of the angels, but I took on the seed of Abraham that I might destroy the works of him that had the power of death; that is, the devil. [Hebrews 2:14] But I also came that I might yield to you and you yield to Me. I have yielded Myself to you in blessing and glory. I have not submitted Myself to your dominion, but I have yielded My Word. Yea, your spirit ravished My heart. [Song of Solomon 4:9] Your spirits have come and called upon Me and rejoiced, and it is not [only] just as [a] bride and [a] bridegroom, for I am also preparing to receive <u>My</u> Bride to Me [when the Rapture occurs].

And this Bride must be separated to Me wholly, undefiled. Yea, My love, My dove, <u>My only one</u>. [6:9a] Who shall be greater than the Bride? Is she not the one that looketh forth in the morning; yea, that is as fair as the moon, and as clear as <u>the sun</u>, and <u>as terrible</u> [awesome] <u>as an army</u> with banners? [See Song of Solomon 6:9a and 10] That is the one that shall ride with Me on white horses! [Revelation 19:14]

<u>O that My people knew this day how far away they are from this place</u>! So many of them claim it and preach it and rejoice in the hope of it, and that shall never do, because they have never donned the very armor of the Lord, the apparel of the Holy Ghost, the baptism with its magnitude and its glories and its personal powers. They have not donned this very white robe. They have not been altogether spotless. [Ephesians 5:27]

But not so with you, and not so with others – <u>if</u> you shall hear My voice this day. You shall now begin to show forth the white-robed ministry: white, pure as Heaven itself, unspotted. [Ibid] Do not condescend to flesh. Do not contemplate in those dimensions, but be in the Spirit.

Note: For more on being "without spot" read Chapter 7, pages 35-44.

A Commentary[33]
By Pastor Ron Auch

Finally the question can be settled once and for all concerning the Rapture of the Church. I will share with you the revelation God gave me regarding this issue.

Since the time Jesus left the earth, there have been different views as to when the Rapture was going to take place. You can find someone that subscribes to your view, whether it is

Pre-Trib, Mid-Trib, Post-Trib, or even "Pan-Trib." The Pan-Trib theory is that of not claiming to know anything other than in the end it will all pan out. There are those who do not believe in a Rapture at all, and those who believe in multiple Raptures.

Now the question can finally be settled. It's as simple as this: No matter which theory you hold to, it doesn't matter, because **the Church in America is going to miss it** – no matter when it happens!

Who are we kidding! We can't even fool the world anymore. They look at us with their worldly eyes and know we are no different than they are.

We have lost a knowledge of the Holy; we can't discern the difference between the holy and the profane. When we go to church, we aren't sure if we should sing a hymn, or rap, or rock and roll. Our "prophets" are so fearful of losing their offerings, they won't deal with the sin in the Church. We are in a big mess, and to top it all off, we can't [even] call the church to prayer! She is not interested in spiritual things and yet foolishly believes she is ready for the return of Jesus Christ!

We read about the parable of the ten virgins [Matthew 25] and think that the five foolish ones must be someone else. We don't even have the basic characteristic of a bride in waiting: a <u>longing</u> for the groom. The next time you hear a prophecy "expert" tell you about when the Rapture is going to happen, will you have to say, "It isn't going to happen for me; I belong to the Church that is rich and in need of nothing." [See Revelation 3:17a]

Disease in the Church[34]

My Church is being destroyed from within. And My people within the Church are being eaten alive, as it were, by a disease called sin. This disease is the result of spiritual harlotry, spiritual adultery. I have stood many times in My Church next to My beloved ones and have pleaded with them to come, to come away with Me to the secret place, to come home to Me, to come to be loved and cherished by Me, to come to be directed and corrected and comforted and married to Me; but they have refused. They have smiled; they have patted Me on the shoulder, as it were, kissed Me on the cheek, said, "I love You" and have gone off to do their own thing. They have gone off to their other loves – their other loves!

As a result of their sin and waywardness, the Church is sick – sick and dying. It is dying from within, from the very inward parts of the Church. My people are dying because the heart is diseased and the heart is broken. The heart is actually cut in two and divided; and **I have so small a portion of the heart of My Church at this time.** For the Church is enamored with her other loves. My people seek them, they follow them, they delight in them; and they hear not My call. They hardly hear Me anymore, calling and calling, calling them to come, to come away.

And it is the time, it is the time to come away. It's the time of the singing of the birds. [Song of Solomon 2:12] It's a time of love, the time of love as the Bride prepares.

On the one hand, there are those who are hearing My call and responding to My call of love, responding to the cleansing process that is taking place for the preparation of the Bride. They are responding. But on the other hand, the Church [at large] and My people [most of them] are **not** hearing the call! The call seems too harsh. The call seems too hard. The call seems too demanding. Surely, surely, they think, **they need to be comforted in all of their grievances and all of their hurts; and all of their appetites need to be fed**... and they are not responding to My call at this time.

But I continue to call. I continue to woo My Church. I continue to call them. I want to heal them. I want to make them perfectly whole. But they are not hearing. They are off in a frenzy of activities. And a flurry of gaiety surrounds them as they whirl and they twirl, as it were, as they dance to another song, another tune; and they hear not My call. They hear not the song of their Lover. They hear not His call. It has been covered over because of the loudness and the blasting of the other things that are calling out to them.

Oh, oh, I call, I call, and I call. I want My Bride prepared. I want those whom I have called and chosen, to come to Me. But they have chosen another way, and it is the path of destruction. **It is the path of death!** But they heed not My call. They heed it not! And My fire which is even now burning out the dross in My Bride, burning out those things that are not right, **will soon be turned in <u>wrath</u> and <u>fury</u> and <u>anger</u> on those who have not heeded My call.** [God is calling them to be cleansed – to get ready for the Rapture.] But they have defiled themselves and have become a part of the world and the world system. [They will miss the Rapture and be here when the Wrath of God is poured out!]

I, the Lord your God, call in love and in mercy. Come, come to Me. Come and be purified, so that I can call you and look upon you as My undefiled one.

The Prophecy that you just read, and the one that begins on page 134, and the Scripture verses that follow, all describe some of the things that are coming soon in the Great Tribulation. Are you prepared for them?

"**And at that time** [during the Great Tribulation] **many will fall away and will deliver up one another and hate one another. And because lawlessness is increased, MOST PEOPLE'S LOVE WILL GROW COLD. And brother will deliver up brother to death** [Christian against Christian], **and a father his child; and children will rise up against parents and cause them to be put to death.** [Mathew 24:10 and 12; 10:21] **But the one who endures to the end, he shall be saved.**" [Matthew 24:13] (NAS)

Question: What you just read will take place during the Great Tribulation. But are you ready for a period of time that is much worse than that – like the outpouring of God's Wrath?

All things considered, wouldn't it be better to be the Bride and make the Rapture, rather than miss it and have to go through the Wrath of God?

Keep pressing in to be that Bride!

Chapter 11

What God Has to Say About Pastors Who Shy Away from End-Time Teachings:

A Word for Pastors[35]

Where are My Jeremiahs? Where are My faithful servants whom I have called forth to serve My people in humility? Where are My prophets whom I have called to sound the trumpet to warn the people in the hour of destruction? Where are My watchmen on the walls? Why will ye not sound the trumpet when you see the enemy approaching? [See Ezekiel 33:6-9]

Has the spirit of slumber fallen upon you? Have you made a covenant of silence with those who refuse to warn My people, lest you lose their respect and honor? Whose honor do you seek? Is it the honor of a fallen race? Or is it the honor of the Saints of all Ages who were faithful – who spoke truth, who warned of sin and judgment to come, who died as martyrs.

Are you afraid of dying for Me? Are you afraid of being accused of madness and error by those whose vain respect you have gained? You say, "I will not be an alarmist. I will not frighten the people. It will cause panic if I speak the truth. Some will

116

get angry. I will lose My congregation! I will lose My pulpit! I will lose My salary."

I say unto you: What is a pulpit? It is nothing but a piece of furniture if the man behind it does not preach My present-day truth — even the message that the Holy Spirit wants him to give for this day and this hour.

What is a congregation? It is only a gathering of people who are unprepared and inefficient in an hour of crisis, if the true Word has not been preached to them. It is even a blind people who will not know which way to go when the End-Time crises come upon them suddenly.

What is a church building? It is only a house of back-sliders who play at religion if they are not warned to repent, forsake their sins, and flee from the Wrath to come!

What is a pastor? Is he a true shepherd of My flock? Or is he a hireling? [John 10:12-13] He must be faithful to warn My sheep and to correct them and to punish them with strong words of warning. He must lay the rod of My Word across their stubborn necks; for My people will go astray as long as you permit them to do so.

There is sin in My Church — gross sin! They bring into My house the earnings of their sin — even the hire of a harlot. [See Micah 1:7] And My pastors accept it and are glad for it. The hour of sorrows has come. [See Matthew 24:8] It is even the hour of My Wrath! But My pastors refuse to warn My people. There is a spirit of compromise upon them.

They promise mercy to those who deserve no mercy.

"For if we sin willfully after that we have received the knowl-edge of the truth, there remaineth no more sacrifice for sins, but a certain fearful looking for of judgment and fiery indig-nation, which shall devour the adversaries. He that despised Moses' law died without mercy ...Of how much sorer punish-ment, suppose ye, shall he be thought worthy who hath trodden underfoot the Son of God and hath counted the Blood of the covenant—wherewith he was sanctified—an unholy thing, and hath done despite unto Spirit of grace? For we know Him that hath said, Vengeance belongeth unto Me; I will recompense, saith the Lord. And again, The Lord shall judge His people." (Hebrews 10:26-30) (KJ)

The pastors preach a message of "unsanctified mercy." They promise peace when there is rioting and death on their streets. They promise peace when the enemy bombs their trade cen-ters [1993], and their homes are full of fighting. They promise blessing when their homes and places of business are col-lapsing in earthquakes, and fires are raging in their suburbs and destroying their homes, and their farms are inundated with the floods of many waters. [1993 was the worst flooding up to that time.]

The rivers overflow because the heavens weep. The fires are lit by madmen whose souls have not found the true Prince of Peace. There is no peace! And there will be no peace as long as there is no peace for the unborn baby who lies in the womb of his mother. All who promise peace, blessing, and prosperity speak a lie!

IT IS A TIME TO WEEP! Call out the mourning women and let them make haste and take up a wailing for us that our eyes may run down with tears and our eyelids gush out with waters. Let the voice of wailing be heard out of Zion, for we are ravaged; we are greatly ashamed of the sin in the land. [See **Jeremiah 9:17-25**]

Hear the mothers weeping for their young sons shot dead in the streets of our cities. Hear them weeping and angry for their little daughters who are pregnant. Hear the forsaken wives who have been left desolate by their unfaithful husbands and lovers, men controlled by demons of lust.

Go to your morgues and count the bodies of your teenagers who have died of drugs. Then count the dollars of the abortionists; see their summer homes, their yachts, their condominiums. See the palaces that gambling has purchased with money "stolen" from foolish people who are controlled by greed and the spirit of chance. See the corruption in government – the misuse of money, of power, and of words (by false promises) – and know the end of all this is come up before Me.

I will not be mocked any longer! I will not allow them to challenge Me any longer! I will not allow them to defy Me to My face any longer! I will show this world one more time – like I did in the days of Noah – that I am God! And nothing will be the same anymore. It will not be "business as usual."

I am, even now, marking those who sigh and cry for the abomination that is done in the midst of My people. And the slaughter weapon is even now in the hands of the destroying angels! [See Ezekiel 9:1-11]

Warn your people, My pastors. For if you refuse to sound the warning, their blood – even the blood of the aborted babies, the blood of the drug addicts, the blood of those who will die of euthanasia, the blood of the suicide victims, the blood of the children who are shot to death on your streets, and the blood of all those who die and will continue to die

**in the coming calamities – will ALL be upon your hands!
[See Ezekiel 3:16-21]**[Bold emphasis by the Author]

[End of Prophecy]

———

The section on pages 51-53 was so important – for anyone who wants to be the Bride – that it is being repeated here on the next three pages: 120-122.

———

Question: I Want to be The Bride
How Can I Know if I "Qualify"?
Answer: **The Hundredfold Will Go:**

Mark 4:20: "And these are the ones sown on good ground, those who hear the Word, accept it, and bear fruit: some thirtyfold, some sixty, and some a hundred."

Romans 12:2: "And do not be conformed to this world, but be transformed by the renewing of your mind, that you may prove what is that good [sixtyfold] and acceptable [thirtyfold] and perfect will [one hundredfold] of God."

1st Corinthians 15:40-42a: "There are also celestial bodies and terrestrial bodies; but the glory of the celestial is one, and the glory of the terrestrial is another. There is one glory of the sun [one hundredfold], another glory of the moon [sixtyfold], and another glory of the stars [thirtyfold]; for one star differs from another star in glory. So also is the resurrection of the dead."

The glory of the sun describes someone who has a hundredfold walk with the Lord. That person would be the Bride of Christ; the sixty and the thirtyfold would **not** be. The Bride is totally filled with Jesus – completely dead to self and matters of the flesh; whereas the others are not.

The glory of the moon is the sixtyfold walk, and the glory of the stars, the thirtyfold walk. Even the stars differ from one another in glory. They can be anywhere from thirtyfold up to sixtyfold. It all depends on how much of Jesus they have in them and how much of their own flesh is there. If they have 30% Jesus and 70% flesh, then they are thirtyfold – star glory. But if they've been growing spiritually and are not baby Christians anymore, they might have 60% Jesus and 40% flesh. Then they are sixtyfold – moon glory. However, if they go all the way and have 100% Jesus and 0% flesh, they are **one hundredfold** – *sun glory!* This is the Bride of Christ.

This one – the hundredfold Christian – will go in the Rapture; the thirty and sixtyfold Christian will not.

They will be **left behind**. However, the thirty and sixtyfold Christian *will* make Heaven. "Marthas" are not the Bride, but they do make Heaven. "Marys" are the Bride, and they make Heaven too, but with a hundredfold reward! And as the Bride they also make the Rapture. They are special – in the Lord. They are the Bride of Jesus Christ.

The Place of Independent Life[10]

A Vision of Those Who Miss the Hundredfold
"Today He [the Lord] spoke to me concerning those elect ones – His chosen instruments that He shall perfect and purify to bring

forth the high manifestation of Himself in that great wave of glory and light that He has already spoken of.

"For many months He had poured out His grace and blessing upon certain people; but in spite of that, they still had not come to the place of independent life – the place of having life in themselves [the life of God, the strong presence of the Lord.] Because of this, they had been *rejected* from being numbered among those chosen instruments that God is preparing in this hour. He said they would not be rejected, not cut off from being His people [they would still make Heaven], and would be taken along their own plane and level of spiritual growth; but they had been rejected from being those choice and elect instruments through whom God will manifest Himself."

(From the book "Visions of the Eternal," Dr. R.E. Miller editor. A compilation of Visions received by Annie Schisler.)

The one who would become the Bride of Christ (1) will prepare her heart; (2) will purify herself; and (3) will make herself perfect in Him. She will then be ready for the Rapture. Read more about these three points on the next page and the one that follows.

1. How Do I Prepare My Heart?
2. How Do I Purify Myself?
3. How Do I Become Perfect?

(1) **1st John 1:7 and 9**: "But if we walk in the light as He is in the light, we have fellowship with one another, and the Blood of Jesus Christ His Son cleanses us from all sin." How? This way: **"If we confess our sins, He is faithful and just to forgive us our sins and to cleanse us from all unrighteousness."**

If we're not confessing our sins at all, or if we're only doing it occasionally, then confessing them on a regular basis will get us started on the cleansing process.

(2) **1st John 3:3**: "And everyone who has this hope in Him purifies himself, just as He is pure."

As we engage ourselves in this process of purification, we are getting closer to reaching the goal mentioned earlier in **Philippians 3:14**: "I press toward the goal for the prize of the upward call of God in Christ Jesus."

(3) And the closer we get to the goal, the closer we get to being counted worthy in Christ. This in turn will allow us to stand before Jesus in the Day of the Lord. **Luke 21:36** says it this way: "Watch therefore and pray always that you may be counted worthy to escape [via the Rapture] all these things that will come to pass [the Wrath of God], and to stand before the Son of Man."

The individual who *seriously* walks out these three Steps and does whatever is necessary *to* walk them out, will be the Bride of Christ, and therefore **will be ready to meet the Lord in the air when the Rapture takes place.**

Chapter 12

What Events Will Occur at the Time of The Rapture?

A dramatic series of events – unparalleled in the history of the world – will take place. It starts with **Matthew 24, verse 29** which tells us: "Immediately after the Tribulation of those days **the sun will be darkened and the moon will not give its light; the stars will fall from heaven**..." In other words, all the natural light in the sky all over the world will be **EXTINGUISHED** at the same moment in time!

Joel 2:31 describes this day also: "Then the sun will be turned into darkness and the moon into blood, before the coming of the great and terrible Day of the Lord."

Revelation 6:12 and 13a state it this way: "And I looked when he opened the sixth seal, and behold, there was a great earthquake; and **the sun became black as sackcloth of hair, and the moon became like blood. And the stars of heaven fell to the earth**,"

Then, going back to **Matthew 24** – in **verse 26**, in response to those who say He is in the desert or at some other location – **verse 27** says: "For as the lightning comes from the east and flashes to the west, so also will the coming of the Son of Man be."

Luke 17:24 describes it this way: "For as the lightning that flashes out of one part under heaven shines to the other part under heaven, so also the Son of Man will be in His day."

This type of lightning does not strike the earth, but flashes from one part of the sky to the other. We have all seen this kind. In the same manner, *without touching the earth*, the Lord will move from one part of a darkened heaven to another part. He will appear in blazing glory in a sky that just moments before was completely and totally pitch black. The Lord Jesus will be like a **MASSIVE BOLT OF LIGHTNING** that travels around the globe in a split second, lighting up the whole world in the process!!!

"And behold, the glory of the God of Israel came from the way of the East. His voice was like the sound of many waters; and **the Earth shone with His glory**." (**Ezekiel 43:2**)

"And then the sign of the Son of Man will appear in heaven, and then all the tribes of the earth will mourn, and they will see the Son of Man coming on the clouds of heaven with power and great glory." (**Matthew 24:30**)

Verse 31 is the **RAPTURE** itself, with the Lord sending out His angels, and "they will gather together His elect from the four winds, from one end of heaven to the other." (**Matthew 24:31**) This triggers or initiates yet another world-wide mega-event – **THE WRATH OF GOD!**

The Rapture and the Wrath of God happen at the same time – almost. The Rapture occurs first, and this triggers the Wrath of God. As the Bride is being taken up in the clouds from earth to her home in Heaven, the Wrath of God then explodes upon the earth with the first of the Seven Bowl Judgments. This is then followed by the remaining six in quick succession. These two events together – the Rapture and the Wrath of God – are called "The Day of the Lord." (The Day of the Lord will officially **conclude** the time of Satan's dominion on the earth which began at the fall of Adam!)

This is described in **verses 37-39 of Matthew 24**: "But as the days of Noah were, so also will the coming of the Son of Man be. For as in the days before the flood, they were eating and drinking, marrying and giving in marriage, until the day that Noah entered into the ark [for his "Rapture"], and [the people] did not know until the flood came [the Wrath of God] and took them all away, so also will the coming of the Son of Man be." [When He comes to Rapture His Bride.] "They were eating, drinking, etc." here would include Gentiles and all Christians who are sleeping, lukewarm, backslidden, or cold; and foolish virgins, who do not have enough oil in their vessels to keep their lamps from going out. [Matthew 25:8] They will all **be left behind** in this period known as the Wrath of God! There will be much weeping, wailing, and gnashing of teeth in this time of intense spiritual darkness and fierce judgment from the hand of Almighty God!

It is a time that no one would want to be here for, but **only the Bride will have the privilege of being absent from it.** As you know by now, she will exit this planet at just the right time, even the right moment, because the pouring out of the Wrath of God will just be getting underway. The next four scriptural references refer to this time of Wrath. The Rapture is not specifically mentioned in those references; nevertheless they are prophesying of a time to come when the Day of the Lord will take place. And, as discussed earlier, the Day of the Lord – by definition – is the Rapture followed immediately by the Wrath of God.

The Rapture is something that will take place in our day. In that sense it is a New Testament "event." It isn't actually mentioned in the Old Testament – although there are several types and shadows, some of which are pointed out in this book.

Either the Wrath of God is stated outright in each reference or the Day of the Lord is. If the Day of the Lord is stated, this would necessarily include the Wrath of God because, as just spelled out two paragraphs earlier, it's one component of, or one part of, the Day of the Lord by definition. The other component is the Rapture. And it's understood that the Rapture will take place first, just before God's Wrath is poured out.

1. **Isaiah 2:12 and 19**: "For <u>the Day of the Lord</u> of Hosts shall come upon everything proud and lofty, upon everything lifted up, and it shall be brought low. They [the people] shall go into the holes of the rocks and into the caves of the earth, from the terror of the Lord [God's Wrath] and the glory of His majesty [the Rapture] when He arises to <u>shake the earth</u> mightily [with the Wrath of God]." Notice the similarity between these two verses in Isaiah to Revelation 6:14-17. (It begins in the middle of page 130.)

2. **Isaiah 13:6 and 9-10 and 13**: "Wail, for <u>the Day of the Lord</u> is at hand! It will come as destruction from the Almighty. Behold, the Day of the Lord comes, cruel, with both Wrath and fierce anger, to lay the land desolate; and He will destroy its sinners from it. **For the <u>stars</u> of heaven and their constellations will not give their light; the <u>sun</u> will be darkened in its going forth, and the <u>moon</u> will not cause its light to shine**. Therefore I will <u>shake</u> the heavens, and the earth will move out of her place [orbit], in the Wrath of the Lord of hosts, and in the day of His fierce anger."

3. **Joel 2:30-31**: "And I will show wonders in the <u>heavens</u> and in the earth; blood and fire and pillars, before the coming of the great and terrible <u>Day of the Lord</u>." **3:14-15**: "... For the Day of the Lord is near in the valley of decision. The <u>sun</u> and the <u>moon</u> will grow dark, and the <u>stars</u> will diminish their brightness."

4. **2nd Peter 3:10**: "But <u>the Day of the Lord</u> [The Rapture followed by the Wrath of God] will come as a thief in the night [for those who are not prepared], in which the <u>heavens</u> will pass away with a great noise and the elements will melt with fervent heat; both the earth and the works that are in it will be burned up." [During God's Wrath]

Revelation 6:12-13: "And I looked when he opened the sixth seal, and behold, there was a great <u>earthquake</u>; and **the <u>sun</u> became black as sackcloth of hair, and the <u>moon</u> became like blood**. And the <u>stars</u> of heaven fell to the earth, as a fig tree drops its late figs when it is shaken by a mighty wind."

If you compare these two verses with verse 29 in Matthew 24, you can see similarities. We already know from earlier sections in this book, that Matthew 24:29-31 is a Rapture passage, and it is as much a Rapture passage as 1st Thessalonians 4:13-17 is. And we know that **verse 29** in **Matthew 24** is talking about the physical appearance of the sun and the moon, and how they will look just before Jesus returns in the air for His elect: "Immediately after the Tribulation of those days **the <u>sun</u> will be darkened and the <u>moon</u> will not give its light**; the <u>stars</u> will fall from heaven, and the powers of the <u>heavens</u> will be shaken." (**Matthew 24:<u>29</u>**)

That's the tip-off. Any time in Scripture you see the sun and the moon radically changing their appearance and stars falling from heaven, know that this is referring to or talking about one thing – the Day of the Lord. And that Day, by scriptural definition, necessarily consists of the Rapture followed by the Wrath of God. In Revelation 6:14-17 the Wrath of God (Wrath of the Lamb) is mentioned, <u>implying that the Rapture just took place</u>. Which in fact <u>it just did</u> – **in verses 12 and 13!** "And I looked when he opened the sixth seal, and behold, there was a great earthquake; and **the sun became black as sackcloth of hair, and the moon became like blood. And the stars of heaven fell to the earth**, as a fig tree drops its late figs when it is shaken by a mighty wind." (**Revelation 6:12-13**)

These two verses are very much like Matthew 24:29, which is the first verse of a three verse Rapture passage:

Matthew 24:29-31: (**29**) "Immediately after the Tribulation of those days **the sun will be darkened and the moon will not give its light; the stars will fall from heaven,** and the powers of the heavens will be shaken. (**30**) And then the sign of the Son of Man will appear in heaven, and then all the tribes of the earth will mourn, and they will see the Son of Man coming on the clouds of heaven with power and great glory. (**31**) And He will send His angels with a great sound of a trumpet, and they will gather together [Rapture] His elect [the Bride] from the four winds, from one end of heaven to the other."

Revelation chapter 6, verses 12 and 13

Three arguments that support the discussion on this page

(1) Read Matthew 24, verses 29-31. Notice that verse 29 mentions several unusual events in the heavens. Then just two verses later, in verse 31, the Rapture takes place.

Also notice that in Revelation 6, verses 12-13, the same unusual events are taking place in the heavens in those two verses! Now since Matthew 24:29-31 is a Rapture passage, then it is understood by the context that verses 12-13 is in, that the Rapture is taking place in those verses as well.

(2) Because verses 12 and 13 in Revelation 6 are very much like verse 29 of Matthew 24, and because just two verses later in verse 31 the Rapture takes place, then the Rapture also takes place in verses 12-13 of Revelation chapter 6.

(3) As mentioned on the previous page, the Rapture is followed by the Wrath of God:

Revelation 6:14-17: "And the sky receded as a scroll when it is rolled together, and every mountain and island was moved out of its place. And the kings of the earth, the great men, the rich men, the commanders, the mighty men, every slave and every free man, hid themselves in the caves and in the rocks of the mountains, and said to the mountains and rocks, 'Fall on us and hide us from the face of Him who sits on the throne and from the Wrath of the Lamb! For the great day of His Wrath has come and who is able to stand?' "

Clearly, 14-17 is about the Wrath of the Lamb, which *is* the Wrath of God. And since the Wrath of God is always preceded by the Rapture, **that means that in verses 12-13 the Rapture just took place,** although it is not explicitly described there as it is in Matthew 24, verse 31. (See page 129.) After the Rapture what event takes place next? As you should know by now, it is the Wrath of God, which was just described in the Revelation 6:14-17 passage.

Summary of Revelation Chapter 6

What we have in the 24th chapter of Matthew with its 51 verses, we also see in Revelation chapter 6 with its 17 verses. But Revelation 6 is much more condensed. First, in verses 1-6 we have the first half of the seven year Tribulation period – the Time of Sorrows. It consists of the first Three Seals: Seal 1 is deception in the name of Christ and it starts with false peace (verse 2). Seal 2 is a time of war which covers the whole earth (verse 4). Seal 3 is a time of scarcity, and this includes world-wide food shortages (verses 5+6). This is followed by the Fourth Seal – verses 7 and 8 – a time in which famine, pestilence, and death wipe out over a fourth of the world's population. This seal includes first the revelation of the Antichrist, followed by his rise, which includes his persecution of the Saints.

All of this, according to Daniel 9:27a, will happen in the middle of the seven year Tribulation. Many Christians will lose their lives at this time – become Martyrs – and this moves us into the Fifth Seal of verses 9-11. This seal marks the end of the 3 1/2 year Time of Sorrows and the beginning of the 3 1/2 year Great Tribulation (minus the time God cuts it short).

While that's going on, we move into the Sixth Seal in verses 12-17 which begins in 12 and 13 with the darkening of the sun and the moon, and the falling of the stars from heaven to earth. We know from other passages in Scripture, some cited on pages 127-129, that these are the astronomical signs that accompany the Rapture and signal that it is taking place.

So in Revelation chapter 6 the Rapture is *understood* to have taken place in verses 12 and 13; and it is then quickly followed by the Wrath of God in verses 14-17. (The wrath of the Lamb is mentioned in verse 16.) That suddenly stops the Antichrist and his forces and puts an end to their persecution and martyrdom of the Saints. These forces and their chief are then immediately subjected to an unimaginable load of severe, escalating judgments from the fierce hand of Almighty God. (Read Revelation 16:1-21) But before that can take place, the Great Tribulation (verses 9-11) is brought to an abrupt halt when it is cut short by the Rapture (verses 12-13). (The Time of Sorrows, (verses 1-6), the first 3½ years, had already ended when the Great Tribulation began.) Then Revelation 16:1-21, the Wrath of God, gets underway.

(Caution: Read the following paragraph slowly and carefully.) Therefore, the Rapture takes place, quite significantly, **after all the events** of the entire seven year Tribulation (verses 1-11) have run their course; and this, obviously, would include those of the Great Tribulation as well. The Great Tribulation, which is 3 1/2 years long, is the last half of that seven year period, but it's cut short by the Rapture in verses 12-13. And right after that, in verses 14-17, God immediately begins to pour out His Wrath.

So again, **the Rapture is Post-Great Trib and Pre-Wrath.**

(Or Post Most-of-the-Seven-Year Trib but Pre-Wrath.)

This Discussion of the Chronology of End-Time Events confirms Arguments #1 (p. 77-82) and #4 (p. 91-94) which state that the Rapture is Post-Great Trib and Pre-Wrath of God.

Again, Scripture confirms Scripture!

———

Note: **The Bride will not depart *until everything* in the seven year Tribulation Period has been fulfilled. Then the Rapture will take place. The Bride will then be taken out, and the Wrath of God will commence.**

Or to put it another way, the Bride escapes nothing that takes place in the seven year Tribulation period. She will be here while all the events are being played out. She will be gone during the time of the Wrath of God, but <u>the Bride will be here for everything else</u>!

(For a condensed summary of the preceding six Arguments, go to page 139.)

Chapter 13

Preface to the Prophecy
that Follows

"**And at that time** [during the Great Tribulation] **many will fall
away and will deliver up one another and hate one another.
And because lawlessness is increased, MOST PEOPLE'S
LOVE WILL GROW COLD. And brother will deliver up
brother to death** [Christian against Christian], **and a father
his child; and children will rise up against parents and
cause them to be put to death.** [Mathew 24:10 and 12; 10:21]
But the one who endures to the end, he shall be saved."
[Matthew 24:13] (NAS)

Soon There Will be a
Great Falling Away³⁶

My children, hear your heavenly Father this day. Soon and
very soon things will change all around you. Yes, darkness is
coming, just as I have warned in My Word. But I do not speak
of this darkness today. Today, I speak of the moving of My
Spirit upon My people.

Soon you will witness outpourings of My Spirit in the most
unlikely places. I will visit My people with My Spirit so that I
may raise up My Last-Day Church. As I have said in My Word,

I am seeking a habitation. And I SHALL inhabit a people in these last days. [Psalm 132:13-14]

Get ready, My children, for soon I will visit with all those that are earnestly seeking Me with all of their heart. I do not speak of those that seek Me merely for what I may do for them, but I speak of those who earnestly desire their heavenly Father. For I am wooing the Bride of My Son to awaken to her destiny. And she shall learn to fast and seek holiness, as I have desired. And she shall make herself ready as she is refined in the midst of the furnace of affliction. [Isaiah 48:10; Revelation 19:7]

Oh, My little ones, do not shrink back from this. For have I not advised you in My Word to buy from Me gold refined in the fire, that you may be clothed in white garments and therefore cover the shame of your nakedness? [Revelation 3:18] So then, My Bride shall be adorned in MY righteousness through this refining and purification. I do not speak of the righteousness that the false teachers speak of; I speak of true holiness and the nature of My Son dwelling within My people.

Now listen to Me this day. **Soon there will be a great falling away.** [2nd Thessalonians 2:3] And many, I say MANY will be offended at Me. Yes, they will desire Me, but they will not be willing to go through the fires of purification in order to obtain the true holiness and righteousness that I require. They will slander and persecute My true ones in their **jealous rage.** For they will witness [see] My love for those who are truly Mine, and it shall stir up a jealousy within them.

Do not contend with these ones, but yet pray for them that they may hunger and thirst for true righteousness. For ONLY with a love for My truth shall one be found seeking true righteousness and holiness in these last days. For I tell you, even now there are many lies and false teachings about My holiness and righteousness. And the lies will only continue to get worse in the days ahead. Many will claim to be righteous and holy while walking in gross sin and darkness.

Therefore, hunger and thirst for true righteousness, and you shall be filled. [Matthew 5:6] For I am now beginning to pour out My Spirit in these Last Days in unprecedented ways. [Acts 2:17-20] And My children, whom I call My own, shall be cleansed and purified. And I shall make these into My habitation in the earth realm [Psalm 132:13-14], for all to witness My glory dwelling within man, the way I have meant it from the beginning.

I love you all with an everlasting love. [Jeremiah 31:3] Now seek Me earnestly with a hunger and thirst for TRUE righteousness, and you SHALL be filled. [Matthew 5:6]

Revelation 19:7: "Let us rejoice and be glad and give glory to Him, for the marriage of the Lamb has come and His Bride has made herself ready."

Hidden Sins and Motives of the Hearts Shall be Exposed[37]

Soon there will be chaos after chaos in the media and on the streets. Do not be shaken when you see these things. Have I not warned of these things to come? Have I not said in My Word that I shall shake everything that can be shaken? [Hebrews 12:27]

Oh yes, many of you know of the tragedies soon to come upon the land. And many of you think that you are prepared.

Well I come to you all this day to declare unto you that many of My children are NOT prepared as well as they may think.

Yes, I shall protect My own, provided that each one walks in My ways and heeds My voice. But I must say unto you all this day that many believe they are covered by the Blood of My Son by their mere pretense of walking in obedience.

I say unto you, one is not obedient unto Me by their religious activities. Nor is one obedient unto Me by their pretense of holiness.

Do you all not know that it is I who discerns and weighs the thoughts and intents of the heart? [Hebrews 4:12-13] Then know that I see ALL things, even those hidden agendas in which many of My children believe to be hidden from all.

I shall expose all agendas and motives of the hearts in these last days. Therefore, I say to you all, repent of your secret sins and hidden selfish motives. For I am full of mercy and compassion upon those with a truly contrite heart.

But for those who think they can continue in sin; they shall be cast out of the camp (the Body of Christ) in these last days. For no longer shall I suffer those who choose to hold onto their sin and [their] secret agendas.

My church shall be spotless and without blemish in these last days and shall declare My will, and My will ONLY, to a broken and dying world.

Oh, My little ones, I do not come to you all this day to be harsh. But I come to you all as a loving father who loves his precious children.

It is the hour in which all that is hidden shall be exposed. Therefore, this is why I must come to you each with a stern warning to repent. For in My mercy, it is not My desire to expose My children of their sins. However, in My holiness, I must cleanse My house.

Therefore, seek Me with all diligence that you may find mercy. And so that I may reveal to each of you your deepest secret motives. For many of My children are self-deceived into believing that all their motives are pure in My sight. But I tell you now, this is not so.

And so, each of you needs My light to shine in the deepest recesses of your hearts that I may reveal to you what is hidden even from your own selves!

I love you all with a deep and everlasting love. Therefore, I say to you all: Seek Me in this, and I shall reveal to you what is hidden in your heart that you may repent and be set free from it once and for all.

Matthew 10:26: "Therefore do not fear them, for there is nothing covered that will not be revealed, and hidden that will not be known." (NAS)

James 3:14: "But if you have bitter jealousy and selfish ambition in your heart, do not be arrogant and so lie against the truth." (NAS)

Matthew 22:11-13: "But when the king came in to look over the dinner guests, he saw there a man not dressed in wedding clothes, and he said to him, 'Friend, how did you get in here without wedding clothes?' And he was speechless. Then the king said to the servants, 'Bind him hand and foot, and cast him into outer darkness; in that place there will be weeping and gnashing of teeth.' " (NAS)

Numbers 5:2: "Command the sons of Israel that they send away from the camp every leper and everyone having a discharge and everyone who is unclean because of a dead person." (NAS)

A Condensed Step-by-Step Summary of The Events that Take Place at The End of the Age

There are six major Biblical events that will take place at the conclusion of this Age, and they will happen in the following order: (1) **The Tribulation** – a seven year period with much deception, false peace, war, scarcity, famine, pestilence, and death. In the middle of that period (2) **the Antichrist will be revealed**. This will contribute to a falling away from the Christian faith (which will already be underway) and will cause it to increase to (3) the **Great Falling Away of many Christians**, some of whom will persecute the Saints.* Next, the Cry of the Martyrs in the Fifth seal marks the beginning of (4) **the Great Tribulation** – the wrath of Satan. At a certain point God will cut this period short with (5) **the Rapture**, followed immediately by (6) **the Wrath of God**. (These last two events together are known as "The Day of the Lord.")

---

*Footnote: There's a falling away going on right now, with some persecution of the Saints taking place. This will lead into **the Great Falling Away** when the Antichrist is revealed, with much persecution of the Saints. Some of it will come from other Christians and some from former Christians who have departed from the Faith.

During the Tribulation

"**And at that time** [during the Great Tribulation] **many will fall away and will deliver up one another and hate one another. And because lawlessness is increased, MOST PEOPLE'S LOVE WILL GROW COLD. And brother will deliver up brother to death** [Christian against Christian], **and a father his child; and children will rise up against parents and cause them to be put to death.** [Mathew 24:10 and 12; 10:21] **But the one who endures to the end, he shall be saved.**" [Matthew 24:13] (NAS)

A Summary of the Summary

1. The seven year Tribulation Period.
2. The Revealing of the Antichrist +
3. The Great Falling Away = the half-way point of the seven year Tribulation.
   This is followed by the Cry of the Martyrs which =
4. the beginning of the Great Tribulation.
5. **The Rapture** cuts the Great Tribulation short.
   This is followed immediately by
6. **The Wrath of God.**
   (5. The Rapture + 6. The Wrath of God =
   The Day of the Lord)

Chapter 14

How Long is the Wrath of God?

Isaiah 34:8: "For it is the Day of the Lord's vengeance, the year of recompense for the cause of Zion." According to this verse in Isaiah, the Day of the Lord – which consists of the Rapture followed by the Seven Bowl Judgments of God (The Wrath of God) – is one year long. Since the Rapture takes place in the "twinkling of an eye," that means that there is essentially a one year period during which the Wrath of God is completely poured out – all seven Vials, according to this verse in Isaiah. But since we do not have a confirming Scripture, this can be left as an open question. But this we do know: According to **Matthew 24:21** it will be a time "such has not been since the beginning of the world, no, nor ever shall be."

Those who miss the Rapture will find themselves in a period when unimaginable destruction is falling upon the whole world. Perhaps it's one year long; perhaps it isn't. We don't have a Scripture that confirms Isaiah 34:8, so we cannot know for sure. But the best thing is to avoid this intense period of God's Wrath altogether. Then we won't find ourselves in the situation where we will have the dubious "opportunity" to check out the length of it.

Better yet – let's keep pressing in to make that Bridal Company. Then we won't have to face the utter horror of being here during the Seven Bowl Judgments of God.

A Word for Those Who Want a Rapture Bail-Out:

There are those who want the Rapture to happen – the sooner the better, so they can escape the hard times that are coming – the Tribulation and the Wrath of God! They want to avoid both! But they have little understanding of End-Time events, and they're not prepared for the Rapture. What does Scripture say about them?:

Amos 5:18: "Woe to you who desire the Day of the Lord! For what good is the Day of the Lord to you? It will be darkness [Wrath] and not light [if you miss the Rapture]." For those who desire this Day because life here on earth is too hard and too difficult and you want to be in Heaven where you can enjoy a trouble-free life: Unless you are paying the price to be the Bride of Christ now and you are that Bride here on earth now, you will not be a partaker of the blessing of escape when the Day of the Lord arrives. That day for you will be "darkness and not light." It will be judgment and not Heaven! "Woe to you!"

What Happens if We Willfully Disobey the Word of God?

No matter what life is like now for a Believer, no matter how hard and difficult it may be, if we willfully disobey the Word of God, we are putting ourselves in a very dangerous situation. Consider the following Scripture verses:

2nd Thessalonians 1, verses 7b-9 warn us: (7b) "when the Lord Jesus is revealed from Heaven with His mighty angels, **(8)** in flaming fire taking vengeance on those who do not know God [sinners, unbelievers], and on those who do not obey the Gospel of our Lord Jesus Christ [that would include an unknown number of Christians and former Christians]. (9) These will be punished with everlasting destruction from the presence of the Lord and from the glory of His power."

This latter group in verse 8 would include someone who was a Christian at one time but who currently is knowingly and will-fully disobeying the Word of God. Then according to verse 9, they "will be punished with everlasting destruction!" Everlasting means eternal – *eternal destruction!* What place does that sound like?

Therefore, before these events begin to take place, it would be wise to take this passage in 2nd Thessalonians seriously; and also be aware of the following admonition in **Luke 21:34-36**: "But take heed to yourselves, lest your hearts be weighed down with carousing, drunkenness [on the things of this world], and [the] cares of this life; and that Day [the Wrath of God] come upon you unexpectedly.For it will come as a snare on all those who dwell on the face of the whole earth. Watch therefore and pray always that you may be counted worthy to escape [via the Rapture] all these things that will come to pass, and to stand before the Son of Man."

Right now in this day and hour we still have a choice. But we need to make the right one while there's still time; because **soon time will be no more.**

Chapter 15

More on Preparing to Be the Bride

The words from the Lord and the Scriptures on the following pages will further help us to prepare.

A Warning to Refill Our Vessels with Oil[38]

Even as it was in the days of Elijah, yea, even in the past Ages, many of the sons of the prophets knew and foreknew that Elijah would be translated – [yet] they did not see him when he went away. [2nd Kings 2:16-17] And behold, even now in the sadness of such a time as this, that in these Ages – even in this very hour, in the time element of God's calendar – there have been many who have known about the coming of the Lord and <u>have looked forward to beholding Him</u>, <u>who would be standing afar off</u>. They would not be permitted to enter into that Bridal Party where all the prophets who have been since the world began were joined in the grand reunion. And even where John the Baptist will stand beside the Bridegroom, even Jesus, that he might declare himself that that is his joy to be beside the Bridegroom. *"He that heareth the Bridegroom's voice will rejoice; and that is my joy,"* says John. [from John 3:29]

Now therefore come, My people, and enter your closets and hide yourselves, as it were, for a little moment until the indignation be overpast [Isaiah 26:20], for I am calling for intercessors now to come in and to fill up this Age which is swiftly passing and will go faster than ever before. And the lightning shall come forth, yea, that He will send upon His intercessors who have waited for Him and who have cleansed themselves from all filthiness of the flesh and the spirit, perfecting holiness in the fear of God [2nd Corinthians 7:1]; for the hour is coming and will soon be past for people to cleanse themselves. And then shall come to pass that great and terrible pronunciation, yea, that [it] will be said to them: *He that is holy, let him be holy still; he that is righteous, let him be righteous still; he that is filthy, let him be filthy still.* [Revelation 22:11] And so it will be that time will be no more.

So prepare thyselves against these great days of doom and degradation. Behold the Bride in the 45th Psalm, and take the admonition from Him to her as the queen in gold of Ophir, that she shall hear the voice of her Beloved. She will forget her own people and her father's house to follow Him who is leading her to the King's palace. And she shall be arrayed in raiment of needlework, and she shall have attendants, even virgins, according to Matthew the 25th Chapter.

But lo, there will be one-half of the virgin company who will not have oil in their lamps. [verse 8] Yea, there will be many turned out into darkness, weeping and knocking on the door of Heaven who won't have oil. They did not have enough of a supply; they did not have that extra, continual flow of oil. [Ibid] It is high time to accept this as a challenge and an index finger pointing to you, My children, to be prepared against that day of the doom of [those] five virgins. [verses 11-12]

Oh beware, saith the Lord, and become humble before Me and refill your lamps. Yea, refill with the Spirit of the Lord, as I have admonished by the apostle to arise and await and fill your lamps. Yea, and trim them and be prepared for the trumpet sound [at the Rapture – Matthew 24:31; 1st Corinthians 15:52; 1st Thessalonians 4:16.]

Much confusion is in the air today. Many of My people who are lukewarm are sluggish, and they are not comprehending and discriminating into things that pertain to the inheritance of the Saints in light. For the Age that thou art now living in hath been the late Age, the late Age of light. Thou hast been duly warned to refill your vessels with oil.

I SHALL have a Bride who is Spotless and without Blemish[39]

In my time with the Lord, He said these words to me:

Son, tell my people to pray...

Word from the Lord:

My children, listen to what I would say to you this day. I have great things in store for many of you. Although, I have this to say: You MUST let go of your <u>OWN</u> preconceived notions of Me and My ways <u>WHICH YOU HAVE ESTABLISHED IN YOUR HEARTS. You must make sure that what you believe truly lines up with My Word</u>, for I shall do a new thing in the earth, of which, if I were to tell you of it, you would not believe it except by revelation of My Spirit.

However, I do tell you this; many have believed on Me for My rewards, healings, promises, etc. Yet, I tell you this day that it is My desire that you also believe on Me to make you sinless and perfect just as your heavenly Father is perfect. Can you trust Me to do this work in you?

Oh, I know that for many of you this is hard to accept. Though have I not given you this promise in My Word? So then, lay down your preconceived notions that full Salvation unto sinless perfection is impossible. I tell you the truth: To only those who do not believe shall this be impossible. **For I SHALL have a Bride who is spotless and without blemish.**

Oh, no longer believe the false teachers and prophets who say that My Bride shall be spotless and without blemish merely because of My Blood covering her sin. For even though I am full of mercy and My Blood DOES cleanse all repented and forgiven sin, this alone does not make My Bride sinless and perfect. For as I have promised in My Word, I shall remove your heart of stone and give you a heart of flesh, and this heart of flesh shall be one with Me. And in this, you shall be holy as I am holy.

Oh, My little ones, do not shrink back from this Word. For just as those who believed not that they could conquer the giants in their promised land, so you too shall not enter into these great promises of Mine if you believe not that you can conquer the giants within your own promised land.

Therefore, I say to you all this day, Stretch forth your faith and receive of Me. Receive My precious promises and seek them as the pearl of great price. For it SHALL be a great price to accomplish this perfection. And that price shall be all that is dear to your self-life including the self-will. But know this: Those who lose their lives for My sake and the sake of My Gospel shall find this abundant life in Me for all eternity. But whoever would seek to save their life, shall lose it.

I love you all, My dear ones. So then, seek Me in this that I may reveal My truths to your hearts and give you each a vision and hope to overcome and live the perfect abundant life with Me in My Kingdom. For truly I say to you: Nothing shall be taken away from those who live this abundant life. But for those of the world, all shall be lost.

I love you all, so heed these words of Mine and seek Me in this. Truly, you shall not be disappointed.

The Bride of Christ

John 3:29a: "He who has the Bride is the Bridegroom; but the friend of the Bridegroom, who stands and hears him, rejoices greatly because of the Bridegroom's voice."

Revelation 19:7: "Let us be glad and rejoice and give Him glory, for the marriage of the Lamb has come, and His wife has made herself ready."

Ephesians 5:31-32: "For this reason a man shall leave his father and mother, and be joined to his wife; and the two shall become one flesh. This is a great mystery, but I speak concerning Christ and the Church."

This mystery in Ephesians is explained in the following verse from **2nd Corinthians 11:2b**: "For I have betrothed you to one Husband that I may present you as a chaste virgin to Christ."

Song of Solomon 8:5a: "Who is this coming up from the wilderness, leaning upon her beloved?"

Song of Solomon 6:8-9: "There are sixty queens and eighty concubines and virgins without number. My dove, <u>My perfect</u>

one, is the only one, the only one of her mother, the favorite of the one who bore her. The daughters saw her and called her blessed, the queens and the concubines, and they praised her."

In verse 8 there are "virgins without number." [In Psalm 45:14 these same virgins follow her into the King's palace.] But only one dove and she is perfect. In **verse 10**: "Who is she who looks forth as the morning? Fair as the moon, clear as the sun, awesome as an army with banners?" Does that not sound like the Bride? Read the Prophecy that starts on page 165 and see what God has to say about this dove in the third paragraph.

Esther 2:17: "The king loved Esther more than all the other women, and she obtained grace and favor in his sight more than all the virgins; so he set the royal crown upon her head and made her queen instead of Vashti."

Psalm 45:9-11: "Kings' daughters are among Your honorable women; at Your right hand stands the queen in gold from Ophir. Listen, O daughter, consider and incline your ear: Forget your own people also and your father's house; so the King will greatly desire your beauty; because He is your Lord, worship Him."

Matthew 25:1-12: "Then the Kingdom of Heaven shall be likened to ten virgins who took their lamps and went out to meet the bridegroom. And five of them were wise, and five were foolish. Those who were foolish took their lamps and took no oil with them, but the wise took oil in their vessels with their lamps. But while the bridegroom tarried, they all slumbered and slept. And at midnight there was a cry made: 'Behold, the bridegroom is coming; go out to meet him!' Then all those virgins arose and trimmed their lamps. And the foolish said to the wise, 'Give us some oil, for our lamps are going out.' But the wise answered, saying 'No, lest there not be enough for us and you; but go rather to those who sell, and buy for yourselves.' And while they went to buy, the Bridegroom [Jesus] came, and <u>those who were ready</u> went in with him to the wedding; and the door was shut. Afterward the other virgins came also, saying, 'Lord, Lord, open to us!' But he answered and said, 'Assuredly I say to you, I do not know you.' "

Psalm 45:13-15: "The King's daughter is *all glorious within* [KJ]; her clothing is woven with gold. She shall be brought to the King in robes of many colors; the virgins, her companions who <u>follow her</u>, shall be brought to You. With gladness and rejoicing they shall be brought; they shall enter the King's palace."

There are many virgins, even wise ones, but only one Bride. The Bride stands next to the Groom and is brought into the King's house. All the other virgins, her companions, **follow her** with gladness and rejoicing. According to verse 9 of chapter 6 of Song of Solomon there are countless virgins but only **one** Bride!

Let us pray that we would be that one; and let us also pray that we would diligently prepare ourselves to be the Bride of Christ – then we'll be "all glorious within" like the King's daughter in Psalm 45.

We also want to be like the one that Jesus was describing in **Luke 11:36**: "If then your whole body is full of light, having no dark part, <u>the whole body will be full of light</u>, as when the bright shining of a lamp gives you light."

This sounds a little like the Lord Himself when He was on the Mount of Transfiguration as recorded in **Matthew 17:2**: "and He was transfigured before them. His face <u>shone like the sun,</u>

and His clothes became as white as the light." Let that be something for us to aim for!

Someone who lived and walked in a rarified spiritual atmosphere, "a man who knew God as few men do," was Smith Wigglesworth. He's an example for us to follow. Read the following account about him from a book by George Stormont:

A Man Who Walked with God[40]

Standing on Holy Ground

"Wigglesworth was the purest man I have ever known, a man who lived daily in the immediate presence of God.

"At one time Wigglesworth was ministering at Zion City in Illinois, founded by John Alexander Dowie. There he called the ministers to a special prayer meeting and was already praying when they arrived. As he continued in prayer, sometimes in English and sometimes in tongues, the awesome presence of God filled the room.

"One by one, the ministers were smitten by the power of God and fell prostrate on their faces. The reality of God's presence so gripped them that they were unable to move for at least an hour. Wigglesworth was the only one who remained standing as he continued in praise and prayer. A cloud, like a radiant mist, filled the room where the ministers were.

"In 1922, Wigglesworth was in Wellington, the capitol city of New Zealand. One afternoon at a special meeting, eleven prominent Christians gathered for prayer at Wigglesworth's request. One after the other they prayed, until all had taken part except the visiting evangelist [Wigglesworth]. He then began to pray for their city and country, and as he continued, the sense of God's presence and power so filled the room that one by one the others left, unable to continue in the blazing light of God's holiness.

"One minister, hearing of this from one who had been there, greatly desired to be in a similar meeting – but with the determination that whoever else left, he would not. An opportunity soon came for him to attend such a meeting. Several people prayed, then Wigglesworth began to pray.

"As he lifted up his voice, it seemed like God Himself had invaded the place. Those present became deeply conscious that they were on holy ground. The power of God in its purity was like a heavy weight pressing on them. One by one, the people left, until only the man remained who had set himself to stay.

"He hung on and hung on until at last the pressure became a compulsion, and he could stay no longer. His own testimony was that, with the floodgates of his soul pouring out a stream of tears and with uncontrollable sobbing, he had to get out of the Presence or die! He added that Wigglesworth, a man who knew God as few men do, was left alone in an atmosphere in which few men could breathe."

It is said of Smith Wigglesworth that he spent all of his waking hours either in active prayer or in the Word, and when he wasn't doing that, he would just wait on the Lord silently. He would stop only if he had the opportunity to minster to someone or if he could talk to them about prayer and the Word.

"Smith Wigglesworth was without a doubt one of the most anointed men of God that has lived in recent times. He was known as the Apostle of Faith, and if anyone deserved to be described as "full of faith and the Holy Ghost," it was him. He lived and walked continuously in the presence of God. And the miracles that accompanied his ministry were of the sort that have seldom been seen since the days of the apostles. People born blind and deaf, cripples twisted and deformed by disease, others on death's door with cancer or sickness of every kind – all were healed by the mighty power of God! Even the dead were raised!"

[The preceding material came from: "Great Healing Evangelists – How God's Power Came," by Andrew Strom.]

––––––––

Revelation 21:9b, 10, and 2: "Come! I will show you the <u>Bride</u>, the Lamb's <u>wife</u>. And he carried me away in the Spirit to a great and high mountain, and showed me the great city, the holy Jerusalem, descending out of Heaven from God. And I, John, saw the holy city, New Jerusalem, coming down from God out of Heaven, prepared as <u>a Bride adorned for her Husband</u>."

When we have done everything we've been exhorted to do, then we, as that Bride, *will* be adorned – properly attired – for our Husband, the Lamb of God.

Woe to the Dilatory Servant[41]

But there will come this thing, the signs of the times. And My dilatory servant, who will not prepare and will eat with the glutton and the drunken and say the Lord has delayed His coming, they will all be given a portion with the hypocrites. As you know, this is My Word [Matthew 24:48-51]; now speak it to everyone that they must prepare for Me. They must don their wedding robes – the white robes of redemption, of justification, of sanctification, and, yea, of glorification *in its entirety*. [See Romans 8:30] And when this is all finished and My chosen ones have fully prepared themselves, I the Lord will break through and I will come [to catch away the Bride]. Now therefore wait for Me; **but wait not to prepare them to receive Me in the day that I shall come**, saith the Lord.

God's People to
Stir out of Their Sluggishness[42]

And will I not do more for this generation than I did for Sodom and Gomorrah – if thou will turn to Me and seek Me in the faith of Abraham, Isaac, and Jacob; the apostles of the Lord Jesus Christ; Paul, the apostle that was born out of due time; all of My leaders and multitudes of My people who are not only on the earth but in the heavens [Heaven], that are seated there in the City of the Great King. Yea, they are there as spectators watching the scenes of Earth, watching the Saints – whether they will be faithful, whether they will be able to overcome the Antichrist that is coming against them. If they are not ready to come out of this, **then they are going to suffer martyrdom!** [The best way to avoid martyrdom altogether is to be the Bride of Christ and thus overcome the Antichrist.]

Listen to My word again. Yea, listen to it. Every Bible student, every teacher of every Bible school, let the Word of the Spirit come and quicken you to reach out and receive it. Let Me send forth in thy way, for I am the Lord thy God. I am He that fainteth not.

Therefore, My servants, My bachelors, My maidens, yea, all of My mothers, and all of the people all over this earth, hear this word: Arise from where you are and do not be so consumed with the things of the world. Be in one accord – all together – because I enjoy days of pleasure for you to fellowship and to glorify. And I want you to know that I'm standing in the fire of the Upper Room. [See Acts 2:1-3] **I'm ready to pour the lightning out upon you with My Latter Rain accompanying.** If you are not ready, I will send it to the heathen. I will send it across the seas. I will send it everywhere. You have the first chance today. But if there is not a great and mighty quickening, then <u>you will not be ready</u> when I shall come in the clouds with glory, in the twinkling of an eye, to **catch away** My beloved [at the Rapture]. [1st Thessalonians 4:17; 1st Corinthians 15:51-52]

O hear Me, hear Me, My children. Awake even now, for it is time for you to awake and receive this mighty power of the Lord your God.

Wonders Will Come Forth[43]

Like a glow of a summer sunset, so will the Lord come forth with His wonders. He will bring wonders at the very darkest hours of mankind. He will bring forth a re-creation, a transformation, and a transportation.

But first there must be a transformation in the life of the person that will be translated [that includes being raptured]. This is the thing that is most important, saith thy God. Become transformed day after day, transformed by the renewing of thy mind – renewing why and how and what with the Word of God, the Word that teacheth all these wonders, all of this inheritance of thine. [Romans 12:2]

I will, therefore, have you cleanse yourselves from all filthiness of the flesh and spirit, and perfect holiness in the fear of

God. [2nd Corinthians 7:1] And in the fear of God have your conversation holy and righteous. [2nd Peter 3:11]

A Place for Preparation[44]

There is a spiritual dimension which I have come to order and to ordain, that you might know this, that you might eat of the fruits of paradise in the Spirit, saith the Lord. There is a paradise spiritual and a paradise literal, and it will bring My people into a place to prepare them for the translation of the Saints [that includes the Rapture]; yea, to come up to the realm of the unknown and the Lord, **where they will see the Angels and the Archangels and saints of old**; and there will be no sorrow, no weeping, no pain, no crying. For I the Lord God will wipe away all tears from their eyes. [Revelation 21:4] Yea, I will bring My people up. I have brought up a very few, but I will bring *all* the congregation – **as many as will be dedicated and sanctified to the Master's use.**

Prepare for
The Soon Coming of the Lord[45]

Remember the ten virgins who went out to meet the Bridegroom, and five were wise and five were foolish. [Matthew 25:1-13] The wise had burning lamps. The foolish had burning lamps, but the foolish took no oil in their vessels with their lamps, and their lamps went out on the way. They cried to the wise ones, who took extra vessels of oil – a custom in those days because the journey was too long and the lamp was small and contained only a small measure of oil. And so it was that the wise stored away the oil, as I want you to do.

I want you not to be satisfied with a status quo and have a mere single infilling, but get closer to God. Remember that in Ephesians the Lord is speaking to you about elevation, being lifted up. He said to be filled with the Spirit; be not drunk with wine wherein is excess, but be filled with the Spirit. [5:18] And did He not also command that you sing psalms and spiritual songs? [verse 19] What did He mean by spiritual songs? He meant to **sing in other languages** as the glory of the Lord is come down. [1st Corinthians 14:15b]

It is the time of the singing of birds, and My dove Bride is making herself ready now to receive Me when I call. [Song of Solomon 2:12] But alas, the foolish ones, who have not kept their lamps burning and their oil replenished, shall go out into the darkness where there is weeping and wailing and gnashing of teeth.... [when the Wrath of God is poured out]. [Matthew 25:30; 24:51]

Therefore, beware and prepare, for the coming of the Lord draweth nigh, and no man knoweth the day nor the hour, neither the angels in Heaven. [But we can know the times and the seasons: 1st Thessalonians 5:1 and 4.] But the Father God is the One who knows, and the command of our Lord Jesus was to watch and pray. [Matthew 26:41; Mark 13:33; Luke 21:36]

The four watches were set for certain events in that time. He spoke of coming at any time, even if it meant the fourth watch. The Lord has been delayed by the neglect of His people to pray and to prepare for His return. [2nd Peter 3:11-12] But now they are coming up and seeking the glory of the Lord. They are crying out to Me and preparing themselves for the last lap of the journey.

So rejoice with Me, O children of God. Rejoice with one another, O people of the Lord, even the people of the Lord of

Abraham. Whether thou be Jew or Gentile, yea, whether thou be bond or free, whether in prison or out of prison, these words will find lodging in your heart; and you shall <u>prepare from this day forward to receive My glory</u>, <u>which shall come any moment that you open your heart to Me</u>.

For behold, I stand at the door and knock, and if any man hear My voice and will open the door, I will come in to him and sup with him and he shall sup with Me. [Revelation 3:20] You shall not be like the person, even the lover of the Song of Solomon, who would not get up in the night to open to her beloved. She said, "I have washed my feet, I've removed my shoes, I've taken off my robe, I am in bed, I am comfortable, I'm well satisfied." But the lover kept knocking and knocking. Soon he disappeared, and when she arose she could not find him. The only thing left was the fragrance of his presence. [Song of Solomon 5:5]

Those Filled with the Oil of the Spirit Will Produce This Glory[46]

Now, before this glory can fully appear, the high priesthood of the Lord Jesus must be completed in Heaven, and simultaneously, the priesthood of His Saints upon the earth, as recorded in the first chapter of Revelation when John cried out that He hath redeemed us, washed us in His Blood, and made us kings and priests unto our God [now]. [verse 6] This is the heritage of the people of the Lord <u>who qualify</u>, who will keep their lamps trimmed and burning and filled with the oil of the Spirit that will produce this glory.

And there as you see in the **25th chapter of Matthew** where the virgins [are] – even the ten virgins who were the accompaniment of the Bride of Christ – five of these were wise and five were foolish. The foolish ones did not have the supply of oil. [verse 3] And this is an admonition and a warning to all of My people now to keep your lamps trimmed and burning. [verses 7-9] But keep a supply – even an extra supply of oil [verse 4] – that at any moment you can be like John, who was immediately in the Spirit when he was called from the upper regions; you can immediately enter into the glory of the Lord. [Revelation 4:1-2]

And just that way will come the Lord for His people to rapture His Church,* and you must be prepared to immediately be translated [raptured]...

*Note: The Lord will come to rapture those in the Church who are ready for Him – the Bride. The rest of the Church will be left behind. Read the prophecy on page 161 – Christ, the Ark of Safety.[49] Notice that the first sentence of the last paragraph says "the Rapture of the <u>Bride</u>." NOT the Rapture of the Church. Most of the Church is not ready for the Rapture. Only the Bride is.

Maria Woodworth-Etter[47]

An Example to Encourage Us

She wrote in her autobiography that before she was called into the ministry "The great desire of my heart was to work for Jesus. I longed to win a star for the Savior's crown. Sometimes when the Spirit of God was striving and calling so plainly, I would yield and say, 'Yes, Lord, I will go.' The glory of God came upon me like a cloud, and I seemed to be carried away hundreds of miles and set down in a field of wheat, where the sheaves were falling all around me. I was filled with zeal and power, and I felt as if I could stand before the whole world and plead with dying sinners. It seemed to me that I must leave all and go at once."

But then Satan came in like a flood and discouraged her. She writes, "I asked God to qualify me for the work. I asked Him to qualify me."

[She continues:] "I want the reader to understand that at this time I had a good experience, a pure heart, was full of the love of God, but was not qualified for God's work. I knew that I was but a worm. God would have to take a worm to thresh a mountain. Then I asked God to give me the power that He gave the Galilean fisherman – to anoint me for service. I came like a child asking for bread. I looked for it. God did not disappoint me. The power of the Holy Ghost came down like a cloud. It was **brighter than the sun!** I was covered and wrapped in it. I was baptized with the Holy Ghost and fire and power, which has never left me. There was *liquid fire*, and angels were all around me in fire and glory."

"It has been recorded that Maria Woodworth-Etter had one of the most powerful ministries and anointings – with astounding healings, miracles, and wonders – that has ever been documented in the history of the Church. Reports state that she would come into a town after sleeping in a tent, and within days there would be approximately 20,000 people in her meetings! At times, God would give people working in the fields in a **fifty mile** radius around her meetings *visions of Heaven and Hell,* and they would fall to the ground under tremendous conviction! It was like a "blanket anointing" would come down upon the whole area. [At other times] it [was] reported that <u>for whole blocks around her meetings, people would be falling to the ground and repenting</u>."

[The preceding material came from: "Great Healing Evangelists – How God's Power Came," by Andrew Strom.]

Christ, the Ark of Safety[48]

Now therefore be quick to hear Him and to obey that which He speaketh unto thee, and He will manifest Himself unto thee in ways that thou knowest not. He will appear to thee in the lonely hours, in dreams in the night. When troubled waters come, He will make Himself known as the great Ark of Safety, yea, the Ark of Prayer, and the Ark of Praise. He will make Himself known to you as the Ark of Refuge that Noah had, and as the Ark of Communion that Moses, Joshua, and others even today have had.

See that ark where the mercy seat was set upon it, and the cherubim (one at either end of the ark), and the Lord who promised, saying, *"I will commune with you from above the mercy seat."* (Exodus 25:22) He will meet you there. For all this is a type of Christ, in His death and burial, and in His resurrection glory. And even as it was manifested in the rod of Aaron to bring forth a dry stick, even into the great truth of the resurrection – and quickened – that word is yours today.

You can live in that quickening so much that when the Rapture of the Bride comes, you will be ready. There will not be any time to prepare at that quickening sound! And this is come to give you a warning of the time to prepare for the greatest event this world has ever seen.

God's Message
to the Church at Ephesus[49]

Throughout the past 6,000 years the Lord hath worked fervently among His people to bring to perfection those whom He had called in each Age. Remember ye not that He has spoken to you of His returning, that He would come in a moment, in a twinkling of an eye, at the last trump? [1st Corinthians 15:52] The trumpet would sound and the Lord Himself would descend with a shout, with the voice of the archangel, and He would come to **rapture** – quicken – to *catch away* <u>those who are prepared to meet Him</u>. [1st Thessalonians 4:16-17]

Transfiguration of My People
Should Come More Abundantly[50]

Oh, that ye would see this and prepare for it and take heed to all that I have spoken in this message [and in all the prophecies before this], even now. And yea, that ye should be ready to be translated [raptured] out of the world into the glory of the Ages and with the triumphant Church* with her Lord and Saviour Jesus Christ throughout eternal Ages, saith the Lord.

*Footnote: The part of the Church that is actually "triumphant" is the **Bride –** <u>not</u> the Church at large. It's asleep.

———

Ephesians 2:6: "and [God] has raised us up together and made us sit together in the heavenly places in Christ Jesus,"

Colossians 3:1-4: "If then you were raised with Christ, seek those things which are above, where Christ is sitting at the right hand of God. Set your mind on things above, not on things on the earth. For you died, and your life is hidden with Christ in God. When Christ who is our life appears, then you also will appear with Him in glory." [At the Rapture.]

God Will Soon Forsake Many, So Be Prepared for the Rapture[51]

Move in Me, and I will take you over the cliffs. I will take you over the mountains. I will take you up from the brush heaps and out of the sand piles. I will take you from the debris of human ingenuity and theologies that I have spoken to you about, that have become corrupt. It has become false psychology, false science. It has become so false that I have left it, saith the Lord.

Now I am getting ready to leave many churches. I am getting ready to depart from many homes. I will not send My angels into homes where I will not send My Blood. I will not send My Blood upon the household where they grieve Me and tempt Me with this stumbling block of **television**, where they center their minds on and view those obscene scenes and look upon them and let their children do so. I will remove My Blood, saith the Lord! I will remove My angel, saith the Lord, and thy prayers cannot stop Me then. Thy prayers cannot change Me then.

So thou hadst better pray now that thou also be changed to the fullest degree and be prepared for the **Rapture**.

[Don't be like those who have the stumbling block of television and trouble the Lord with it – so much so that He has removed His Blood and His angel from their homes, and He will not hear their prayers or change His mind on the matter.]

The following two prophecies were used earlier, in Chapter 10, and are being repeated here because the warnings in them

163

are so important that the Bride-in-the-making needs to read them again.

A Warning to Those
Not Ready for the Rapture[31]

Now is the time to tell My people to prepare to escape this thing [the Wrath of God]. Did I not say to My children **"to pray always that you may be counted worthy to escape** [via the Rapture] **all these things** [the Wrath of God] **and to stand before the Son of Man?"** [Luke 21:36]

O fear not to declare it. Yea, by all My ministries declare that My coming is at hand and that the five foolish virgins will not go into the Marriage Supper. But there will be weeping and wailing and outer darkness and gnashing of teeth [Matthew 24:51; 25:30] when the Great Wedding is on, when it is spread out, when it is in full sway. Then shall the King see that a guest has come that has not on the wedding garment. This is the parable that I spoke through My servant Matthew [chapter 22:11-14] and others about this great consternation, that some will come right up to the hour of the Rapture and right up to the hour of being caught away, and because they have indulged in foolishness, and in jesting and joking, and television filth – yea, **television** scenes corrupted by Hollywood and satanic forces – even these will not go with Me [in the Rapture].* And I have foretold it.

Yea, I have prepared this escape, and that is by the great moving of the Rapture, and that will come suddenly [to those who are not prepared]. No man knoweth the day nor the hour. [1st Thessalonians 5:2-3]

*Note: This Word from the Lord was given over 40 years ago when television was somewhat innocent and had fairly high standards. Swearing was not even permitted. Imagine what God thinks of TV today!

Many Have Missed This Calling[32]

Send out this truth, that I am the Word that in the beginning was with God and became flesh. Yea, I became flesh, and now I am glorified, that <u>My people shall go through the same process I went through</u>, figuratively; and they shall come into My presence as they follow Me to the cross and they are identified with Me in My crucifixion, in My burial, and in My resurrection, of the means of baptism and the glorious outpouring of the Spirit.

I will know you after the flesh; for that is why I came in the flesh – to know you after the flesh. I took not on the nature of the angels, but I took on the seed of Abraham that I might destroy the works of him that had the power of death; that is, the devil. [Hebrews 2:14] But I also came that I might yield to you and you yield to Me. I have yielded Myself to you in blessing and glory. I have not submitted Myself to your dominion, but I have yielded My Word. Yea, your spirit ravished My heart. [Song of Solomon 4:9] Your spirits have come and called upon Me and rejoiced, and it is not [only] just as [a] bride and [a] bridegroom, for I am also preparing to receive <u>My</u> Bride to Me [when the Rapture occurs].

And this Bride must be separated to Me wholly, undefiled. Yea, My love, My dove, <u>My only one</u>. [6:9a] Who shall be greater than the Bride? Is she not the one that looketh forth in the morning; yea, that is as fair as the moon, and as clear as <u>the sun</u>, and <u>as terrible [awesome] as an army</u> with banners? [See Song of Solomon 6:9a and 10] That is the one that shall ride with Me on white horses! [Revelation 19:14]

165

O that My people knew this day how far away they are from this place! So many of them claim it and preach it and rejoice in the hope of it, and that shall never do, because they have never donned the very armor of the Lord, the apparel of the Holy Ghost, the baptism with its magnitude and its glories and its personal powers. They have not donned this very white robe. They have not been altogether spotless. [Ephesians 5:27]

But not so with you, and not so with others – if you shall hear My voice this day. You shall now begin to show forth the white-robed ministry; white, pure as Heaven itself, unspotted [Ibid]. Do not condescend to flesh. Do not contemplate in those dimensions, but be in the Spirit.

[Note: For more on being "without spot" read Chapter 7, pages 35-43.]

A Warning
Concerning the Five Foolish Virgins[52]

Yea, tell My people about Chapter 25 of Matthew... The five wise ones had burning lights because they kept the Word of the Lord in them, because they depended upon the principles of righteousness and the Word of God.

And the foolish virgins were doing what many ministers today are doing – relying on past experiences. They feel they only have to come to God and get forgiveness, and they make of it a light thing, as Samson did. But they shall not prosper in such things. Show them very clearly that at the rate they are going, they will NOT be ready to meet the Lord. And that is the **ultimatum**!

Chapter 16

Our Authority in Christ

Philippians 4:13: "I can do all things through Christ who strengthens me."

2nd Corinthians 2:14a: "Now thanks be unto God, which always causes us to triumph in Christ," (KJ)

Romans 8:37: "Yet in all these things we are *more* than conquerors through Him who loved us."

Romans 8:31b: "If God is for us, who can be against us?"

Romans 5:17b: "those who receive abundance of grace and of the gift of righteousness will reign in life through the One, Jesus Christ."

Isaiah 54:17a: "No weapon formed against you shall prosper,"

Colossians 2:9-10: "For in Him [Jesus] dwells all the fullness of the Godhead bodily; and you are complete in Him, who is the head of all principality and power." Jesus is the head of all principalities and powers, and that includes the devil himself, as the following Scripture reference states:

Luke 10:17-20: "And the seventy returned with joy, saying, 'Lord, even the demons are subject to us through Your name.' And He said to them, "I saw Satan fall from heaven like lightening. Behold, I give you authority to trample on serpents and scorpions [demons, evil spirits] and over <u>all</u> the power of the enemy, and nothing shall by any means hurt you. Nevertheless do not rejoice in this, that the spirits are subject to you, but rather rejoice because your names are written in Heaven.' "

And because our names are written in Heaven and we are "complete in Him who is the head of all principality and power" (**Colossians 2:10**), <u>we</u> have all power over the enemy, including Satan himself – as these verses in Luke chapter 10 tell us, and the following four scriptural references unequivocally confirm:

(1) **Revelation 12:11a**: "They overcame him [Satan] by the Blood of the Lamb and by the word of their testimony," Satan and his angels were just kicked out of Heaven and cast down to earth.

(2) **1st John 4:4**: "Ye are of God, little children, and have overcome them, because greater is He that is in you, than he that is in the world." (KJ) From the context of that section, it is understood that "them" refers to those individuals who have the spirit of Antichrist.

(3) **James 4:7**: "Therefore submit to God. Resist the devil and he will flee from you." Do this in our own walk with the Lord first; that is, grow in the area of our own deliverance. Once we've done that, *then* we can help others in the area of deliverance and do even more than that, as the following verses in Mark indicate:

(4) **Mark 16:15-18**: [Jesus speaking]: "These signs will follow those who believe: In My name they will cast out demons;

they will speak with new tongues; they will take up serpents [demons]; and if they drink anything deadly, it shall not hurt them; they will lay hands on the sick, and they will recover."

And, as just mentioned on the previous page, according to **Luke 10:17-20** we have all power and authority in Christ to do this.

(This authority is illustrated in Steps 5 and 6 of "The 7 Step Healing Program" in the book "How to be Healed of Sickness and Disease.")

Philippians 4:13: "I can do all things through Christ who strengthens me."

Ephesians 6:10: "Finally, my brethren, be strong in the Lord and in the power of His might."

Proverbs 28:1b: "...the righteous are bold as a lion."

John 20:23: "If you forgive [remit] the sins of any, they are forgiven them; and if you retain the sins of any, they are retained."

Chapter 17

The Bride

Part 1
Special Dominion of the Bride
Over Her Enemies and Circumstances

Psalm 144:1-2: "BLESSED BE the Lord my strength, which teaches my hands to war and my fingers to fight: my goodness and my fortress, my high tower and my deliverer, my shield and He in whom I trust, who subdueth my people under me." (KJ)

2nd Samuel 22:30: "For by You I can run against a troop; by my God I can leap over a wall."

Daniel 11:32b: "the people who know their God shall be strong and carry out great exploits."

Judges 7:7: "Then the Lord said to Gideon, 'By the three hundred men who lapped I will save you, and deliver the Midianites into your hand. Let all the other people go, every man to his place.' " Over 31,000 men were sent home. God got the job done with just three hundred men against a whole army of Midianites and Amalekites!

Hebrews 11:32b-35a: "For the time would fail me to tell of Gideon and Barak and Samson and Jephthah, also of David and Samuel and the prophets: who through faith subdued kingdoms, worked righteousness, <u>obtained promises</u>, stopped the mouths of lions, quenched the violence of fire, escaped the edge of the sword, out of weakness were made strong, became valiant in battle, turned to flight the armies of the aliens. Women received their dead raised to life again."They all stood on the promises of God and obtained them by faith – exactly what we must do today, if we want to be like these heroes of the faith.

Psalm 149:5-9: "Let the Saints be joyful in glory; let them sing aloud on their beds. Let the high praises of God be in their mouth and a two-edged sword in their hand, to execute vengeance on the nations and punishments on the peoples; to bind their kings with chains and their nobles with fetters of iron; to execute on them the written judgment.This honor have all His Saints. Praise the Lord!"

Song of Solomon 6:8-9: "There are sixty queens and eighty concubines and virgins without number. My dove, <u>My perfect one</u>, <u>is the only one</u>, the only one of her mother, the favorite of the one who bore her. The daughters saw her and called her blessed, the queens and the concubines, and they praised her." Clearly, this is talking about the Bride. **Verse 10**: "Who is she who looks forth as the morning, fair as the moon, clear as the sun, <u>awesome as an army</u> with banners?" Still the Bride, and it doesn't sound like someone who is going to be taken down by anyone – including the Antichrist – does it.

The Book of Esther: Being queen, Esther had protection from the king, so she was able to deliver and spare her people from annihilation. In the king's house Esther was safe from the wrath of the enemies of the Jewish people, and even had authority over them through the king. As bride and queen (co-ruler), Esther was safe in a type of Father's House.

Micah 4:8: "unto thee it shall come, even the first dominion; the Kingdom shall come to the daughter of Jerusalem." (KJ)

Malachi 4:2-3: " 'But to you who fear My name, the Sun of Righteousness shall arise with healing in His wings; and you shall go out and grow fat like stall-fed calves. You shall trample the wicked. For they shall be ashes under the soles of your feet on the day that I do this,' says the Lord of Hosts.'"

Exodus 7:1a: "So the Lord said to Moses: 'See, I have made you as God to Pharaoh,' "

———

Revelation 3:10: "Because you have kept My command to persevere [the Bride], I also will keep you from the hour of trial which shall come upon all the world, to test those who dwell on the earth." According to Revelation 13:8a "all who dwell on the earth will worship him [the beast] whose names have not been written in the Book of Life;" that is, all people who are not truly Born-Again will worship him, and also those who were once true Christians but who fell away from the faith. And because of that, are part of the great falling away of the Last Days. (Refer to 2nd Thessalonians 2:3) **Verse 7b** of Revelation 3 states that "authority was given him over every tribe, tongue, and nation." These are the ones that the beast will have authority over, and they will not be kept from the "hour of trial" to come.

On the other hand, those who "persevere" – the Believer in the church at **Philadelphia** – *will* be kept "from the hour of trial which shall come." Since this particular church represents the Bride, this is the same as saying that the Bride will be kept from the hour of trial which shall come upon the whole world. She will not be controlled by the beast in any way nor come under his authority. And she will not suffer harm from the wrath of the devil, even though he will be enraged with God's people and the bridal remnant in particular. Read on:

"Therefore rejoice, O heavens, and all you who dwell in them! Woe to the inhabitants of the earth and sea! For the devil has come down to you, having great wrath, because he knows that he has only a short time. And the woman was given two wings of a great eagle that she might fly into the wilderness to her place, where she is nourished for a time and times and half a time from the face of the serpent. And the dragon was enraged [full of wrath] with the woman [God's people in the Great Tribulation]." **(Revelation 12:12, 14 and 17a)**

————

But not to worry. We have all the promises listed in this Section, and we close with those mentioned in **Deuteronomy 28:1 and 7 and 10: "the LORD your God will set you high above all the nations of the earth. The Lord will cause your enemies who rise against you to be defeated before your face; they shall come out against you one way and flee before you seven ways.Then all the peoples of the earth shall see that you are called by the name of the Lord, and they shall be afraid of you."**

[Note: The prophecies that begin on pages 219, 221, 223, 225, 226, 231, 235, 237, and 242, and the dreams on 185 and 245, and the vision on 98 have sections in them that describe in detail the dominion and authority that are coming to the Bride very soon. She has a good measure of that dominion and authority already, but that is about to increase *significantly* in the very near future.]

Part 2
Overcomers — The Bride

Revelation 21:7: "He who overcomes shall inherit all things, and I will be his God, and he shall be My son."

Revelation 2:26: "And he who overcomes and keeps My works until the end [here on earth], to him I will give power over the nations" This will also happen in the Millennium, but this power will begin before that, as the Bride-in-the-making becomes the overcomer that God has destined her to be.

Revelation 3:5: "He who overcomes shall be clothed in white garments [like Jesus in verse 4] ...I will confess his name before My Father and before His angels."

Revelation 3:21: "To him who overcomes I will grant to sit with Me on My throne, as I also overcame and sat down with My Father on His throne."

When man's dominion on this earth ends, the 1000 year Millennium will begin, when Jesus and His overcomers will rule and reign with Him for 1000 years. (**Revelation 2:26 and chapter 20: verses 4 and 6**)

Revelation 12:11: "And they overcame him [Satan] by the Blood of the Lamb and by the word of their testimony, and they did not love their lives to the death." "Death" in this verse is referring to death of self and things pertaining to the flesh, areas that the Bride has learned to put under her feet. This is something we can learn too, and when we do, it will be all Jesus and none of us; our flesh will be under *our* feet, and we'll be one of those overcomers that this verse is referring to.

Galatians 2:20 puts it this way: "I have been crucified with Christ; it is no longer I who live, but Christ lives in me; and the life which I now live in the flesh I live by faith in the Son of God, who loved me and gave Himself for me."

Revelation 13:7a: "And it was granted him [the beast] to make war with the Saints and to overcome them." He does not, however, have any power over God's true overcomers. We know from what we just read on the previous page in Revelation chapter 12 verse 11, that the Bride overcomes him! You cannot overcome an overcomer!

Verse 13:7b: "And authority was given him over every tribe, tongue, and nation." The tribes, tongues, and nations mentioned here are the people of the world, over which Satan is king, but it also includes worldly Christians and can include some of those who do not make the Bride. But Satan does not have authority over the Bride of Christ. He has to go through God to harm her. What do you think the chances of that are?

Revelation 7:3: "Do not harm the earth, the sea, or the trees till we have sealed the servants of our God on their foreheads." [For their protection in the Tribulation]

Part 3
Protection for the Bride and Outright Deliverance from Her Enemies:

Jesus passed through the midst of those who were going to kill Him with stones. Peter was led out of prison by an angel. Paul and Silas were set free from prison by a divine earthquake. David was delivered by God from King Saul and many other enemies. Lot was led out of Sodom and Gomorrah by angels. Not one of Joshua's enemies laid a hand on him in all of the battles that he fought with them – in countries which they, Joshua's enemies, had possessed for generations! Three young Hebrew men did not perish, but survived inside of a fiery furnace. Daniel was not harmed by hungry lions during his overnight visit in their den. Gideon overcame two enemy armies, an innumerable host, with just three hundred men!

Jesus escaped death from His enemies three times: "Then they took up stones to throw at Him; but Jesus hid Himself and went out of the temple, going through the midst of them, and so passed by." (**John 8:59**) Similar situations are recorded in Luke 4:28-30 and John 10:39. In like manner we can be protected by the Lord before the Rapture, even if we're surrounded by extreme danger. God can and will protect us – especially if we're part of His bridal remnant.

Psalm 91 sheds additional light on how we can be protected in dangerous situations while still here on earth:

PSALM 91, all 16 verses: "He who dwells in the secret place of the Most High shall abide under the shadow of the Almighty. I will SAY of the Lord, 'He is my refuge and my fortress; My God, in Him I will trust.' [Speak it out!]

"Surely He shall deliver you from the snare of the fowler and from the perilous pestilence. He shall cover you with His feathers, and under His wings you shall take refuge; His truth shall be your shield and buckler. You shall not be afraid of the terror by night, nor of the arrow that flies by day, nor of the pestilence that walks in darkness, nor of the destruction that lays waste at noonday.

"A thousand may fall at your side, and ten thousand at your right hand, but it shall not come near you. Only with your eyes shall you look and see the reward of the wicked.

"Because you have made the Lord, who is my refuge, even the Most High, your habitation, no evil shall befall you, nor shall any plague come near your dwelling; for He shall give His angels charge over you to keep you in all your ways. They shall bear you up in their hands lest you dash your foot against a stone. You shall tread upon the lion and the cobra; the young lion and the serpent [Satan] you shall trample under foot.

"Because he has set his love upon Me, therefore I will deliver him; I will set him on high because he has known My name. He shall call upon Me, and I will answer him; I will be with him in trouble; I will deliver him and honor him. With long life I will satisfy him and show him My salvation."

The Psalm 91 Christian – the one who takes the Psalm seriously – will dwell in the secret place of the Most High. He or she spends so much time drawing close to the Lord and being in His presence that they never leave His side.

The Psalm 91 Christian has made the Lord their habitation. They have moved in with Him!

The Psalm 91 Christian has set their love upon the Lord. It sounds like the kind of love that a bride would have for the groom. It sounds like a bride, because it is *the* Bride! That's why there are so many statements in the Psalm about protection, deliverance, and long life. The Lord protects, and will continue to protect His Bride here on earth as He will no one else.

The 91st Psalm in War[53]

"World War I soldiers of the 91st Brigade agreed to recite the 91st Psalm daily. The 91st Brigade was engaged in three of the bloodiest battles of WW1 – Chateau Thierry, Belle Wood, and the Argonne. While other units similarly engaged had up to 90% casualties, the 91st Brigade did not suffer a single combat-related casualty!" Oh, by the way, a Brigade usually has between 3,200 and 5,000 men!

If God can protect soldiers in combat, many of whom were not Christians, would He not protect His people and keep them from harm, especially someone like the Bride of Christ?

The Bride of Christ

When there is someone as valuable for the advancement of God's Kingdom as the Bride, wouldn't God keep her here on earth for the entire Tribulation so that He can use her to carry out His work? The Bride hears from God freely and does exactly what He wants her to do. But with those who are not the Bride, some measure of the flesh can get in the way and interfere with and compromise the way God's will and plans are carried out. Souls are lost; valuable Kingdom projects are partially completed, abandoned, or even ignored. But with the Bride that doesn't happen. Everything God assigns to her to do, she does – according to His instructions.

Therefore, is it any wonder that Almighty God will NOT let her be martyred or even harmed in any way? When the Great Tribulation is over, and the Bride is no longer needed here on earth to do God's work, He will take her to Heaven in the Rapture, just before His Wrath breaks out.

Think about it.

—Four Prophecies about the Blood—
Apply My Blood![54]

The enemy is always planning to enter – to steal, kill, and destroy. [John 10:10a] He is always plotting. He shoots his arrows and fiery darts to burn and destroy. But if he can enter through the door or windows, he plunders and kills!

KEEP YOUR MIND COVERED WITH THE BLOOD! Apply it. It is your only safeguard against him. Apply My Blood to the areas of the enemy's strongholds. Let the Spirit reveal to you, in your life and in the lives of those you are praying for, where the enemy is robbing, killing, destroying, and paralyzing. Many he has tied up, as it were. They are helpless and are being destroyed!

Cleanse your houses with My Blood. My people perish for lack of knowledge! They know not the power or workings of My Blood.

Overcoming the Enemy[55]

Prepare yourself against enemy attack. Cover yourself, your house, your family, with My Blood. The enemy is always working, preparing, and planning. Be ever on the alert! Be prepared! You overcome him with My Blood and the word of your testimony. [Revelation 12:11a] You defend yourself with:

1. The covering of My Blood.
2. Knowing and speaking what I am and do and have done.
3. Defending yourself with My Word.
4. Soaking yourself in My Word:

Think on It.

Practice It.
Arm yourself with it.
Use It.

If you wait until you feel his hot breath and hear his cries, it will be too late! Casualties and even death will occur to you and yours. Be sure all are in the Ark of Safety. PRAY MUCH IN THE SPIRIT. [1st Corinthians 14:18] How else will you know what to do? How else will you know the plan? I have the plan – the plan of attack. I know his maneuverings and his advancements, for I am all-knowing. I will show you things to come. Otherwise you will be surprised and overcome – time and time again!

It is not enough to only lock your doors against his attack. You must be strong in Me. His fire will burn your house down if you have not planned, prayed, and protected! The enemy has spies, as it were. They will come in and find out your where-abouts and your plans and the lay of the land. Confer only with Me. **Keep secret** those things you possess: the lay of your land.

Remember the Blood is a protection – *a wall of fire around you!* The enemy cannot enter it or touch you in it. Know it also, its power and workings. It is your greatest defense against him. I overcame him with it. Use it, My children, use it! Do not be overcome with his wiles and stratagems. It is so important! My people do not realize or know the importance of it. Study and acquaint yourself with it. Stand in it. It is alive! It speaks!

Get on your horse, My children, and ride. Ride into battle with My Plan. You shall overcome! But you must know My Plan and be prepared. Remember these orders:

1. The Blood
2. The Word

3. The Spirit*

Pray much! Be on the alert, ever prepared, and ye shall not be overcome.

*And 4. The Name (Jesus).

(Note: See page 206 of THE LAST CALL for more on the Blood and the Name.)

The Blessing Is in the Blood[56]

To be blessed by Me is to have the Blood covering on you. This is absolute, divine covering and protection from every kind of evil, seen and unseen... For everything that is Blood-covered is protected. Satan cannot touch anything [or anyone] that is covered with the Blood. **It is as safe as though it were in Heaven!** Put your possessions, your loved ones, and yourself under the divine covering of My precious Blood. Remind Satan that that is where they are. <u>Let him know, together with his evil demonic spirits, again and again that you are under My Blood covering</u>. [See Revelation 12:11a]

The same is true of works done for Me. Those precious souls I have given you are under My Blood covering. All your **works**, your **ministry**, your **buildings**, [your **homes**], your **family**, your **equipment**, all the works of your hand are blessed because they are included under My Blood Covenant [See Hebrews 12:24] – therefore they are under My Blood covering...

The School of the Holy Ghost[57]

Everywhere you go there is demon activity. The forces of evil are everywhere. That is why I instructed you and My disciples to pray, "Lead us not into temptation, but deliver us from evil." [Matthew 6:13a] The Holy Spirit is sent as your Paraclete: One sent alongside to help, to instruct, to teach and to lead you into truth, to lead you in the right ways and paths, and to alert you to danger. [John 16:13] If you will stay in close communion, you will be directly led, warned, and delivered. My Blood and My Name bring the deliverance. **My Word spoken as directed will send the enemy fleeing.** You must be under a constant covering of My Blood! Sometimes you need it as a cleansing – ask for it. Sometimes as protection – ask for it. Sometimes as deliverance – ask for it. Speak it out!

My people are so ignorant of this. They walk around without this covering. They are an open target for the enemy! <u>You hide in My Blood and My Name</u>. It is a covering. You cannot stand without it! You cannot be victorious without it!

BE IN MUCH PRAYER. As you continue to pray, you will, with the Holy Spirit's help and enabling, sense in your spirit and know the whereabouts of the enemy, his lurkings and hiding places. **Keep pleading the Blood!** Cleanse things in the world with My Blood – do not be a partaker of other men's sins. [1st Timothy 5:22b] Ask Me; I will show you. This is warfare! The weak will not stand. The uninformed will perish!

Come to Me daily for strength to stand. Come to Me daily for cleansing. I will use pure vessels for My Kingdom glory. Do as I instruct you to do in all areas of your life. Keep checking with Me. You are in the School of the Holy Ghost! Be sure you do your homework each day. STUDY AND PRAY. Meditate on the things of God, the things you are being taught.

Concluding Comments on The Blood From the Preceding Four Prophecies

(1) Let the Spirit reveal to you, in your life and in the lives of those you are praying for, where the enemy is robbing, killing, destroying, and paralyzing. (2) Remember the Blood is a protection – <u>a wall of fire around you</u>! The enemy cannot enter it or touch you in it. (3) You hide in My Blood and My Name. It is a **covering**. You cannot stand without it! You cannot be victorious without it! (4) Let Satan know, together with his evil demonic spirits, again and again that you are under My Blood covering. For everything that is Blood-covered is protected. Satan cannot touch anything or anyone that is covered with the Blood.

(5) PRAY MUCH IN THE SPIRIT. Cleanse your houses with My Blood. You must be under a constant covering of My Blood! **Keep pleading the Blood!** [End of the section on the Blood.]

The Two Witnesses

Revelation 11, verses 5 and 6 say this about the two witnesses of the Last Days: "And if anyone wants to harm them, fire proceeds out of their mouth and devours their enemies. And if anyone wants to harm them, he must be killed in this manner. These have power to shut heaven so that no rain falls in the days of their prophecy; and they have power over waters to turn them to blood and to strike the earth with all plagues, as often as they desire."

These two verses about the two witnesses in Revelation and what they're going to do, serve as a testimony and an inspiration for the Bride. What these witnesses are going to accomplish for God is an example for her to follow and to imitate right now. And God will use that overcomer-Bride to thwart and cripple Satan's kingdom, yet she herself will not be harmed in any way by the devil or by the beast and the forces that are allied with him against God's people.

When the two witnesses "finish their testimony" (verse 7) for others to behold, the beast will be permitted by God to kill them. But this will not happen to the overcomer-Bride. According to **Revelation 12:11** it will be quite the opposite for her: "And they overcame him [Satan] by the Blood of the Lamb and by the word of their testimony, and they did not love their lives to the death." This is referring to death of self and things pertaining to works of the flesh – that in her walk with the Lord the works of her flesh are quickly disappearing from her life and soon they will be gone! The word of *her* testimony refers to the words that she speaks. The Bride will do these things and be perfected in them; and when the Rapture occurs she'll be taken to Heaven! She will be "taken to," not taken out. She won't even be here on Earth during the Wrath of God. And for the whole time that she is here before the Rapture, she will be *completely* protected by God.

Luke 21:36 explains how to escape this period when God's Wrath is being poured out: "Watch therefore and <u>pray **always** that you may be counted worthy to escape</u> [via the Rapture] <u>all these things</u> that will come to pass [God's Wrath], and to stand before the Son of Man." If we pray in this fashion, it will play a part in helping *us* to be ready for the Rapture, which means we won't be here during the outpouring of God's Wrath. We'll be gone!

Another example: "By faith Enoch was translated so that <u>he did not see death</u>, and was not found because God had translated [raptured] him, for before his translation he had this testimony, that <u>he pleased God</u>." (**Hebrews 11:5**) And it won't be any different for the Bride – she will please God and thereby be translated; that is to say, raptured. She will never see death! In the meantime, right now God has work for her to do here on earth – work that only the Bride is able to do and carry out.

Revelation 3:9: "Indeed, I will make those of the synagogue of Satan, who say they are Jews and are not ...I will make them come and worship before your feet, and to know that I have loved you." The enemies of the Bride will one day come and worship at her feet! We will find out more about this in the very near future.

Two Witnesses Power Revival[58]

I saw a large picture frame on a wall that came to life like a stage-play, with different scenes on it.In the first scene I saw dark foreboding clouds with death and sorrow and pain throughout – a state of panic, war, and misery was in the air. People were walking with their heads down, depressed, and seeming to go to and fro in chaotic fashion, as if looking for something to relieve their pain and confusion. Black-uniformed soldiers were chasing and killing ordinary people without hesitation; they were chasing the Saints too. Death was in many places. People were not burying their dead but leaving them in the streets. It was horrible.

Then appeared [on] the bottom half of [the picture frame] two men dressed in all white – one on each side of the picture frame facing towards the center. Their garments were sparkling with light. They were standing on the left and right side of the picture frame, each holding a pure gold bucket. They then simultaneously started to pour the contents of the bucket into the middle of the picture scene. The liquid that came out was *pure white light*. Once the liquid light hit the Saints on the ground, they were **immediately** transformed! They now had intense boldness and determination in their faces, and their eyes were like flames of fire! They started pointing their fingers and commanding, and the whole scene started to change. The dark clouds started to flee. They would point at the dead bodies in the streets, and the dead would arise. This put the people witnessing this in shock and awe. [The two witnesses] would point and speak, and **people would be healed of diseases, injuries, and other calamities**. People were dropping to their knees and pleading with these Saints.

The Saints would speak to the black-uniformed soldiers, and some of the soldiers would drop dead in masses. Others would flee in utter terror. **Whole armies with advanced weaponry were being stopped and put to flight by these Saints**, as they marched on, not breaking rank.

I awoke screaming and rejoicing. I was so full of awe and joy that my wife had to calm me down. Later on, the Lord would emphasize that fact that there were two men pouring out two buckets of pure white liquid light, and it was a **double-portion.** (Note from David Eells: The pure white liquid light is the river of living water, the Word of God, coming out of the two witnesses to restore the Saints...)

Cities of Refuge[59]

In the coming holocaust, I will again be establishing "cities of refuge," as it were, for the safety of those I know and those who have taken time to know Me. These spiritual Cities will be havens of rest, provision, and safety for My Bride for the season of change before My return [for the Rapture of the Bride]. Unseen walls of protection, holy nourishment, and sweet refreshing will be available to those who have learned to feed on the Source of real life. My Holy Spirit will guide My chosen children to these places in time of need.

Do not limit Me by your carnal understanding as to the nature of what I am saying. Go to My Word: I have confused the enemies of My people that they might escape. [2nd Chronicles 20:23] I have blinded the eyes of aggressors so paths of safety could be seen. [John 8:59] I have opened the eyes of My people to heavenly warriors, that they might see alliances stronger than their foes. [Elisha in 2nd Kings 6:17]

Nothing is too hard for Me. [Jeremiah 32:17b] Safety is not where you are, but who you are with. <u>When you are truly with Me</u>, **NOTHING OR NO ONE** <u>can touch what I call sacred</u>. Come to Me. I am your place of safety, your ever-present City of Refuge forevermore.

Part 4
Only the Bride Goes in the Rapture: A Summary of Types and Examples

The examples used here, and later in **Part 5**, come from Scripture and from prophecies used in this book. All of the prophecies came from the book, "The Last Call." Also included are examples of individuals in the Old Testament (types and shadows) who entered the Promised Land, both spiritually and literally:

NOAH escaped God's Wrath in Genesis 7:1-23 through a type of Rapture – in the Ark, the Ark being a type of Christ. Noah and his family were raised up (the Rapture), just as God began to pour out a flood of destruction (His Wrath) upon the earth.

Psalm 45:9-11, 13-15: "Kings' daughters are among Your honorable women; at Your right hand stands the queen in gold from Ophir. Listen, O daughter, consider and incline your ear: Forget your own people also and your father's house; so the King will greatly desire your beauty; because He is your Lord, worship Him. The KING'S DAUGHTER is *all glorious within* [verse 13, KJ]; her clothing is woven with gold. She shall be brought to the King in robes of many colors; the virgins, her companions who <u>follow her</u>, shall be brought to You. With gladness and rejoicing they shall be brought; they shall enter the King's palace."

There are many virgins, even wise ones, but only one Bride. The Bride stands next to the Groom and is brought into the King's house with the Groom – a type of the Rapture. All the other virgins, her companions, "<u>follow her</u>" with gladness and rejoicing. They do *not* go in to Father's House hand in hand with the Groom. This is supported by chapter six of Song of Solomon which says that there are countless virgins but only <u>one</u> Bride!

Let us pray that we would be that one; and let us also pray that we would diligently prepare ourselves to be the Bride of Christ – then we'll be *"all glorious within"* like the King's daughter in verse 13 of Psalm 45; then we'll be ready for the Rapture!

ESTHER was selected by the king to be his bride. She was chosen over hundreds of other beautiful virgins who lived in the king's domain at that time but were not allowed to go into his personal quarters. Esther prepared herself to be a bride <u>first</u>, and then in Esther 2:17, the king chose her to live with him. She was elevated by the king to be by his side and rule and reign with him on his throne. (See Revelation 3:21.)

Let Esther be an example for us in our day of the proper time and place that preparation has – it's to be done before we meet the Groom, <u>before</u> He comes for us in the Rapture. Then, on that great and glorious Day when the Rapture does take place, we will take our seat next to Jesus on His throne! But let us be like Esther and know how important royal apparel is and <u>when</u> to put it on. Let us know how to prepare to meet our King. Then, when He does come for us, we'll be ready.

ENOCH: "By faith Enoch was translated so that <u>he did not see death</u>, and was not found because God had translated [raptured] him, for before his translation he had this testimony, <u>that he pleased God</u>." (**Hebrews 11:5**) Out of all the people living on the earth at that time, God chose only Enoch to take to Heaven with Him without having to experience death first – a type of Rapture – because he pleased God. The Bride must also please God in the same way.

ELIJAH went directly to Heaven in a chariot of fire without seeing death, in 2nd Kings 2:11. This is another example of a type of Rapture.

JOSHUA AND CALEB – advanced in years but alive and well; and because they pleased God, they went into the Promised Land, which is a type of Heaven. (**Numbers 14:30**) They made Heaven when many others around them did not. Yet another example of a type of Rapture.

MARY of Mary and Martha chose the good part – to sit at the feet of Jesus. (**Luke 10:39-42**) She will be in the Rapture, not Martha. The prophecy on pages 68-69 has more to say about this.

1st John 3:2: What follows is a possible interpretation of this verse: When Jesus is revealed as He comes for His Bride in the

Rapture, if we are like Him, then *we* shall actually see Him as He is, and we will then go to Heaven with Him. If we are not like Him, we will not see Him as He is when He comes for His Bride, and we will miss the Rapture. We can still make Heaven, but not as the Bride of Christ. We would then go into that period known as the Wrath of God.

The Hundredfold Will Go*

Mark 4:20: "And there are those sown on good ground, those who hear the Word, accept it, and bear fruit: some thirtyfold, some sixty, and some a hundred."

Romans 12:2: "And do not be conformed to this world, but be transformed by the renewing of your mind, that you may prove what is that good [sixtyfold] and acceptable [thirtyfold] and perfect will [one hundredfold] of God."

1st Corinthians 15:40-42a: "There are also celestial bodies and terrestrial bodies; but the glory of the celestial is one, and the glory of the terrestrial is another. There is one glory of the sun [one hundredfold], another glory of the moon [sixty-fold], and another glory of the stars [thirtyfold]; for one star differs from another star in glory. So also is the resurrection of the dead."

The glory of the sun describes someone who has a hundredfold walk with the Lord. That person would be the Bride of Christ; the sixty and the thirtyfold would *not* be. The Bride is totally filled with Jesus – completely dead to self and matters of the flesh; whereas the others are not.

The glory of the moon is the sixtyfold walk, and the glory of the stars, the thirtyfold walk. Even the stars differ from one another in glory. They can be anywhere from thirtyfold up to sixtyfold. It all depends on how much of Jesus they have in them and how much of their own flesh is there. If they have 30% Jesus and 70% flesh, then they are thirtyfold – star glory. But if they've been growing spiritually and they're not baby Christians anymore, they might have 60% Jesus and 40% flesh. Then they are sixtyfold – moon glory. However, if they go all the way and have 100% Jesus and 0% flesh, they are **one hundredfold** – *sun glory!* This is the Bride of Christ.

This one – the hundredfold Christian – will go in the Rapture; the thirty and sixtyfold Christian will not. They will be left behind.

*(Taken from material used earlier on pages 51-53.)

Will You Rise in the Rapture or Will You be Left Behind?[60]

Come to Me poor – not hanging on to the things of this life, not clinging to them. Give them all to Me – like the widow that cast in all she had. [Mark 12:43-44] Come and stand before Me empty-handed, as it were, with only yourself to offer and give. Come meekly and humbly. I will not refuse you. I will give you what you need, what you lack. [Philippians 4:19]

You will rise in the Rapture as you are free of earthly entanglements, earthly weights, earthly baggage. **If you cling to anything here, it will tie you down!**

You are still holding on very tightly to the things of this life. Loosen your grip; let go! The things you hold so tightly with your hands are in reality what your heart loves and treasures. For where your treasure, there will be your heart also. [Matthew

6:21] It is imperative that you let go of all earthly loves and treasures, for they will tie you down and weigh you down and keep you from rising to meet Me in the air when the last call is given.

You will not rise to meet Me if your hands are holding onto any other love or treasure. You must let go now; you must become unencumbered now. You must seek and desire Me as your only love and greatest treasure. You must cling to Me alone. Let go and abandon all else now. Rid yourself of all that your heart and hands are tied to, or you will not be ready for My soon return – **you will not rise in the Rapture!**

Part 5
Only the Bride Goes in the Rapture—
As Told in Words from the Lord

The following four prophecy excerpts and one prophecy are all saying the same thing: When the Rapture takes place, only the Bride will go:

You Are Not Ready to Go[12]

Excerpt: So prepare yourself <u>now</u> to be My Bride, for soon the call will go out: *"Behold, the Bridegroom cometh; go ye out to meet Him,"* and then only the wise virgins who have prepared for that event, will be taken out. [Matthew 25:4,6-10] The foolish virgins [3,11-12] will be **left behind** to taste the sorrows and sufferings that shall befall as darkness closes in upon a sin-cursed world" [in the time known as the Wrath of God].

Mary or Martha?[21]

Excerpt: **It is My Marys who will be an important part of the out-working of My Plan in these Last Days.** It is My Marys who will hear My voice – the voice of their beloved Bridegroom calling them to Myself and the Marriage Supper of the Lamb. My Marys are even now in preparation, for "the Bride has prepared herself." [Revelation 19:7] For she shall be arrayed in a fine garment, clean and white. [verse 8] She is preparing her heart. She is dying to herself and the things of this world. She is willingly laying down her life in preparation. She is becoming humble, meek, and merciful; and in doing so, her love for Me is being purified. This process is taking place in My Marys as they pull away from the din and clamor of the world, and answer My call of love to come and sit and listen and learn.

It is My Marys that I come to. It is My Marys who will be ready. They will hear My final call. They will be **raptured** from this world – **raptured** to meet their First Love, **raptured** to be with Me forever! O My Marys, My precious Marys. I can hardly wait!

(Note: This prophecy in its entirety is on pages 68-69.)

Many Have Missed This Calling[32]

Excerpt: Your spirits have come and called upon Me and rejoiced, and it is not just as [a] bride and [a] bridegroom, for I am also preparing to receive My Bride to Me [when the Rapture occurs].

And this Bride must be separated to Me wholly, undefiled. Yea, My love, My dove, My only one. Who shall be greater than the Bride? Is she not the one that looketh forth in the morning; yea, that is as fair as the moon, and as clear as the sun, and as terrible [awesome] as an army with banners? [See Song of Solomon 6:9a and 10] That is the one that shall ride with Me on white horses! [Revelation 19:14]

(Note: This prophecy in its entirety is on pages 110-111.)

The Rapture Call[1]

"The call to come as Jesus returns and comes for His Bride will be familiar to the Bride. The call to come away is the call that the Bride has heard and responded to many times: *'Come away, My love, My fair one. Rise up, My love, and come away.* [See Song of Solomon 2:10b and 13b] *Come with Me from Lebanon, My spouse.* [4:8a] *Come, My beloved, let us go forth into the field.* [7:11a] *The Spirit and the Bride say come! Let him that is athirst come, and whosoever will, let him come and drink of the water of life freely.'*" [From Revelation 22:17]

"The Rapture call will be a clear, loud, clarion call; and the heart of the Bride will respond to it. *'Come away, My love, My dove, My undefiled one.'*" [From Song of Solomon 5:2]

(Note: Used earlier on page xxiii.)

Are You Prepared?[61]

Excerpt: So My word to you, My children is: Watch for My coming with expectant and believing hearts. For as you are faithful and believing, you shall also see Me revealed. You shall see the outpouring of My Spirit, the reviving of My people; and you, My Bride, shall behold Me, your beloved Bridegroom.

You shall hear Me call you unto Myself: *'Rise up, My love, rise up.'* " [to meet Him in the air]

This short section of Prophecies alone is sufficient to establish the fact that only the Bride will go in the Rapture. But there are many other prophecies in this book and they all in one way or another come to the same conclusion, and that is:

When the Rapture takes place, only the Bride will go. All other Christians will be **left behind.**

The Final Call[28]

As the days draw to a close and the plan of the Ages is fulfilled, I will come to My precious, purified, and spotless Bride. [Ephesians 5:27] Oh, how I long for her. Oh, how I long to have her close to My side, forever with Me, her Bridegroom and the Lover of her soul. Everything is ready; the call has gone forth: *"Come, come, all things are ready. Come to the feast. Come to the Marriage Supper of the Lamb. Do not delay!"* [see Revelation 19:7-9]

Answer the call of the Bridegroom to prepare and make yourself ready. Respond to His call of love. Respond to His wooing. Make no excuse! Set not your heart on other things. Do not be indifferent to this call. Come, come to the secret place and prepare your heart to be My Bride. Cut all ties to earthly desires and loves so that you will be ready when you hear My final call to come – to come up and be with Me forever.

The wedding day draws near. Final preparations are being made. There is much excitement in Heaven! Oh, My love, My dove, hasten to the place of love and intimacy. *Daily* answer My call of love to prepare your heart. Listen, watch, and wait for the final call to arise, My love, My fair one; and come away. [Song of Solomon 2:10]

(Note: Used earlier on pages 75-76.)

Chapter 18

A Final Warning and Exhortation to ALL Christians

Yet Seven Days[62]

The Lord would say to thee: Prepare for the coming days of trial and hardship. Prepare for the day of My judging the world. I am coming down and I will speak. For a long time I have been silent. The world has not heard My voice. They have heard the voices of My prophets, My intercessors, and My singers, but I warn you to get ready to hear MY VOICE!

You will hear My voice in the clouds, in the thunder. It won't be normal thunder; it will be thunder on a cloudless day. You will hear the belly of the earth roar as the earth shifts and moves at My coming. It will be a fearful time, and the sinners shall tremble in great fear. For they shall know that I am God.

"Yet seven days!" That is what I said to Noah. [Genesis 7:4a]

"And I say, I will do nothing, but I will reveal it to My servants, the prophets." [Amos 3:7]

Sodom: Before I destroyed Sodom, I told Abraham what I was about to do. [See Genesis 18:17-22]

Ninevah: I warned Ninevah of impending overthrow in forty days. [See Jonah 3:4]

Jerusalem: I wept for Jerusalem because I saw its coming destruction. [See Luke 13:34-35; 19:41-44] Before the Roman Army destroyed Jerusalem, I allowed great persecution to come upon the early Church in the Holy City so that they would be scattered all over Judea and Samaria. [See Acts 8:1] This is what saved their lives.

My people did not want to leave Jerusalem. They had read the prophecies that had spoken of My return on the Mount of Olives, and they were daily expecting Me to come back. [See Zechariah 14:4] They did not want to go even as far away as Galilee, lest I would return while they were gone. Many of them had been on the Mount of Olives when I ascended to Heaven. They remembered the promise of the angels, *"Ye men of Galilee, why stand ye gazing up into heaven? This same Jesus which is taken up from you into heaven shall so come in like manner as ye have seen Him go into heaven."* [Acts 1:11]

They expected to see My return in their lifetime. But I knew I would be delayed, so to save them from slavery and death by the Romans, I sent them from the destruction that was coming on the city.

Today again, many shall leave their cities. Persecution, sin, crime, pollution, high taxes, economic collapse, shall drive them out. And some shall go because they heard My voice telling them to go. The wise ones are selling out and moving <u>now</u>. The not-so-wise will leave later, but they will not be able to sell. And last of all, **the foolish shall stay until it's too late and lose their lives!** Obey the voice of the Holy Spirit when He tells you to come into the Ark!

First you will see the political and the religious upheavals. Then you will see the upheaval of the earth as I come down, bringing retribution. **This coming judgment will destroy whole cities!**

Believe Me, on that day you won't have time to pack up. You won't be able to return into the house to get anything [See Matthew 24:16-17] because the earthquake will destroy many houses; and what the earthquake doesn't destroy, the fires will; and what the fires don't destroy, the floods will!

So hasten to come into the Ark.

Yet seven days.

Seven is the perfect number. It will come in the perfect time, the appointed time. And nothing shall hinder Me. The gross sins of the people, the murder of the innocents, the perversion of the sodomites, the blasphemy of the rebellious to My face, will all STOP in one moment of time!

I am coming down. The earth shall know it! The mountains shall cleave asunder.

Yet seven days!

It's time for the move.

I give you just enough time to get ready now.

Come into the Ark!

A Time of Reflection and Preparation[63]

"And in the day that he goeth into the sanctuary, unto the inner court, to minister in the sanctuary, he shall offer his sin offering, saith the Lord GOD. (Ezekiel 44:27) (KJ) Be ye enraptured unto Me, come unto Me, would say the Lord.

"But it came about in the same night that the word of the LORD came to Nathan, saying, 'Go and say to My servant David, "Thus says the LORD, 'Are you the one who should build Me a house to dwell in? For I have not dwelt in a house since the day I brought up the sons of Israel from Egypt, even to this day; but I have been moving about in a tent, even in a tabernacle. Wherever I have gone with all the sons of Israel, did I speak a word with one of the tribes of Israel, which I commanded to shepherd My people Israel, saying, "Why have you not built Me a house of cedar?" ' " (2nd Samuel 7:4-7) (NAS)

In this season, I want many of you to come unto Me in a special way. Let it be a time of reflection, would say the Lord. Let it be a time of giving and not receiving. For those who give unto Me spend their time with Me. They come into the sanctuary of My presence.

Come into the inner court, would say the Lord. For too long, many of you have just come into the outer court. You have beheld My presence from afar. Come past the candlesticks. Come past the walls that have separated you from Me, says the Lord. Behold, there are many others who have beheld Me from afar. They have just touched My robe. But come and sit at the table with Me. [Revelation 3:20] For the table is prepared for you and Me and our time together. Come behind the curtain that has separated us. Come through the open door. For before you, My courts are always open to you.

For as this is a season of reflection, it is also a time of preparation for what is ahead. You may ask, "What may we be preparing for?" I say, to have your temples prepared within. For when I say to come into My sanctuary, I don't mean a place. For it has always been this way with some. You build great houses of worship for Me, but I reside in that secret sanctuary within you. You want to build something great for Me? Then build that abode <u>within you</u>. Then you will come into the most beautiful sanctuary of all. For My courts are to be filled with the sounds of praise, would say the Lord. [Psalm 135:1-2]

Behold, the many altars that some of you have set up for Me have a pretense [of] a reverence for worship, but the real altar is set upon your hearts.

The time will come when your houses of worship will be destroyed. Where will you meet Me then, would say the Lord? When the land is scourged and taken over, surely this is because we didn't build Him a beautiful place to worship in. And then on that day I will say that I never knew you. [Matthew 7:23] For if you knew Me you would have known about these things.

Those that Hold to the Rapture Lie Shall be Beaten Down by the Truth[64]

Oh My people, why, why do you still believe the lies of the serpent? Many still believe in the lies of the devil that you will be raptured away and not face the persecution to come. Oh My people, how I weep for you – all who have put your trust in lies. For the day approaches when the overwhelming scourge will cover the lands and peoples. And many of My people shall be overtaken and beaten down when it comes. Have I not said this in My Word? [Isaiah 28:18] (NIV) <u>Then why do many of you</u>

still believe the false shepherds who tell you that you shall not see the Tribulation to come?

Prepare yourselves, My people. Prepare your hearts before Me, and seek Me for your repentance in believing such lies. It is not too late for you. If you would seek Me now in this, I will show you My truth and show you how you may escape the scourge to come. But it will not be by a Rapture in the sky as you have been told. For have I not shown you in My Word how I have protected My people in the midst of their tribulations? Was I not in the midst of the fire with Shadrach, Meshach, and Abednego? [Daniel 3:25] Did I not shut the lions' mouths when My servant Daniel was thrown into their den? [6:22a] Then why do you still think that I have somehow changed and will not cause you to go through the Tribulation with My protection upon you?

Oh hear Me, My people. You have been made fools of by the false shepherds. They have sold you a lie, and many of My people love it so. Why do you not seek Me in this? Is it because you are afraid of learning the truth? Why, My people, do you choose to believe a lie over My Word? How can you sit in contentment, thinking that I will take you out of this world, when I prayed to the Father to NOT take you out of this world, but to protect you from evil? [John 17:15] Oh why, My people, can you not discern the error of your ways? Do I not care for all those that are Mine? Then why do many of you still believe that I shall take you out of this world and leave Mine that are still lost for the wolves to devour?

I tell you now: **I shall have a people to walk in <u>My authority</u> in the earth realm during this Tribulation to come**, and they shall speak My truth to the masses. They shall be a judge to those that sit in judgment and a word of love and rebuke to those that will hear and turn to Me. But for those that have chosen to hold on to their lie of the Rapture, woe unto you. For you shall be beaten down by the truth day and night, and you shall not escape. <u>Many of you shall even lose your lives because you chose not to have a love for My truth</u>.

Oh, My little ones. I do not come to you to be harsh this day. But I come to you with a sincere and yet broken heart. Hear My heart crying over you all to come out of the lies you have believed, and seek the true Shepherd who will protect you with truth. Do you not see that the false shepherds fatten themselves with your money and live lives of luxury as they fleece My sheep? Well I tell you now that their judgment shall be ten-fold when the Tribulation takes over the earth. And they shall suffer My Wrath far more than those whom they have deceived, because they have taken My sheep captive with their lies and caused My people to put their trust in lies and not My truth, so that they might escape the over-whelming scourge that shall try those on the earth. [So these false shepherds think.] [See Ezekiel 34:1-10]

My people, hear Me this day. I am about to do a wonder in the earth realm that will astound the masses. Have I not said in My Word that I shall save the best wine for last [John 2:10]; and the glory of the latter house shall be greater than the former? [Haggai 2:9a] Therefore, those that have ears to hear, get ready. For I shall now begin to seek out those that are Mine and have a love for My truth. These ones <u>have</u> <u>prepared their hearts to go through the Great Tribulation</u>, and I shall now begin to do a mighty work in these ones, and **they shall become My great army in the land**. **They shall do many mighty miracles in My Name**, saith the Lord.

But for those who have chosen to believe THE LIE instead, get ready for great destruction that you shall not escape from. Oh, My little ones, do not take this as too harsh. For I have warned you in My Word of the Last Days. Did I not warn you that there would be many to come in My Name, and they shall deceive many? [Matthew 24:5] Then why have you not tested these ones against My Word? And it is for your lack of knowledge of My truth that many of you shall now be destroyed, though it did not have to be this way. [Hosea 4:6]

[End of prophecy]

1st Chronicles 28:9 "As for you, my son Solomon, know the God of your father, and serve Him with a loyal [perfect] heart and with a willing mind; for the Lord searches all hearts and understands all the intent of the thoughts. If you seek Him, He will be found by you; but if you forsake Him, He will cast you off forever."

Author's note: If this could have happened to King Solomon – and it might have – it could happen to any Christian. If for any reason we forsake the Lord, He will forsake us and cast us off forever!

This is the Way of Escape that I have Provided for My Children[65]

In my time with the Lord this morning, the Lord said these words:

Son, tell My people to hear Me this day. Many run to and fro and do not sit at My feet.

Word of the Lord:

Oh, My people, do you not understand that it was Mary who chose what I preferred rather than Martha. [Luke 10:42] Yes, there is a time and season for every good work under the sun. But hear Me, My children, when I say come unto Me this day.

Many of you do not know what is at your doorstep. And <u>only those hidden in Me shall be protected</u>. Oh, My little ones, it is not My desire that any of you should perish. But hear Me well when I say that many shall lose their lives in the short days ahead when disaster strikes. I do not want My children walking in fear when this thing happens. Therefore, I say come unto Me, My little ones and sit at My feet. For those that dwell in the secret place shall abide under the shadow of the Almighty. [Psalm 91:1]

My children, oh My children. You are entering the days [when] I shall fulfill every jot and tittle of My Word. You shall see a thousand fall at your side and ten thousand at your right, but it will not come nigh thee [Psalm 91:7], if you would abide under My shadow [verse 1]. And for you to abide under My shadow, you MUST be obedient unto Me and sit at My feet and listen to My still small voice [1st Kings 19:12]. For I shall protect you in the days ahead, provided that you obey what I say unto you.

Do not think that you can do your own thing and have My protection upon you simply because you call yourself by My Name. For I tell you now, <u>the days ahead shall be the most dangerous days any of you have ever lived in</u>. **Destruction, death, pestilence, and calamity shall be everywhere.** Do not think that you can hide yourself from those things without My protection upon you. For your sins shall surely find you out in these last days. And <u>ONLY those abiding in Me through their obedience to Me shall have My protection upon them</u>.

Oh, My little ones. Have I not warned you of these last days? Many shall be running to and fro and men's hearts will fail them for fear of what they see coming upon the world. But for those abiding in the secret place of The Most High, they shall not be harmed by what is coming. This is the way of escape that I have provided for My children in these last days – **NOT**

the escape from [the] Tribulation through a Rapture. And for those that have believed this lie and have not prepared your hearts before Me to <u>go through the Great Tribulation</u>, I say woe unto you. For you do not know what is coming for those that believe not in My Word. It shall not be a pleasant thing for those not abiding under My shadow in the secret place. For the authorities shall take many of you, even by force. And many of those that call themselves by My Name shall turn from Me and deny Me!

Think not that all this is too hard a thing to bear. For I have warned you all in My Word. For if they persecuted Me, My little ones, they shall persecute you. [John 15:20] And because of My Word that shall be released in power throughout the earth in these End-Times, persecution shall be great.

Oh, My little ones, do not fear. For this life cannot even compare to what I have stored up for those that are faithful to Me to the end. But for those that think that they shall be raptured out of the earth and not face the Great Tribulation, I say come unto Me now and pray to be found worthy to escape the things to come. [See Luke 21:36] For many of you that have believed the lie and have not prepared yourselves shall find it very difficult to continue to call yourselves by My Name.

And for those that have prepared your hearts to go through My Tribulation upon the earth, I say to you, prepare, My little ones. I do not say prepare for your doom as those not prepared. But I say prepare to be tested in all ways. But know this: The trial of your faith, being much more precious than gold that perishes, though it be tried by fire, will be found unto praise and honor and glory at My appearing. [1st Peter 1:7] And <u>as you go through My refining fires, you shall find it easier to follow Me in all truth</u>. Whereas, those in darkness will find it too difficult. For it shall be like the two opposing forces of magnets.

The light and the darkness shall repel against one another. And those walking in My light shall find the darkness more and more repulsive as the days grow darker.

But for those that have not prepared themselves for this day, **they shall find it more and more difficult to cross over to My Kingdom of light as the days grow darker.** For the darkness in people shall repel against the light. But not all hope is lost for those who do desire to cross over to My light. For I shall have mercy on any that will desire My light in the days ahead. And My light shall shine bright in those that are Mine for all the world to see. [Matthew 5:16] And any that desire My light shall be given mercy to cross over from the kingdom of darkness. But as I warned, it shall become more and more difficult as the days grow darker. For the light and darkness shall repel against one another in intensity, thus creating My true Kingdom of light amidst a world of darkness and decay.

Oh, My little ones. Hear Me when I say to you all, to come unto Me now and separate yourselves from the things of this world. For the enemy of your soul is doing all he can <u>through the workings of man</u> to fill My children with the things of this world. So that when this great separation begins, many of My children will be found on the side of darkness. And I tell you now, many of My children are already on the side of darkness and know it not.

Therefore, I say come out from among all that is unclean and separate yourselves unto Me. Sit at My feet and allow Me to wash you through My Word to you, My little ones. For you do not understand the gravity of the gross darkness that is coming. And this gross darkness shall fill all hearts and minds that are already darkened. And <u>many that thought themselves to be My chosen ones, shall find themselves on the side of darkness.</u>

Do not take My words lightly this day, My children. For none of you has faced this kind of darkness before. Therefore, once again, I cry unto you all to come unto Me and sit in My presence, and do it often. Do not think that you already stand in My light. For have I not declared in My Word, he who thinks he stands, let him take heed lest he fall. [See 1st Corinthians 10:12]

I love you all, My dear ones, and do not desire that any of you perish. Therefore, it would be wise for all of you to heed these words of Mine this day.

Only Those Close to Me Shall Survive[66]

I am coming so very, very soon. Yea, stay very close to Me, saith the Lord God, for terrible times are on the way. Terrible times are coming to this nation, saith the Lord God. For I have put a curse on this nation. I have put a curse upon this nation for what it is doing to My name, saith the Lord God. Yea, I shall soon pour out My Wrath upon this country and upon this nation, and I am calling My people to come close to Me, saith the Lord God. I'm calling My people to stay very close to Me.

But not all hear. Not all are listening to My voice, saith the Lord God, for they have turned Me aside. They have turned Me aside, saith the Lord God. They have pushed Me away from them. Yea, but they shall soon see that My Words are truth and My Words are power. For I will pour out My Spirit upon those who are drawing close to Me, and only those. *None other,* saith the Lord God

For My Wrath is coming against this nation in a fierce way, saith the Lord God. And I am the Lord, and I am God Almighty, and I shall do as I have said in My Word, saith the Lord God. For those who do not hear My Word or listen to My Words, yea, **they shall go down,** saith the Lord God. **But only those who have drawn close to Me shall survive.** They shall call upon Me, and I shall answer them, saith the Lord God. The others shall call, but I will not answer them – only those who are drawing close to Me. For My anointing shall fall upon them, saith the Lord God, and they shall go forth in a *mighty way* to do My works.

But My wrath, My anger, is waxing hot, saith the Lord God, and I am soon to pour out this Wrath upon this nation. So stay close to Me. Stay in the Word, stay in the Word. Read My Word daily, and pray daily, and stay close to Me, saith the Lord God. For it is soon, so very soon to happen, saith the Lord.

Jesus Corrects His People[67]

Oh, My people, hear Me this day. Why do you still not heed My warnings? Time is short, My people. And soon I will not be weary with you any longer, but I shall pour forth My judgments upon the lands and peoples. And hear Me, My people. My judgments shall begin with My house. [See 1st Peter 4:17] I am rising up this day to judge all that call themselves by My Name. I shall judge each one according to My Word. [John 12:48]

Woe unto those that have believed the lies of the false prophets and teachers. For there will be a great falling away as I separate the sheep from the goats – those that are truly Mine from those that are imposters. [Matthew 25:32-44] And I shall call My own out from among the heathen and the imposters, and they shall be healed from their backsliding as I purge them through the fires of My purification.

Oh, My people, hear Me this day. I am jealous for My Bride. For My Bride shall make herself ready as I take her through the fires of purification to bring her forth without spot or blemish. For I am a holy God, and I shall have a holy people. [See Deuteronomy 28:9]

Oh, My people, why? Why do you not take My warnings to heart? Many are going to and fro with business as usual and not seeking what I desire. Each one seeks his own. Oh, My people, the days are short, and very soon there will be distress of nations <u>like never before</u>. But I shall have a people that will be a light in a darkened and corrupt world. [Philippians 2:15] **My beautiful Bride shall do great exploits in ushering in her Bridegroom and King.** Oh, My people, how I desire that each one of you could be part of My beautiful Bride. **But not all that call themselves by My Name shall take part as My Bride. Only those that OVERCOME shall be allowed to sit with Me on My throne** to rule the nations with a rod of iron. [See Revelation 2:26-27]

Oh hear Me, My people. Why do you listen to the hirelings and false teachers and prophets? Did I not say in My Word that not all that say to Me "Lord, Lord" shall enter into the Kingdom of Heaven, save those that do the will of the Father who is in Heaven? [Matthew 7:21-23] Then why do you still go about doing your own will and [then] tell yourselves that you are My Bride? My people, you have been lied to by the enemy of your soul. Seek Me in these things. Surely I will reveal My truth to you. I love you, My dear children, and it is My desire that each of you share My throne with Me. But unfortunately <u>only a Remnant shall overcome</u>. [Chapters 2 and 3 of Revelation]

For too many have listened to the lies told by the false shepherds and prophets. THEY SPEAK OF HOW YOU EACH ARE ALREADY CLEANSED AND ADORNED IN RIGHTEOUSNESS SIMPLY BY YOUR BELIEF ON MY NAME. These are all lies, My people. For does not My Word say that he who DOES righteousness is righteous? Yes, My people, you are made righteous by your faith in Me, but it is fulfilled by your obedience to My voice. IT IS NOT IMPUTED TO YOU BY A ONE-TIME CONFESSION OF MY NAME.

Oh, My people, you have been lied to. Read My Word for yourselves. Why listen to those that fatten themselves by fleecing My sheep? [Ezekiel 34:2-8] I have not sent many of the shepherds that are out there. They have sent themselves for their own glory and their own profit. Oh, My people, did I not say in My Word to judge them by their fruit? [Matthew 7:16-20] Then where is the fruit, My people? Oh, but those that have itching ears care not about the fruit. [2nd Timothy 4:3] They want to be told all is well, and that they shall prosper if they simply believe on My Name and My promises. Lies, lies, lies, I tell you.

Oh, My people, why do you not study My Word to show yourselves approved? [2nd Timothy 2:15] Why do you go about from doctrine to doctrine seeking what will make you feel good? Can you not see that there is no healing in the dead churches? Not [just no] healing of the physical body, but [no] healing of the soul and spirit. This is because there is no life in them. For where My Spirit is, there is liberty. [2nd Corinthians 3:17] Not liberty to gratify or tingle the flesh; but liberty *from* the flesh.

Oh, My people, how I wish to take you all with Me now into My chambers. But you are not ready, and many of you never will be. For you do not test the spirits of those you follow, and so you have chosen to believe their lies. [1st John 4:1] I will and I shall have a Bride that is spotless and without blemish. [Ephesians 5:27] Do you take My invitation this day to come away with Me and be cleansed of all filthiness of flesh? [2nd Corinthians 7:1] Oh, My people, come away with Me, and we shall ride together on the heights of the earth. For I shall rise

211

with healing in My wings [Malachi 4:2], and I shall heal all that have called out to Me with a pure heart. I shall heal and I shall cleanse with My cleansing fire.

Oh, that I wish you all would call out to Me for My cleansing fire. For not many of you will, because your desire is for your flesh. But for those that choose to call out to Me for this fire, I will answer thee and <u>pour upon thee both My glory and cleansing fire</u>. And **I shall purify you to be My Bride if you do not shrink back.** For I am now choosing those that choose Me, and we will walk together and be one as I take each of you through My fires of purification. And My Bride shall be purified and come forth refined as silver and purified as gold. [See Malachi 3:2-3] And I shall be her God, and she will be My Bride to be shown forth to all nations.

Now choose this day, My people. Will you let Me take you through the fires, or will you cling to the lust of your own flesh? The choice is yours, My people. For I am no respecter of persons [Acts 10:34], and I offer this opportunity to all.

Be Very Careful
Some Saints Lost Everything—
Even Heaven![68]

In these Last Days you will be tested in every way possible, for Satan will seek to cause you to lose your reward. You have wondered why I have permitted these very great trials. They are even like the trials of Job. Satan wants you to lose everything in the last hours that remain before I come for you.

So I warn you to be very careful. Many of My greatest Saints lost everything in the very last hours and days of their lives. You have wondered how it could have been that someone who was so greatly used of Me could have fallen so deeply into sin in the latter part of their lives. Now you know. They were terribly tested and tempted by Satan, and in the end died without honor and lost their great inheritance. Some even lost Heaven!

So take care, My beloved one. Keep your eyes on Me. Every day will become a testing day. Every day will become a day when you must stay very close to Me, because the devil is going around like a roaring lion, seeking to devour the Saints in these Last Days. [1st Peter 5:8-9] And if he can't get them to lose their Salvation, he certainly will do all he can to get them to lose their rewards.

So stay close to Me. Stay filled with love. And be honest with yourself. It is one thing to be honest with others, but it is another thing to be honest with yourself. That is a state which few can attain to. **But if you are not honest with yourself, you cannot deal with the weaknesses in yourself, which will rob you of your crown.**

Eternal greatness is only obtained during your temporal life on earth, through your godly response to the hours of trials and testings which you are going through, even now.

I love you. You are My precious treasure. And on the Day of Judgment all who have tried to ruin your character or destroy you will know that I have loved thee, and they will be ashamed. Hold fast to your crown! [Revelation 3:11] Don't lose it in these last hours of fiery trials. [1st Peter 4:12-13] If you overcome, *"I will make you a pillar in the temple of my God, and you shall go no more out: and I will write upon you the name of my God, and the name of the city of my God, which is New Jerusalem, which cometh down out of Heaven from my God: and I will write upon you new name."* [Revelation 3:12]

Many Christians Will Fall[69]

Many are those who sit neglectful, loving the world and the things of the world. Many seek the life of the earth, but they do not prepare themselves to meet the Holy One. Jesus is coming. Do not be lazy! Terror and great pain are coming upon the earth! The devil will take upon himself power, and he will attempt to make war with the holy. But Christ, the Victorious One, will come and save His people.

Proud men – all those who pretend to be teachers and never living the life, all those who say they worship Me, yet their hearts are far from Me. [Matthew 15:8-9a] Says the Lord: I will make them part of the suffering, torment, and terror, that they may call upon Me, but I will NOT answer.

Those that today humble themselves and seek Me with a clean heart, in that day – the hard day – will be glad and will rejoice. The power of the devil will increase in this country, and many Christians will fall in [his] chains because they have dishonored Me in their lives – in their pride, their arrogance, and their vanity – thinking they are holy and are worshipping Me, *yet never really worshipping Me.*

———

The winds and the storms that will begin against the Christians in this country will take many. **Those who remain standing will be very few!** Humble yourselves. Be holy. Seek Me more than ever, kneeling before Me often, that in the hard days I may save you, says the Lord.

Many of My People
Have Gone Their Own Way[70]

Can America stand against My judgment? No, it cannot stand against My judgment, for I am judging the sins of this nation, saith the Lord God. It is a sinful and corrupt nation. It is a nation that has not done My will. It has come against My Word and come against My Name. Therefore it has sealed its own doom, and it is soon coming, it is soon coming, saith the Lord God.

And many of My people have fallen into the trap of the wayside, have fallen into the trap of the world. The world is pulling them into a net of its own. It is a snare and a trap. And they have not heeded My Word as I have spoken it in the past to them. They have laid My Word aside, and they have gone their own way. They are called by My Name, and they are My people, saith the Lord God.

And if they continue in that realm, they will lose their life completely, saith the Lord God. **In all phases – body, soul, and spirit – they shall go down,** saith the Lord God. For I am serious in calling them in a strong way in these last of the last days. And if they do not heed My calling, they shall perish, saith the Lord God!

Intercede for Those
Who Have Fallen by the Wayside[71]

Last days, the last days – they are here, they are here. The last of the last days are here, saith the Lord God. And many, many are falling by the wayside, for they do not walk with Me. They have chosen other Gods, and they walk with these other gods. And they entertain these other gods, saith the Lord God, and some of them are My people.

Yea, some of them are called by My Name. And they have entangled themselves with these false gods and their false teachings. And darkness has overtaken their minds, saith the Lord God.

But if My intercessors will pray, if My intercessors will pray for **an opening** – <u>for light to come in</u> – then I will break through. But I'm putting this call upon My intercessors to pray for these people that are falling by the wayside, these people that are called by My Name, saith the Lord God.

And I will hold you accountable if you do not pray for them, saith the Lord God.

There Will be Some Who Hear Because You Have Interceded[72]

Do you hear the wind blowing, saith the Lord? Yea, hear the wind blowing. Listen to that wind. It is not My Wind, but it is the wind of Loadicea, saith the Lord. For that wind is blowing upon My people and drawing them into a Loadicean relationship. They think that they are saved and that they are well in doing the things that they do. But it is a lost section, a lost section of a church that I have spoken about in My Word, and it is called Laodicea.

And that wind is blowing strongly upon My people, saith the Lord, and drawing many away from the truth that I have spoken in My Word. They have shunned My Word, and they have turned in the direction of the wind that is blowing upon them, and that wind is Laodicea.

And I have been calling you to intercede for the lost, and you have done that in this moment. [Two men were praying together.] And you have been praying for those people who are caught in that wind. Yea, and now My Wind shall blow upon them and change them and push them in another way, saith the Lord God. And I will blow with **MY** Wind, saith the Lord, upon that Church, upon the Laodicean Church, and I will say to those people, "Come out! Come out and follow Me. For these are the last moments, the last times, saith the Lord God."

Yea, and there will be some who hear because you have interceded. And you have moved darkness away from them, saith the Lord, and I can blow with My Wind upon them. And they shall feel My Wind and say, "Let's turn, let's turn into this new Wind," because it is the Wind of My Spirit, saith the Lord God. And I will blow and move them on out and draw them to a closer relationship with Me, saith the Lord God, because you have taken this time – this time that has seemed like only a few minutes to you, [45 minutes] but much has been done in the Spirit realm.

Yea, My sons, stay close to Me, for I expect more of you. I expect more of your interceding prayers – not the prayers that are lukewarm but the deeper things that are upon My heart, saith the Lord God. It will be done according to My Spirit. My Spirit shall pray through you. So Stay close to Me, saith the Lord. There is much more to be done.

[Note: The man who received this Word and the Author of this book were praying together, mainly in tongues, when this Word from the Lord came forth. We were both surprised at its spiritual impact because while our praying was sincere and focused, it was not especially fervent. So be encouraged. Even if your prayers are not very fervent at some prayer meetings, they can still bear fruit. Nevertheless, press in with those prayers of intercession that are fervent. And watch what is accomplished by the Holy Spirit then!]

Intercede on a Daily Basis for Lost Souls, For I Will Hold You Accountable[73]

Last days, last days, saith the Lord God. My people are perishing and fallen, saith the Lord God; yea. But I have called My intercessors to pray and to intercede for those lost souls, saith the Lord God. Only some are doing it – only some, saith the Lord God.

But take heed to the words that I speak to you this day. For if you do not pray and intercede on a daily basis, I will hold you liable. For the time is short – is coming to a close, saith the Lord God.

And you are only thinking of yourselves when you do not intercede for others, saith the Lord God. But be faithful to the calling of My commission that I have given to you, and intercede on a daily basis for lost souls, **for I will hold you accountable to do it,** saith the Lord.

One Hour of Travail Every Day[74]

My food, said Jesus, is to do the will of Him who sent Me and to finish His work. [John 4:34] Your food, says Jesus, is to do My will, [the will of the one] who is sending you, to finish My work in you. My will is that you abide in Me, become one with Me: I in you and you in Me [John 15:4] – that you may do the greater works [John 14:12] , that I might be lifted up in you to draw all men unto Me. [John 12:32] For the harvest is great, and the workers are few. [Luke 10:2a]

Will you work with Me? Will you pray and travail in prayer until My Man-child is birthed in My people? Will you travail until I am fully formed in My people [Galatians 4:19] and My people grow up into My full stature? [See Ephesians 4:13]

Make it your **priority** – fit it in first. Don't let it be crowded out. It doesn't have to take hours. Even watching and praying with Me for one hour [Matthew 26:40-41] produces a significant eternal harvest. *Then* as you go about the business of the day, **pray in tongues without ceasing** [1st Thessalonians 5:17; 1st Corinthians 14:18], **making your life a life of prayer.** And in Eternity you will be glad for the harvest of souls!

My Remnant Church[75]

I am not an adulterer. I will not be married to a harlot church! My eyes rove to and fro over the earth, looking for one who will stand in the gap; for through the prayers of one, I will take the poorest, dirtiest, bloodiest, almost-dead one, and clean her up with My gifts of repentance and Salvation. As she turns to Me, seeking the face of her Master, I will create in her a clean, pure heart and give her holy hands to lift in surrender and worship to her Lord. [1st Timothy 2:8] I will take her with Me into the wilderness, and she will come out leaning on the arm of her Beloved. [Song of Solomon 8:5]

My Bride shall come from My Remnant Church... It is My Remnant Church that shall do greater works than I did. **It is My Remnant Church that shall do mighty exploits.** My new thing shall be done by My Remnant Church. To them alone shall I tell what is to come before I do it, and to them only will I reveal the deepest secrets of My Word.

Seek Me, My Bride. Call out to Me. Long for Me; yearn to come into My heart. Desire Me to possess your heart to its very center. Oh, cry out for Me in the night hours, My Bride.

Learn of Me as Marys at My feet. Follow Me wherever I lead you. Surrender your will and all the desires of your heart unto Me. Be My faithful, true, and loyal Bride. Have eyes only for your Jesus. I suffered and died and rose to life for love of you, My precious, pure, beautiful Bride.

I Must Have Overcomers[76]

O My children, there is a way that I would lead thee that is not easy for the flesh to bear. It is not a pleasant way, nor in accord with the desires of the carnal nature. I have not purposed to please the self-life, but rather to bring it to crucifixion; for it can never be a help, but only a hindrance to thy spiritual progress and to My working through thee.

Ye have faith in Me, this is good, but faith without works is dead. [James 2:20] Faith I can give thee as a gift, but the works I can do through thee only as your own ego is moved out of the way. For they are not your works, but My works, even as Jesus said, *"I must work the works of Him that sent Me."* [John 9:4a] And as Paul said, *"The life that I now live in the flesh, I live by the faith of the Son of God who loved me and gave His life for me."* [Galatians 2:20b] And again in another place it is written, *"It is no more I that live, but Christ liveth in Me."* [verse 20a]

I will cause the tears to flow through thee <u>in a flood</u>, and I will purge out thy self-life, and I will give thee My love; and with My love, I will give thee My power, and ye shall walk no more in your own way, but ye shall reign with Me in the throne life.

FOR I MUST HAVE OVERCOMERS THROUGH WHICH I MAY OVERCOME. There is an enemy to be contested and defeated, and to do this, there must be more than resolve in thy heart, **there must be power!** This power cannot operate until self-will is put out of the way. Yea, My new life shall become thine in direct proportion to the amount of thy self-emptying.

This I know ye cannot do for thyself, but ye must will it to be done, and as ye will it, I will work with thee and in thee to bring it to pass. Ye shall know joy as never before and as never possible any other way. Ye shall have rest from inner conflict; yea, **ye must be delivered of the inner conflict in order to engage in this outer conflict with the enemy**.

Learn to Reign[77]

Call My people to repentance. Yea, call them to their knees for prayer and fasting, for confession and vigilance. For this is a strategic hour. The enemy is rejoicing already over his anticipated victories. Ye can disappoint him and thwart his evil designs <u>if ye lay hold upon the throne of God in **steadfast, believing prayer**</u>.

Yea, I say unto thee, ye must do even as the devil has done and anticipate your victories in advance. Ye can do MORE than the enemy at this point. For ye can claim the victories in the Name of Jesus, and all that ye claim in that all-powerful Name is sealed in Heaven before it comes to pass on earth; and the enemy is defeated, yea, even **PRIOR** to the actual battle!

<u>Lay hold upon this, My people</u>. This is not only a glorious truth in which to rejoice, but it is *absolutely vital* to thy victory. How go the troops to battle in carnal warfare? Not without due preparation, ample ammunition, and intensive training. I do not expect you to meet your adversary unequipped, unarmed, undisciplined.

Do not count upon Me to deliver by some kind of magic. I give you orders and ye must obey, otherwise ye shall suffer intolerable defeat. Ye do not face light skirmishes in which you can look for easy victories. I remind you that you are not contending with flesh and blood and matching wits with men, but ye are being ambushed and facing open attack from the very enemy of your souls, Satan himself. [Ephesians 6:12] He is not out to torment. He is out to destroy. Not to hurt you, but to crush you. Your strength is no match against him. Ye *must* learn how to lay claim to the throne of God. I have met him and won already as I hung on the Cross. **Now YOU must find the way of victory yourselves – each one individually** – so that My victory already won can become a present victory in operation for you.

Do not cry to Me in the hour of crisis and distress as though I would extend some miracle in answer to prayer. Of course, I <u>do</u> answer prayer, and I can perform miracles and bring deliverance, but if I do this, I have only rescued one of My own out of trouble while you yourself have won no victory at all! **I want to teach YOU how to actually circumvent the enemy, to drive him out of the arena, to subdue kingdoms, and to truly reign in the Kingdom of Heaven.** I want you to experience Jericho's – not Ai's. [Joshua chapter 6 and 7] Ye *must* be OVERCOMERS if My work is to be accomplished.

Ye are not qualified to be used for My purposes as long as ye are being harassed by the enemy and I keep needing to rescue you from a constant parade of distressing predicaments. Ye are MORE THAN CONQUERORS, Paul said [Romans 8:37], and it was by My Spirit that Paul was taught to speak thus.

Rise up, then, and lay claim to the power that is yours, because I am in you and ye are in Me, and as I was in the world, even so are ye. I was victorious, and you too can be victorious. I withstood every encounter with the devil, and you too can stand against him. I healed the sick and wrested tortured bodies out of the grip of evil forces, and <u>you too can do the same</u>!

LEARN TO REIGN, for lo, I have made you to become kings and priests. [Revelation 1:6] I have purposed that ye should come into that place where ye share My authority, and thus I will be able to manifest forth My glory through you. This is My greatest joy – to lift man out of enemy territory and seat him in the heavenlies with Me. [Ephesians 2:5-6]

And where am I? Even at the right hand of the Father who sitteth upon the throne [Mark 16:19, Ephesians 1:20], and He has invested in Me all power in Heaven and Earth and under the earth [Philippians 2:9-10]; and ye are seated with Me, far above all principalities and powers. [Ephesians 1:20-23] Through Me ye have inherited all. And ye can lay claim to that inheritance *now* because I have already died. Because I have already died, ye can enter in *now*.

You do not gain an inheritance when *you* die, but when the testator dies. [Hebrews 9:16-17] <u>Take it</u>, My people. It is yours NOW! It is yours because of Calvary. When ye think of Calvary, ye think of My love; and this indeed is the tie-in between Calvary and this sharing of My throne life. I want you with Me. I want you seated beside Me because I want you near Me. Because I love you.

You are Joint Heirs with Me[78]

"I believe that many of us don't fully realize how God sees us when we are accepted into Him, forgiven, and given new life. Oftentimes our sins, our weaknesses, cause us to believe that we are less than what we are. I'm not talking here about viewing ourselves too highly, but that we would know how God sees us and views us as His children, but also as heirs with Him in His Kingdom." (Stephen Hanson)

"And if children, then heirs; heirs of God and joint-heirs with Christ; if so be that we suffer with Him, that we may be also glorified together." [Romans 8:17] (KJ)

The Prophecy begins:

"And in the beginning was the Word, and the Word was with God, and the Word was God." [John 1:1] For My Son springs forth from My Spirit. [The Father speaking] We are One, and we have always been One from the beginning. [John 10:30] If you worship the Son, then you worship Me [the Father]. For how can you separate One who has always been in you? [Ibid]

There was no beginning, for We have always been. And I called My Son to be a ransom for many; that in the coming Ages you would then reign with Us. [Revelation 5:10] For I have called you to be kings and princes in My Kingdom. [1:6] But few know this for they do not see through My eyes. For they would continually put Me back up on the Cross.

For if you are children, then you are heirs, and then heirs in My Kingdom. For you are entitled to all the things in My Kingdom. But you must first accept the work that I have done for you. When I have forgiven you, then accept that forgiveness. [IF we have stopped practicing that sin.] For I then no longer see that sin; it is you that sees it.

And I have said that if you have faith as a mustard seed that you would say to this mountain, "Be removed into the sea." [From Mark 11:23] But because you doubt and because you waver, it does not happen. [James 1:6-7]

You don't realize the power that you have "in Me," says the Lord. For as I have come into this world and died for you, I came that your old life would be done away with, but I also came that you would reign with Me in the heavens.

For I have set you upon this earth that you would glorify My Son. That means that you would do even greater things than what He did. [John 14:12b] For you see, you have My Spirit that abides within you. **That creative force that I spoke the world into existence [with] dwells within you.** That force can literally move mountains in your life. That force can cause the blind to see. It can cause the lame to walk. For in these coming days you will see miracles wrought that you would never have thought possible before. For My Spirit is giving you more and more revelations of Me. [End of Prophecy]

[Stephen Hanson's prayer]: I pray that your eyes will be enlightened to the hope of glory that is in you.

Keep My Commandments[79]

For I say unto you, as you say you adore Me, you will adore Me when you keep My commandments. [John 14:21a] Because My promises to you are yes and Amen [2nd Corinthians 1:20] – when you keep My commandments.

In the days that are coming – and they are here now – but as they crescendo into a place of great darkness, those of you who have kept My commandants, **My promises will be unleashed unto your lives.** You will not have worry or be concerned, for I will take within Me those that have been obedient to My Word. I will comfort them with the Spirit of comfort. **I'll bring them to a high place in glory.**

They shall not be touched, saith the Lord, by the evil that surrounds them. Many will come in that day and want to do harm to My beloved ones, but those who have kept My commandments will be brought up into that mountain top of Zion. [Hebrews 12:22] They will have the words of life within them, and when they speak the words of life, **Satan cannot come near them, he cannot touch them;** there will be a wide berth around My precious ones, saith the Lord.

They will be **My Bride,** they will be **My sons** [and daughters], they will be **My overcomers,** they will be **the manifested ones** in the earth. [See Romans 8:19, 29, 37] For I have said in My Word this is so, and therefore My Word is true, saith the Lord. Come now unto Me and remember, remember, remember: Keep My commandments in this day, for your trials [and how you respond to them] will show your heart.

The Truth Must be Spoken[80]

The truth must be spoken without leaven or compromise. The hour is truly late and the DAY is at hand. The truth is, beloved, that trying times are increasing and the walls of your nation are about to crumble. The political and social agitations are destroying the foundations of your country. There is no true UNITY in your nation and the offense against the Lord is great.

Read the list of abominations and then try to justify your cause: **Children being kidnapped and taken to places of isolation for pornography; murder, rape, hate, deception, lies, manipulation, homosexuality, lesbianism, religious pride, gossip, backbiting, finger pointing, child abuse, drugs, alcohol, promiscuity, defilement, debasement, corruption, vulgarity, abortion, sensuality, witchcraft, rebellion, stubbornness, division, and more.**

How can these things exist in any measure without being severely punished? These things do not only exist in the world in which you live but in your own churches and in your own homes! Many have mistaken My kindness, patience, and mercy for blindness, deafness, and light-heartedness. I tell you that My heart is not light concerning the things that are going on in your country. **I tell you that terrible destruction is coming to your shores!**

This is the truth, yet it is one side of the truth. The other side of the truth is that a tremendous revival is coming to your shores, America. A revival that has not been known, recorded, or witnessed by any since the creation of the world!

What is this revival? It is the REVIVING of a humanity that was sown into the earth two thousand years ago. [The Church Age] A humanity whose origin is from above and not beneath. A humanity whose image, nature, and character is that of the Father's. A humanity of overcomers, conquerors, triumphant and victorious sons [and daughters]! The old humanity has kept the creation in bondage until now! The new creation humanity is going to destroy the yoke and execute righteous judgment upon the old. Though many will lose their lives and the casualties be great, all who stand in the newness of life and have been separated from the old system of things shall be taken into Eternal Glory beyond the comprehension and imagination of many!

Yet **a Remnant** – 144,000 redeemed warriors and over-comers – will be standing upon the Mount called Zion, which is an elevated place in the Spirit [Revelation 14:1; Hebrews 12:23], ready to make war with the beast and the Harlot system. **These 144,000 have overcome death and have been translated, raptured** [in a sense]**, and transformed in their spirits, souls, and bodies. These shall come against unseen principalities**

and overcome them. THESE SHALL HAVE FIRE COME FORTH OUT OF THEIR MOUTHS and shall take back what has been lost! [Revelation 11:5] **These shall come forth in the likeness of their God and will bring transformation to the earth. These shall take the dominion and exercise their rights as sons and overcomers.**

This is what the devil and a fallen humanity fear and war against the most. It is not true that the wars in the world are due to political maneuvers but are direct results of a seed coming to fruition. The reality of this revival is a coming together among Saints! A joining together! I have seen this company, called THE BODY OF CHRIST FILLING THE EARTH! They are unseen to the eyes of men, but in time shall be revealed from that heavenly place in which they are now seated [in Christ Jesus]. [Ephesians 2:6]

I am building them up on the inside and teaching them not to fear man or devils, witches or warlocks, casters of spells or chanters of evil. [Deuteronomy 18:10-11] **I am training them to speak direct words of truth that will be as piercing swords. Their weapons shall destroy the Dragon in the sea and Leviathan, that twisted serpent!** [Isaiah 27:1] **These will confront with ABSOLUTE POWER those who are religious and pious with their own piety. These will tear down the facade of religion and will walk into large churches and call down their walls! These (1) shall walk the streets of the damned and shall bring life to those who are dead, and (2) death to those who are alive (apart from Me).***

Yes, this is the Remnant of which the enemy is terrified! Your ground will become a battleground, America! There will not be one brick upon another until all that has been spoken be fulfilled. There will be ONE KINGDOM, and <u>My chosen shall rule it with divine wisdom and mastery</u>, for they have been granted the right [to] because they have chosen the way of righteousness and truth over the way of selfish ambition and greed. These have been brought to the lowest place and have been willing to thrust away all they have for Me.

You have heard the words TORA! TORA! TORA! before, America, and I tell you now that My eyes are not blind, My ears are not deaf, and My Spirit not far off. The truth is that the larger part of your country has already been prepared for slaughter. Most of your citizens are walking their streets waiting for the next terrible event. Most have placed their hope in the arm of flesh, whose arm I will break and make of no use. This will be done according to each decision made that advances the cause of evil, selfish gain, and manipulation of the masses. Your nation is marching towards the cliff and is about to be thrown down. Your eyes will behold these things in their time. Patriotism is not sufficient for the present crisis! Only a nation that will change their course will be spared the things I have spoken. The truth is clear! It is balanced! It is light for My Saints and darkness to all the rest. The abounding reality is that your war is not against flesh and blood. You are battling evil spirits, principalities and powers that have been set up in high places. [See Ephesians 6:12]

*[Note: There are two groups: (1) Those who are lost who will be saved. And (2) those who are lost who refuse to be saved. This latter group will be judged.]

A Flood of Filth is Coming to America[81]

Son, tell My people to pray hard. Pray hard for the leaders and for your land called the United States of America. For I declare unto you that a great flood is coming upon your land. I do not speak of a flood of rain or waters; no, I speak of a flood of filth!

For your recent supreme court ruling legalizing same-sex marriage has prepared the way for the gates to be opened allowing a great flood of filth and perversion of every kind. And I have allowed this because I am a God of justice and mercy, and I will not stand by and allow men to continue in their sinful ways without reaping what they have sown.

This country which you call great is not great in My eyes. No, this country is worse than Sodom and Gomorrah. For in the days of Sodom and Gomorrah they were not as advanced and blessed as the United States of America has been.

So then, I shall allow this great deluge of evil and darkness to be poured out upon your land. And just as it was with Lot, many who are called by My Name shall be sorely vexed in their souls by this great evil. And there shall be blood spilled in the streets all across the land when this flood comes. For with this filth there shall be death and darkness of all kinds to come with it.

But know this: The day shall soon come afterwards where My people will say, "No More." And they shall rise up by the power of My Spirit and drive the darkness out of their cities and regions. And then, there shall be **Goshens** established in diverse places. [Goshen was a land that God protected from judgments while He rained them down on the evil areas and regions surrounding Goshen. Read Genesis 47:27; Exodus 8:22 and 9:26.] And in these cities and regions there shall be great light which the darkness cannot overcome. And My chosen ones shall live in peace and righteousness with My protection, while outside these **Goshens** there shall be great darkness and weeping.

But I will not allow this to go on for too long. For just as in the days of Sodom and Gomorrah, I shall send my messengers to survey the United States of America to determine if there is any righteousness in her; that is, in the outer dark regions outside of My **Goshens.** And then, if there be none found righteous, I will then destroy this land you call great. But it shall not be utterly destroyed. For My **Goshens** shall be protected from this destruction. And My chosen ones shall worship Me in Spirit and in truth. And then, I will once again visit this land to bring healing and restoration.

But know this. Even after I restore, this country shall never again be great as she once was. And this shall be a sign to all who dwell upon the earth that I am a righteous God and I shall not be mocked. For whatever man sows, he shall also reap. For he that sows to his flesh shall of the flesh reap corruption; but he that sows to the Spirit shall of the Spirit reap life everlasting. [Galatians 6:7-8]

A Word to the Remnant[82]

Beloved, the time of refreshing and restoration has come! A new season for the remnant of My chosen ones has dawned, and a new season of Fruitfulness and Forgetting has arrived. The troublesome past shall be just that – PAST! You shall now come to a place of fruitfulness in the very land you experienced your greatest suffering and trial. It is the birthing of Manasseh (MY FORGETTING) and Ephraim (FRUITFULNESS IN THE LAND OF TROUBLE)! [Genesis 41:51-52] This is Joseph's reward for his faithfulness.

And you too, My beloved, have been faithful with little, and now you shall be given much! Are you ready? **Your eyes and ears will hardly believe what is about to happen to you and in you. You will hardly believe that such prosperity and favor could have ever been designed for you,** for even those great words of prophecy shall pale in comparison to the receiving of what you are about to embrace!

This is your hour of EXPONENTIAL GROWTH! This is your time of coming forth QUICKLY out of the dungeon into the palace! [Genesis 41:40-44] Are you ready? I ask you this because you, My people, are living in the prophetic Third Day, and I have revealed in this day a people that are ready! It is time for you to experience the reward of your readiness. And what is that?

It's an encounter with your God in a new and living way! Now is the time! Let the words of the Spirit raise you up to new heights in this season, and allow the breath of My mouth to lift you out of your present circumstances to new dwellings beyond the earthly and mundane things of this earth! I am calling you to an even greater inheritance than that of Joseph. I am calling you into MY KINGDOM! I am calling you to rule within the halls of My justice! I am calling you to reign in the courts of My praise and glory!

Yes, you are coming to the place of your inheritance and that is a place of GOVERNMENT. This is the difference between the First Two Days and the THIRD DAY. The Third Day is A DAY OF GOVERNMENTAL POWER! **It is time for you to take the mantle of My Divine Authority and execute judgment upon that which is contrary to My will!** It is time for you to take your place within My Kingdom and **govern the nations of the earth!**

For My Kingdom is an everlasting Kingdom and an everlasting dominion that shall never pass away. My Kingdom has been INCREASING since the onset of its birth! My Kingdom has been spreading its rule, dominion, and authority over all the earth; and the peace of My Kingdom has been established in the hearts of those who are Mine.

I say to you now, Arise and come forth into your REST! There still remains a REST for the people of God [Hebrews 4:9], and this is the SEVENTH DAY – the day that I have chosen for you to REST in. From this place of rest and peace you shall rule and reign! **You shall speak the word, and it shall come to pass.** You shall execute the judgment that has been written.

Now listen! These words are for the renewed in mind and spirit, for these words that I am about to say to you are foolishness to the carnal mind and will have no place in the man of earth. These words are for the regenerated, Born-Again, and spiritually-minded men and women that have entered into the chambers of Council at My throne. I say unto you that a great honor has been bestowed upon you. I have given this honor to the Saints. What is this honor? It is that **you will destroy the yoke, pull down the stronghold, and <u>possess the land</u>. I have given you divine weapons to CAST SATAN OUT OF THE EARTH!** [The Bride is already playing a vital role in casting Satan out of the earth right now, but she will do even more as we rapidly approach the end of the Age.]

He has been sent into the Earth with great wrath. Yet the power of My Spirit within the Saints [those who are the Bride of Christ] is greater! **You have been given the legal mandate and right to CAST SATAN OUT OF THE EARTH, to take away his dominion and power and to consume him out of the Earth, thus bringing forth a new heaven and a new Earth!** Here is where the elements shall melt with fervent heat, and all the works in the earth that are and have been inspired by the kingdom of darkness shall be BURNED UP! [2nd Peter 3:10] I AM A CONSUMING FIRE!

Hear what the Spirit is saying to the REMNANT! YOU SHALL EXECUTE THE JUDGMENT THAT HAS ALREADY BEEN WRITTEN AND SPOKEN! Take now the KINGDOM BY FORCE! [Matthew 11:12b: "the Kingdom of Heaven suffers violence, and **the violent take it by force**."] Begin where you are to speak forth My KINGDOM into your dwelling place! **SPEAK THE WORD OF THE LORD!! SATURATE YOUR HOME WITH PRAISE AND WORSHIP! KEEP THE ENEMY OUT!!! From that spiritual environment that you have created, with <u>the breath of your mouth</u> shall go forth great hailstones of truth! Release the judgments written in My Word! Release the plagues! ...Release the earthquakes and storms of Glory!**

Release My judgments, oh remnant, and you will see things turn in a moment, even in the twinkling of an eye! My two witnesses strike the earth as often as they will! Why? Because I have given them power to rule! I have given all who would believe this same power [as the two witnesses], but many have refused the power and given the enemy great ground.

But to you, beloved remnant, I have given this power with a DOUBLE-PORTION ANOINTING! Do not play with this power; it is not for light things. Do not be frivolous with this power, for **it is greater than Nuclear weapons! Receive this power and exercise it over ALL the power of the enemy!** [Luke 10:18-19] **This is My Dunamis power given to My CHURCH for the destruction and overthrow of the Satanic kingdom. Now do it!! I have given you RESURRECTION POWER to disarm your enemies! I have given you all that I have. Now utilize it! Change the world!** [Matthew 28:18-20] **Do not let the world rest until the CHANGE IS COMPLETE! Do not let evil hide anymore, anywhere!**

Oh, My remnant, I know you so well. I know your faith. I know your trials. **I know all about you and how you have longed to destroy the evil out of the earth. I am with you in this matter, and I will have a people who hate evil as I do, and will confirm their words with signs and wonders following.** [Mark 16:20] **Let now nothing sway you from the course I have called you to. Rule now, oh kings, in the earth, even My sons [and daughters] of glory!**

[Note: The prophecies that begin on pages 209, 219, 221, 223, 225, 226, 231, 235, 237, and 242, and the dreams on 185 and 245, and the vision on 98 have sections in them that describe in detail the dominion and authority that are coming to the Bride very soon. She has a good measure of that dominion and authority already, but that is about to increase *significantly* in the very near future.]

Take the Land[83]

Take the Dominion! Take the Kingdom! Take back what was given to you! I say that VIOLENT MEN TAKE THE KINGDOM BY FORCE! [Matthew 11:12] This is the APPOINTED DAY! THE TIME HAS COME! This is the FULLNESS OF TIMES! I GIVE YOU JUDGMENT! EXECUTE THE JUDGMENT WRITTEN! **CAST DOWN THE BEAST!** You HAVE OVERCOME! YOU ARE VICTORIOUS! YOU ARE MORE THAN A CONQUEROR! [Romans 8:37]

I AM not speaking to an individual, but to a BODY! I AM calling to My people all over the earth! I say ARISE! DO NOT LOOK BACK! You have made great progress! You have come a long way! You have overcome much! Keep your focus! Stay on top! Do not be threatened by the roar of the enemy! Do not turn to the left or right, just keep going straight ahead. Walk through! Keep pressing in! Come up and out of the realm of darkness.

Put on the MIND OF CHRIST! Be renewed in the spirit of your MIND! Breakthrough! Win the Battle! Do not turn away! Do not go around the mountain one more time! Stand your ground and fight even unto death! Do not go back to the prison that the Lord God Almighty has delivered you from! Do not go back! You have come into marvelous victory, and I am in absolute love with you. Know My Spirit, and sense My Breath! I Am with you! Do not look about with doubtful expectation! Stand ready, for I Am bringing you to the High Places of the earth. You shall walk in your destiny, and oh won't you be so blessed and so filled with My joy as your harvest comes into full view!

Yes, you shall shout, for you shall know that this is your DAY, the DAY of JUBILEE! [YES!] This is the DAY of your release! Only do not look back! Do not give into the same old tricks that your enemy shall throw at you! NO! NEVER! FIGHT! I say **FIGHT!** Lift up your sword! Unsheathe your weapons of war! Take the battle to the enemy, and you will see him flee! Your obedience is come to completion, and therefore you are given the right to revenge all disobedience! Let the energy of My Spirit quicken you.

The enemy has sought to mock and scoff at My sons. He has sought to afflict them with doubt and discouragement. I say NO! You cannot give place to the DEVIL! [Ephesians 4:27] You are My witnesses upon the earth today. My light and My glory shall shine forth to the nations through you! You are My house, My habitation! The eyes of the nations must be drawn away from the deceptions in the earth! They must see Me in you!

Satan IS BOUND! I SAY HE IS BOUND! LET ALL THE SAINTS EXECUTE THE JUDGMENT WRITTEN AGAINST

HIM! SAY IN ONE VOICE, "SATAN YOU ARE BOUND!"
This is written in My Word and is revealed in the Scriptures,
that in the Seventh Day SATAN WOULD BE CAST INTO A
PIT, A PRISON! [Revelation 20:1-4] CAN YOU BELIEVE
IT? All your eyes are seeing is the residual effects of what he
has planted. BUT HE IS BOUND!

ERASE THE LIES FROM THE MINDS OF THE WORLD!
Let them see that SATAN HAS NO POWER OVER YOU!
Give them the assurance of what I have written so I have performed! I have performed in you what no man could have ever
done. Give up the glory to Me! Ascend with Me to the highest
heights, and watch the favour I will pour upon you. You are a
new creation in Me! [2nd Corinthians 5:17a] You have no past,
you have no weakness that has not been made strong. For I Am
your strength! You are walking into unchartered areas that have
been waiting for you. The **DOMINION IS GIVEN TO YOU.
TAKE IT! TAKE IT!**

I will say again, TAKE THE DOMINION! Though the enemy
roars, he shall only roar from his prison! Fear him not. My
crucified ones the time is now! The DAY is here. TAKE IT!
Take it within, and all the outward events in your life shall be
completely directed and guided by Me. You will find your life
in this hour, for it has been hid in Me, and **I AM COMING
FORTH IN YOU,** and your life is coming forth with Me.

OH TASTE AND SEE THAT THE LORD IS GOOD!
[Psalm 34:8a]

A Message to the Saints in America[84]

**TO MY ELECT: I will gather you together and fill you with
the anointing that breaks every yoke.** [Isaiah 10:27] **I will**

go before you into every battle and destroy your enemies. [Deuteronomy 28:7] **I will stir in you a revolution that has been planned and designed for this hour. For you, My elect ones in the earth, have been destined to be a generation that will usher in the Kingdom of My dear Son.**

I will bless you in every area of your life and more than satisfy you with long life [Psalm 91:6a]; **I will increase even the span of your days as you are transformed into an indestructible priesthood after the order of Melchisedec.** [See Hebrews 7:1-3] **You will have no end of life!** [verse 16]

I will cause your enemies to bow at your feet [Isaiah 49:23], and they will know that I have loved you. Your enemies will talk to one another behind closed doors of the power surrounding your life. They will confess to one another that their words could not prevail against you, and therefore will have no other course but to acknowledge the Living God within you. **I will raise you up and take you to your high place and will cause you to walk upon the high places of the earth** [Deuteronomy 32:13; Isaiah 58:14]; and I will give you a name among men and will lighten your path and guide you and direct you into opportunities that will further advance My cause in the earth.

Yes, **MY ELECT ONES** know that there is a cause in the earth today, and they have given themselves wholly to that cause. This is the company of DAVID, the HOUSE OF DAVID, WHO SHALL BE AS GOD in this final hour. [According to Zechariah 12:8] These are they who are willing to yield and submit their lives to the call of My Spirit. These are they who have become ONE in unity and purpose. These are the ones who forsook their own cause and entered into Mine. These are they who have become the bone of My bone and the flesh of My flesh. [See Genesis 2:23] These are the ones who overcame the spirit of division and disunity and humbled themselves under

My mighty hand. Now I will exalt them! [1st Peter 5:5-6] **Now I will lift them up and fill them with My eternal consuming fire, and all who come into contact with them <u>will either be made holy by the fire</u> <u>or will be consumed and wither away</u>.**

Those who said they were Mine but did not respond to the call of My Spirit but continued in their debate and division, will suffer greatly and be beaten with many stripes. [Luke 12:45-47] Those who refused to unite and seek reconciliation with the brethren but continued in their own cause will experience the fire, but this fire will consume all their works. What they have labored and striven for will vanish by the flame. Ministries will be burned up. The people will be like chaff, and the leaders will not be able to put out the fire. The people will be burned as those who are bundled and cast into the fire. [Matthew 13:30] This will happen because these who were too proud to release and forgive became arrogant. Their judgment shall be just!

The fire shall surely fall: **to one it shall be the fire of My Spirit, perfecting, healing, restoring, renewing, transforming, and delivering from every bondage.** To the other it shall be suffering, pain, bondage, death, imprisonment, and agony. I will mock those who have mocked Me, and I will not hear when they cry unto Me, as they did not hear when I cried unto them. [Zechariah 7:13] The wretched shall talk to one another seeking comfort, but there will be no comfort! The word of the wicked shall perish from the earth, and their words which they have spoken against the upright shall turn upon themselves. Judgment is determined upon those who have refused My call. Mercy is determined upon the elect who have responded to My call.

Surely I come says the Lord, surely I come to take what is Mine. **For this is the DAY of the TAKEOVER! I am taking over all things! I am taking over the governments of this earth and**

establishing My own. In My Government I will elect those who have been without name, those who have sought not their own glory but only Mine, those who were despised in the eyes of the great, and those who were seen as the weakest among men. I will refuse the house of SAUL, the self-sufficient ones whose strength is in their own hands. **I am taking over the military might of the nations and establishing My own power in the earth. I am sending forth weapons of mass destruction into the earth, and these weapons shall destroy forever the power of the kingdom of darkness.**

I am taking over the airwaves wherein the prince of the power of the air has ruled; but now I Am taking it over. I am taking the Television back! I am taking the radio back! I am taking the arts back! I am taking the stadiums back! I am taking the forests back! I am taking the rivers back! I am taking the oceans back! I AM taking the earth and the heavens back! For all these things have I made, and no longer will the unrighteous rule over these things, but **I will place MY ELECT ONES over all My creation.** I will take the ONE NEW MAN in the earth and **<u>cause him to have dominion over all the earth</u>**.

I will remove those who refused My voice. Their works once again shall be shattered to nothing. There will be no regathering of these things! There will be no more second chances! There will be no ability to restore and fix what I have broken. For I have warned and I have called, but you have refused! You have broken covenant with Me by breaking covenant with those who are Mine. You have been proven unfaithful in the least of things, and you will not partake of that which is great. You would not love one another as I have pleaded with you to do [John 13:34], but have chosen the way of self-righteousness and haughtiness. Therefore you shall be brought low.

America is divided, and she will not stand beneath the pressure that I am sending! America shall be broken, and the nations shall see it from afar. Those who have eyes to see are not deceived but are even now witnessing the dismantling of this nation. No scheme of the enemy will prevail. No trick will be able to cover the truth of what is taking place in America. The enemy has sought to confuse the masses by counterfeiting and moving around what the Sovereign Lord has said, but his demise shall be seen in his own inability to UNITE ONE NATION UNDER GOD!

It is too late! The line has been crossed by America, and she will continue down the wide road that leads to destruction. The elect have prepared themselves for the downfall [of it]. They know that their time has come, for they are Mine and they know My heart and they know My voice. I have given time for this nation to REPENT, but she did not, but became more vile in her ways.

Suddenly America shall be broken without remedy! I will settle all disputes. I will settle the disputes! I have drawn a line, and it is a matter of time that the division will be complete! Those who are Mine will be known by their fruit, and those who are not will be seen for who they are. Many wolves in sheep's clothing have gone from house to house in order to devour the flock of My inheritance, but I have given My Shepherd DAVID to rule over My people. He shall not allow one to be lost! As the shepherd has been struck in times past, so now will I strike the wolves! **I WILL STRIKE EVERY ENEMY WITH MY CURSE!** Choose this DAY whom you will serve! No longer halt between two opinions! The line is drawn! CHOOSE THIS DAY! [See 1st Kings 18:21]

Judicial Authority Released from The Throne of God[85]

The Right to Give Commands

This Day, I am releasing you – My beloved church, the called-out ones who have been sanctified by My Blood through faith in Me – to command the seas! The nations are in an uproar, and the waves of adversity do mount. A storm has risen in the East and is coming against the walls of the cities. The watchmen have seen afar off and have blown the trumpet. EUROCLYDON COMES!

Know that in this storm, you My chosen ones, shall arise to the high place where you will take the reins of control. Your voice will be heard among the nations for the wisdom you possess and because of the God you serve. For I AM and there is none other! **America will be struck by a mighty tempest in order to shake loose the vile from their high places.** I will bring low every mountain and exalt every valley, says the Lord of Hosts whose name alone is Holy.

When the storm hits is when you will understand the depths of the authority I have given you. There is a spiritual storm raging already, and those who know it are even now learning to command the winds and the seas! These spiritual storms are preparations for what is about come in the natural. *If one does not possess authority in this spiritual battle, they will not have the ability to stand when all Hell breaks loose against them in the natural.* [In order to have authority in the natural realm, one must first have authority in the spiritual realm.]

By the voice of your commands the winds and the seas shall obey you! [see Mark 4:39] As you are being beat upon by the storms of life, you will find that your house, your life, will stand

and remain! For you have built your life upon the ROCK, says *the* ROCK, Who is steadfast and immovable. [Matthew 7:24-25] I have given you entrance into the unshakeable Kingdom! [Hebrews 12:28]

Now **command** the seas! **Command**, I say, that which has been an offense to you! **Command** that which has been an offense to Me! **Command** the walls to come down! **Command** the valleys to be exalted! **Command** the mountains to be brought low! **Command** your harvest to come forth! **Command** your health to spring forth! **Command** your thoughts to be filled with righteousness! **Command** your enemies to be at peace with you! **Command** the winds to blow at your back in order to thrust you forth into your place of destiny! **Command** the accuser to flee! **Command** the lion to whelp! **Command** the adversary to take flight!

This is just the beginning of what you shall face. As you wage your war and give command to all things spiritual, you will move into a place wherein you shall give voice to those about you, and the voice you give will be one of divine authority!

Enforce Obedience

You must enforce obedience upon all that resists your entrance into eternal life! I am speaking of the ways of your flesh, your worldly desires, and the cares of the things of this earth. [see Mark 4:19] For I would have you undistracted in this time, in order to bring you forth into My plan and purpose for your life. I have given you the right to enforce My will upon your enemies, the enemy within your gates. Again, the resistance you are experiencing at this time is of a spiritual nature. There are internal obstacles and activities that are thwarting your progression into the Kingdom.

243

It is here, on the inside, that you must enforce My will! You have the right to enforce obedience upon the activities of your lower nature and the motions of sin within you. You may enforce obedience upon the thoughts you possess and the tears you may have. I am giving you an unction at this time to create a new spiritual environment within you. Here you will reverse the tide and come into havens of peace and rest. Not until you enforce obedience upon yourself will you have the peace and abundance you so deeply desire. This ability to enforce righteousness is going to be a very joyous experience for you, one that is free from legalism and bondage.

For you shall know what it is to walk in divine authority, ruling and reigning over your own lower nature. You will begin to see the manifestation of a BRAND NEW CREATURE ARISING WITHIN YOU WITH ALL THE FRUITS AND ATTRIBUTES OF THE ONLY BEGOTTON SON OF GOD! After this inward transition, you will come to a place wherein you shall enforce obedience upon all who are against themselves and against Me.

Take Action

It is time for you to take action against long-held territories within your soul realm that the enemy has occupied. It is time to take action against all unrighteousness within you! Again I say that this taking of action is for the purpose of spiritual transition so that you may take action in the natural in the very near future. **For if you will not take action against all ungodliness <u>within you</u> now, then you will not be able take action against all ungodliness around you, thus leaving yourself wide open for destruction when it comes.**

Judge the things, I say, by the fruits of your life already. Where have you left off righteous judgment? There will find the enemy in operation to steal, kill, and destroy your life! [John 10:10] The time will come when you shall be called upon to take action in national ways. Some will take action in difficult situations where the lives of many will be at risk. The action you will take will be with regard for their lives, and you will know what action to take because you have been trained in your self-discipline season. There are too many today that desire to move against natural forces but find themselves unable to because they would not take action against the issues of their own heart.

Final Decisions

Today you must decide who will you serve? [Deuteronomy 30:19] The final decision lies within your ability to choose. <u>You</u> make the final decision concerning the course of your life. As you choose to serve Me with all your heart, you will be led into **glorious realms of eternal glory!** You must arise within and make the final decision for righteousness! You must finalize all things concerning your walk with Me. As you make final decisions for doing what is right in every area of your life now, you will be the one making final decisions in the days ahead concerning many lives. You will lead those who are unable and weak, to make decisions that will not be thwarted or undermined by any. These decisions will have accuracy <u>because of the time you spent finalizing and making right decisions now</u>.

Latter "Reign" Anointing[86]

I dreamed I was in the Spirit, looking at a group of men. They were standing in a small thick "doughnut" formation that looked similar to the shape of a bunt cake, about four people deep all the way around, and there was a small hole in the center of the formation. They all seemed to be facing outward but were tightly packed together. While I was in the Spirit, all the surroundings around these men were whited out by very bright light, and the entire formation was ablaze with *very hot blue fire*. Each individual looked like a large blue flame of fire.

After this, the scene changed, and I was then inside the formation with these men, and I too was ablaze with this blue fire! **It was like Pentecost, only it wasn't a little flame on our heads;** *it engulfed our whole bodies!* **It was incredible! It is very hard to describe, but we all had so much power that it seemed to be coming right from the very core of our being, and boldness like I've never experienced before, and faith like I've never experienced before – <u>undaunted, unwavering, the complete and total absence of any fear or doubt</u>! The power we had was such that nothing could stand against us, and it was so powerful,** yet [it was] absolutely and completely under control. [Also] it was like there was no evil in the midst of us that could possibly abuse the power or twist it for wicked purposes.

We were all united in this formation, and we were all speaking in different mathematical terminologies and equations...We were speaking to crowds of people. I could see them through the blue flames, and somehow they were receiving and understanding what we were saying! The people were falling to their knees, repenting in droves, and everything we spoke would happen immediately. We would speak healings to people, and we would command deliverance. *Not one thing we spoke failed to happen instantly!*

The signs that came from this mathematical speech that was flowing out of our mouths from our very core were unable to be opposed or fought against by any demons or gain-sayed by man. **No one could stand against the power we had.** I could see the words in mathematical equations blowing on the wind of our breath outward toward the people like musical notes, and they [the notes] would pass into them. None of the equations or words fell to the ground! It was the most exhilarating feeling I have ever had! The closest thing I can compare it to would be the constant feeling of going downhill on a [very] tall rollercoaster.

The Anointing of the First-Fruits[87]*

I would like to share a dream I was given in the fall of 2006. I was standing in a plain (wilderness) all by myself. I looked off into the distance, and I could see someone or something coming towards me. As it got closer I could make it out as a cloud. Within seconds it was right beside me, and on this cloud sat a messenger from God. He had an invitation for me. It was in the form of a large golden telegram that was reminiscent of the golden tickets in a Willy Wonka movie. (A ticket to visit a wondrous land.) He said this was in invitation to attend a revival that was taking place in the mountains of the Yukon. (Meaning "great river;" i.e. of the waters of life.)

As soon as I took the golden invitation I found myself high above the earth, flying over North America to the far left corner of the continent. This only took a matter of seconds, as I flew thousands of miles across the nation, and I found myself at the foot of a snowy white mountain. I began to walk up this mountain, and as I walked, I looked down and saw that I had no shoes on! (We are to climb the mountain of God, which in Daniel 2:45 is a mountain. God demands that we take off our shoes when we are on holy ground [see Exodus 3:5] so that we are not separated from holiness.) I could not believe it! I had no shoes, walking in the snow, but my feet were not cold at all; so I kept walking up the mountain.

After a long trek up, I made it to a stream and began to walk through the stream that flowed from the top of the mountain. (Walking in the waters of life, the Word of God, cleanses our walk.) There were large square stones that were placed in the middle of the stream for me to walk on. These stones were crafted and had a decorative border on them. (The foundations laid by the apostles and prophets.) They were massive in size – must have weighed tons for just one of them. I continued to walk on these stones until I made it to the beginning of the stream in a small clearing at the top of the mountain. (The source of the "river of the water of life" is "the throne of God and the Lamb," as Revelation 22:1 says.)

On top of the mountain I saw a group of people who were standing on the bank of the stream. They were all lined up in a straight line, and something very, very supernatural was happening to them. (These are the first-fruits to be anointed with the latter rain at the beginning of the Tribulation. Revelation 14:1 and 4: "And I saw, and behold, the Lamb standing on the Mount Zion, and with Him, a hundred and forty and four thousand having His Name, and the name of His Father written on their foreheads. These are they that were not defiled with women; for they are virgins. These are they that follow the Lamb whithersoever He goeth. These were purchased from among men to be the first-fruits unto God and unto the Lamb.")

Something was being poured on them from the heavens. (The coming of the Lord in His people through the Latter Rain. Hosea 6:3 ...He will come unto us as the rain, as the latter rain that watereth the earth.) It was like water that glittered and shone brightly. It was so glorious. It seemed like the water was *liquid glory*. (**2nd Corinthians 3:18**: "But we all with unveiled face, beholding as in a mirror the glory of the Lord, are being transformed into the same image from glory to glory, even as from the Lord the Spirit.") As I watched, each one of these people receiving this water was transformed into a more powerful being receiving his own special gift. I even saw one grow what seemed like angel-type wings. (Ability to move supernaturally: underline(translation). They will be able to pass these gifts on to disciples, as Jesus did. Phillip was translated.)

I know this sounds crazy but they resembled superheroes. (More like **"Christ in you, the hope of glory."**) [Colossians 1:27] Then I fell on my face and started praising God. Next, I heard one call out to the rest, "The world hates us now. They hate us." (**John 15:18**: "If the world hateth you, ye know that it hath hated Me before it hated you.")

He seemed very troubled by this. I got this feeling that this hatred came on so quickly that he could not understand why it was happening. That is when I was given the understanding that these people were to be sent back out into the world with their power and gifts to overcome the world. (Just as their Master, who was a type of them, did.) That's when I became bold and full of faith and said back to him in complete confidence, "Why do you question this? Did not the Master tell us this was supposed to happen?" [John 15:20] (This is the beginning of the great revival at the beginning of the Tribulation.) End of dream.

*Footnote: The comments in parenthesis are from another individual, as given to him by the Lord. The Scriptural references in the comments are from the 1901 ASV Bible.

[Author's note: The two verses quoted earlier on the previous page, Revelation 14:1 and 4, would seem to place this event at the beginning of the Great Tribulation, not at the beginning of the seven year Tribulation.]

One Hour of Travail Every Day[74]*

My food, said Jesus, is to do the will of Him who sent Me and to finish His work. [John 4:34] Your food, says Jesus, is to do My will, [the will of the one] who is sending you, to finish My work in you. My will is that you abide in Me, become one with Me: I in you and you in Me [John 15:4] – that you may do the greater works [John 14:12] , that I might be lifted up in you to draw all men unto Me. [John 12:32] For the harvest is great, and the workers are few. [Luke 10:2a]

Will you work with Me? Will you pray and travail in prayer until My Man-child is birthed in My people? Will you travail until I am fully formed in My people [Galatians 4:19] and My people grow up into My full stature? [See Ephesians 4:13]

Make it your **priority** – fit it in <u>first</u>. Don't let it be crowded out. It doesn't have to take hours. Even watching and praying with Me for one hour [Matthew 26:40-41] produces a significant eternal harvest. *Then* as you go about the business of the day, **<u>pray in tongues without ceasing</u>** [1st Thessalonians 5:17; 1st Corinthians 14:18], **<u>making your life a life of prayer.</u>** And in Eternity you will be glad for the harvest of souls!

*(Used earlier on pages 218-219.)

Characteristics of the Remnant – Spiritual Growth[88]

Some are coming to [realize] the possibility that before the Second Coming of Christ, this Gospel of the Kingdom will be victorious throughout the entire world. We call these disciples "the Remnants." The Remnants carry a subduing spirit as the Scripture confirms. "And when all things shall be subdued unto

Him [the Father], then shall the Son also Himself be subject unto Him [the Father] that put all things under Him, that God may be all in all." (**1st Corinthians 15:28**) [KJ] [Note: The Scriptures in this article are either KJ or NKJ]

The Remnants know they are destined for dominion. When building churches, preachers come to a decision: they either draw the multitudes or the Remnants. Today those that gather the multitudes water down their message, refusing to address sin and idolatry. Many issues are not confronted such as: homosexuality, pornography, adultery, and national influence of corrupted politicians, failure of the public school system, and worldly music that is impinging [invading] the Church. Regardless of this withdraw [on the part of the compromised Church], others stand boldly like John the Baptist as a voice of one crying in the wilderness, "Make straight a highway for our God." These are the Remnants.

The uncompromised Gospel still convicts of sin and confronts the demonic powers of darkness. This Gospel of the Kingdom is a stumbling stone for some and the cornerstone for others. In every generation the Holy Spirit anoints remnant Believers, for it is the Remnant that goes first, carrying the banner of Christ's victory.

After a grand house is carpeted there are a few pieces of carpet left. These left-over pieces are known as the remnant. No one knows what to do with them because they don't fit anywhere. Some are discarded and others placed at doorways. The remnant carpet sits at the doorway and used to clean the bottom of someone's shoes before entering. Have you ever felt like you [don't] fit anywhere? The reason for that is because you really [don't] fit. You are probably part of the Remnant. Remnant Believers are different because they carry a different spirit.

251

The Remnants play a major role in the restoration of all things. (**Acts 3:19-21**) To them belong many "go first" apostolic opportunities because they carry a dominion spirit. A dominion spirit is one that is ready to take over for Christ. The Remnants reject a fatalistic world view that Christ will rescue the Church right before the world is overrun by demon powers. They understand their apostolic call to build and restore. Scripture declares, "And they [the Remnants] shall build the old wastes, they shall raise up the former desolations, and they shall repair the waste cities, the desolations of many generations." (**Isaiah 61:4**)

The Remnants believe the spiritual man is strong in the Lord and the power of His might. (**Ephesians 6:10**) To be a spiritual man means to be led by the Holy Spirit for it is written, "For as many as are led by the Spirit of God, they are the sons of God." (**Romans 8:14**)

The Remnants are doers of the Word not just hearers. James makes it plain: "But be ye doers of the word and not hearers only, deceiving your own selves. For if any be a hearer of the word and not a doer, he is like unto a man beholding his natural face in a glass: For he beholdeth himself and goeth his way, and straightway forgetteth what manner of man he was." (**James 1:22-24**)

As "repairers of the breach" the Remnants carry the culture of the Kingdom of God into a dark world separated from the love of God. Every kingdom has a culture, so too the Kingdom of God. The Remnants understand their duty to carry the light of Christ's truth into the world. As already said, the Remnants make a highway for Christ. Scripture says, "And they [the Remnants] that shall be of thee shall build the old waste places: thou shalt raise up the foundations of many generations; and thou shalt be called, the Repairer of the Breach, the Restorer of Paths to Dwell In." (**Isaiah 58:12**)

The Remnants believe the Word became flesh, was anointed by the Holy Ghost, and was crucified for our sins, rose from the dead, defeated Satan and all his demon hoards. To the Remnants the devil is defeated! They see the devil subdued under their feet and sing, "O clap your hands all ye people; shout unto God with the voice of triumph. For the LORD most high is terrible; he is a great King over all the earth. He shall subdue the people under us and the nations under our feet." (**Psalms 47:1-3**)

OVERCOMING ALL OPPOSITION

The Remnants believe they can overcome the world through faith. "For whatsoever is born of God overcometh the world: and this is the victory that overcometh the world, even our faith." (**1st John 5:4**) To overcome means to subdue. In the Genesis mandate is the blessing to be fruitful, multiply, replenish, subdue, and take dominion. These are five blessings, expectations, empowerments, and responsibilities. The word subdue in Hebrew is "kabash," meaning to tread down, subjugate, subdue or bring into subjection. In the New Testament, the Greek word is "nikao," meaning to subdue. The Remnants believe they are born of God and through faith subdue the world for Christ. These Scriptures confirm this belief. Let's read these Scriptures, exchanging the word "overcome" with the word "subdue."

"For whatsoever is born of God overcometh [subdues] the world: and this is the victory that overcometh [subdues] the world, even our faith." (**1st John 5:4**)

"I write unto you, fathers, because ye have known Him that is from the beginning. I write unto you, young men, because ye have overcome [subdued] the wicked one. I write unto you, little children, because ye have known the Father. I have written unto you, fathers, because ye have known Him that is from the beginning. I have written unto you, young men, because ye are strong and the Word of God abideth in you, and ye have over-come [subdued] the wicked one. Love not the world, neither the things that are in the world. If any man love the world, the love of the Father is not in him. For all that is in the world, the lust of the flesh, and the lust of the eyes, and the pride of life, is not of the Father, but is of the world. And the world passeth away, and the lust thereof: but he that doeth the will of God abideth for ever." (**1 John 2:13-17**)

These verses are clear. Christ gave His disciples the power to subdue the earth and bring it into subjection to Christ. As you can see the Remnants are destined for dominion. Other prom-ises include:

———

PEACE

"These things I have spoken unto you, that in me ye might have peace. In the world ye shall have tribulation: but be of good cheer; I have overcome [subdued] the world." (**John 16:33**)

"Ye are of God, little children, and have overcome [subdued] them: because greater is He that is in you, than he that is in the world." (**1 John 4:4**)

———

TREE OF LIFE

"He that hath an ear, let him hear what the Spirit saith unto the churches; To him that overcometh [subdues] will I give to eat of the tree of life, which is in the midst of the paradise of God." **(Revelation 2:7)**

NO HARM IN THE SECOND DEATH

"He that hath an ear, let him hear what the Spirit saith unto the churches; He that overcometh [subdues] shall not be hurt of the second death." **(Revelation 2:11)**

HIDDEN MANNA

"He that hath an ear, let him hear what the Spirit saith unto the churches; To him that overcometh [subdues] will I give to eat of the hidden manna, and will give him a white stone, and in the stone a new name written, which no man knoweth saving he that receiveth it." **(Revelation 2:17)**

POWER OVER NATIONS

"And he that overcometh [subdues] and keepeth My works unto the end, to him will I give power over the nations." **(Revelation 2:26)**

CLOTHED IN WHITE RAIMENT

"He that overcometh [subdues], the same shall be clothed in white raiment; and I will not blot out his name out of the Book of Life, but I will confess his name before My Father, and before his angels." (**Revelation 3:5**)

––––––––

PILLAR IN THE TEMPLE OF GOD

"Him that overcometh [subdues] will I make a pillar in the temple of My God, and he shall go no more out: and I will write upon him the name of My God, and the name of the city of My God, which is New Jerusalem, which cometh down out of Heaven from My God: and I will write upon him My new name." (**Revelation 3:12**)

––––––––

SIT WITH CHRIST ON HIS THRONE

"To him that overcometh [subdues] will I grant to sit with Me in My throne, even as I also overcame [subdued], and am set down with My Father in His throne." (**Revelation 3:21**)

––––––––

DEFEATED SATAN

"And they overcame [subdued] him by the Blood of the Lamb, and by the word of their testimony; and they loved not their lives unto the death." (**Revelation 12:11**)

––––––––

VICTORY

"And I saw as it were a sea of glass mingled with fire: and them that had gotten the victory [subdued] over the beast, and over his image, and over his mark, and over the number of his name, stand on the sea of glass, having the harps of God." **(Revelation 15:2)**

———

From these verses we read the Remnants understand their call to invade, influence, and subdue the world with the Gospel of the Kingdom of God. St. Athanasius saw the Remnants ability to carry the Word of God into society and bring glorious change: "When the sun has come, darkness prevails no longer; any of it that may be left anywhere is driven away. So also, now that the Divine epiphany of the Word of God has taken place, the darkness of idols prevails no more, and all parts of the world in every direction are enlightened by His teaching."

The Church can only lose the battle to Satan when it is overcome with doubt and unbelief. How you see yourself determines how the devil sees you: "And there we saw the giants, the sons of Anak, which come of the giants: and we were in our own sight as grasshoppers and so we were in their sight." **(Numbers 13:33)** The Remnants see themselves walking in victory. Like Caleb they see the enemy subdued and under their feet: "And Caleb stilled the people before Moses, and said, 'Let us go up at once, and possess it; for we are well able to overcome it.' " **(Numbers 13:30)**

Be Very Careful
Some Saints Lost Everything—

Even Heaven!⁶⁸*

In these Last Days you will be tested in every way possible, for Satan will seek to cause you to lose your reward. You have wondered why I have permitted these very great trials. They are even like the trials of Job. Satan wants you to lose everything in the last hours that remain before I come for you.

So I warn you to be very careful. Many of My greatest Saints lost everything in the very last hours and days of their lives. You have wondered how it could have been that someone who was so greatly used of Me could have fallen so deeply into sin in the latter part of their lives. Now you know. They were terribly tested and tempted by Satan, and in the end died without honor and lost their great inheritance. Some even lost Heaven!

So take care, My beloved one. Keep your eyes on Me. Every day will become a testing day. Every day will become a day when you must stay very close to Me, because the devil is going around like a roaring lion, seeking to devour the Saints in these Last Days. [1st Peter 5:8-9] And if he can't get them to lose their Salvation, he certainly will do all he can to get them to lose their rewards.

So stay close to Me. Stay filled with love. And be honest with yourself. It is one thing to be honest with others, but it is another thing to be honest with yourself. That is a state which few can attain to. **But if you are not honest with yourself, you cannot deal with the weaknesses in yourself, which will rob you of your crown.**

258

Eternal greatness is only obtained during your temporal life on earth, through your godly response to the hours of trials and testings which you are going through, even now.

I love you. You are My precious treasure. And on the Day of Judgment all who have tried to ruin your character or destroy you will know that I have loved thee, and they will be ashamed. Hold fast to your crown! [See Revelation 3:11] Don't lose it in these last hours of fiery trials. [See 1st Peter 4:12-13] If you overcome, *"I will make you a pillar in the temple of my God, and you shall go no more out: and I will write upon you the name of my God, and the name of the city of my God, which is New Jerusalem, which cometh down out of Heaven from My God: and I will write upon you my new name."* [Revelation 3:12]

*(Used earlier on pages 212-213.)

The Righteous Remnant[89]

Hear Me, O My people, and listen to My words. You give attention continually to the words of men. You listen, read, you study and ponder multitudes of words that express only the thoughts of others who, like yourself, are searching for truth. To search is not evil, but if you desire understanding, come directly to Me. Ask of Me. As the Scriptures teach, if any seeks wisdom, let him ask of God, for He gives liberally. [James 1:5]

Wait upon Me, and I will clarify things that are dark and puzzling to you. [see Luke 8:17] Israel is My Chosen People, now as truly as in the days of old. But as My Church has failed Me, even so has My people, Israel. There is, as there has always been, a wide discrepancy between what I have taught them, yes, even between what they believe and what they experience;

259

[between] what they accept as My commandments and what they do. You have both fallen short – Church and Israel alike!

But I shall have a people... I shall have those in whom I can rejoice – as I found pleasure in the devotion of David and in the integrity of Job, yes, in the faith of the Shunammite and the courage of Elijah. These lived in times when those who were truly dedicated to Me were in the minority, even as today. Goodness has never been a common commodity. Devotion and self-sacrifice have always been at a premium.

I shall have a people, but it will be <u>the righteous remnant</u>. **It will be no larger percentagewise than the family of Noah in the days of the flood!**

When the Devastation Begins[90]

As time as you know it draws to a close, things around you will accelerate. It is imperative that you come away to the secret place right now – that quiet, peaceful place of love. I resorted there often. Go to it often. Leave the hustle and bustle and clamor around you, and hide in the "secret place of the stairs." [See Song of Solomon 2:14] Seek it out, desire it, yearn for it – *now*. Familiarize yourself with it now, **or you won't know how or where to find it when the devastation begins!**

The Final Call[28]*

As the days draw to a close and the plan of the Ages is fulfilled, I will come to My precious, purified, and spotless Bride. [Ephesians 5:27] Oh, how I long for her. Oh, how I long to have her close to My side, forever with Me, her Bridegroom and the Lover of her soul. Everything is ready; the call has gone forth: *"Come, come, all things are ready. Come to the feast. Come to the Marriage Supper of the Lamb. Do not delay!"* [See Revelation 19:7-9]

Answer the call of the Bridegroom to prepare and make yourself ready. Respond to His call of love. Respond to His wooing. Make no excuse! Set not your heart on other things. Do not be indifferent to this call. Come, come to the secret place and prepare your heart to be My Bride. Cut all ties to earthly desires and loves so that you will be ready when you hear My final call to come – to come up and be with Me forever.

The wedding day draws near. Final preparations are being made. There is much excitement in Heaven! Oh, My love, My dove, hasten to the place of love and intimacy. *Daily* answer My call of love <u>to prepare your heart</u>. Listen, watch, and wait for the final call to arise, My love, My fair one; and come away. [Song of Solomon 2:10]

*(Used earlier on pages 75 and 195-196.)

A Closing Word

Write the vision,

And make it plain on tablets,

That he may run who reads it.

For the vision is yet for an appointed

time;

But at the end it will speak,

and it will not lie.

Though it tarries, wait for it,

Because it will surely come.

It will not tarry.

Habakkuk 2:2-3

Footnotes

1. The Rapture Call xxiii+194
Received by Barbara Bloedow (12 of THE LAST CALL)

2. The Power of Your Words 16-17
Written by Thurman Scrivner

3. The Power of Your Prayers 18
Given by Anita Lee Riddell
New Wine Ministry Church
Bella Vista, Arkansas
858-864-8712NWMglobal.org

4. Cherish My Words 44
Received by Francis J. Roberts
From the book, "Come Away My Beloved" by
Francis J. Roberts

5. Will ALL Christians Be in The Rapture? 45
An article by Rudolph C. Schafer

6. Who Will Be in the Rapture? 47
Received by Pastor B.H. Clendennen
During an all-night church prayer meeting

7. Only Those Who Have Come Close to Me
Will be Raptured Up 48
Received by Daniel Lundstrom

18. The Last Hours 64
Received by Barbara Bloedow (256 of THE LAST CALL)

19. Stay Pliable in My Hand 65
Received by Frances J. Roberts
From the book "Come Away My Beloved"

20. Dynamos of Praise 66
Received by Frances J. Roberts
From the book "Come Away My Beloved"

21. Mary or Martha 68
Received by Barbara Bloedow in a time of prayer.(90 of THE LAST CALL)

22. I Want You as My Bride 69
Received by Barbara Bloedow (97 of THE LAST CALL)

23. You Are Very Precious to Me 70
Received by Barbara Bloedow (93 of THE LAST CALL)

24. This is Marriage Love 72
Received by Barbara Bloedow (97 of THE LAST CALL)

25. You Need Love Times 73
Received by Barbara Bloedow (98 of THE LAST CALL)
(97 of PROPHECIES of the END-TIMES)

26. Listen to the Silence 73
Received by Frances J. Roberts
From the book "Come Away My Beloved"

27. Find Solitude 74
Received by Frances J. Roberts
From the book "Come Away My Beloved"

39. I SHALL have a Bride who is Spotless
and without Blemish 146
Received by Kevin Barrett

40. Standing on Holy Ground 151
From the book "Smith Wigglesworth,
A Man Who Walked with God" by George Stormont,
pages 69-71.

41. Woe to the Dilatory Servant 153
Received by Anna Schrader (213 of THE LAST CALL)

42. God's People to Stir Out of Their Sluggishness 154
Received by Anna Schrader (216 of THE LAST CALL)

43. Wonders Will Come Forth 155
Received by Anna Schrader (218 of THE LAST CALL)

44. A Place for Preparation 156
Received by Anna Schrader (218 of THE LAST CALL)

45. Prepare for the Soon Coming of the Lord 156
Received by Anna Schrader (219 of THE LAST CALL)

46. Those Filled with the Oil of the Spirit
Will Produce This Glory 158
Received by Anna Schrader (220 of THE LAST CALL)

47. Maria Woodworth-Etter 159
From her autobiography and quoted in "Great Healing
Evangelists – How God's Power Came" written by Andrew
Strom. His website is www.revivalschool.com.

48. Christ, the Ark of Safety 161
Received by Anna Schrader (224 of THE LAST CALL)

57. The School of the Holy Ghost 182
Received by Barbara Bloedow
(114 of PROPHECIES of the END-TIMES)

58. Two Witnesses Power Revival 185
A dream from Kevin R. From "Unleavened Bible Study,"
a ministry headed up by David Eells.

59. Cities of Refuge 186
Received by James P. Corbett (28 of THE LAST CALL)

60. Will You Rise in the Rapture
Or Will You be Left Behind? 191
Received by Barbara Bloedow (14 of THE LAST CALL)
12. You Are Not Ready to Go 72+194
21. Mary or Martha 82+195
32. Many Have Missed This Calling 120+170+195
1. The Rapture Call 16+196
Received by Barbara Bloedow (12 of THE LAST CALL)

61. Are You Prepared? 194
Received by Barbara Bloedow (17 of THE LAST CALL)
28. The Final Call 89+197+256

62. Yet Seven Days 197
Received by Gwen Shaw (229 of THE LAST CALL)

63. A Time of Reflection and Preparation 200
Received by Stephen Hanson
From "The Word of the Lord to Stephen Hanson—Volume 1"
By Stephen Hanson

64. Those that Hold to the Rapture Lie
Shall be Beaten Down by the Truth 201
Received by Kevin Barrett.

65. This is the Way of Escape
That I have Provided for My Children 204
Received by Kevin Barrett.

66. Only Those Close to Me Shall Survive 208
Received by Daniel Lundstrom (77 of THE LAST CALL)

67. Jesus Corrects His People 209
Received by Kevin Barrett

68. Be Very Careful, Some Saints Lost Everything—
Even Heaven 212+258
Received by Gwen Shaw (238 of THE LAST CALL)

69. Many Christians Will Fall 214
Received by Dimitru Duduman (29 of THE LAST CALL)

70. Many of My People Have Gone Their Own Way 215
Received by Daniel Lundstrom

71. Intercede for Those Who Have Fallen by the Wayside 216
Received by Daniel Lundstrom

72. There Will be Some Who Hear
Because You Have Interceded 215
Received by Daniel Lundstrom

73. Intercede on a Daily Basis for Lost Souls
For I Will Hold You Accountable 218
Received by Daniel Lundstrom

74. One Hour of Travail Every Day 218+250
Received by Barbara Bloedow

75. My Remnant Church 219 (100 of THE LAST CALL)

76. I Must Have Overcomers 220
Received by Frances J. Roberts
From the book "Come Away My Beloved"

77. Learn to Reign 221
Received by Frances J. Roberts
From the book "Come Away My Beloved"

78. You are Joint Heirs with Me 233
Received by Stephen Hanson

79. Keep My Commandments 225
Received by Patricia Joy Xavier
New Wine Ministries Church
858-864-8714NWMglobal.org

80. The Truth Must be Spoken 226
Received by Pastor Vincent Xavier
New Wine Ministries Church
2262 Forest Hills Blvd
Bella Vista, Arkansas 72715
858-864-8712NWMglobal.crg

81. A Flood of Filth is Coming to America 229
Received by Kevin Barrett

82. A Word to the Remnant 231
Received by Pastor Vincent Xavier

83. Take the Land 235
Received by Pastor Vincent Xavier

84. A Message to the Saints in America 237
Received by Pastor Vincent Xavier

Author's Bio

Rudolph C. Schafer is the author of five books since 1989, including his latest, "The Rapture," which is currently available on Amazon. Four of the five books address the End-Times and the spiritual aspect of preparing for it.

Schafer has 9 years of college. He was accepted at Harvard twice – the first time as an undergraduate and the second time as a graduate student. Schafer has a B.S. Degree in Geophysics from The University of Wisconsin (the main campus in Madison). He attended the University of California at Berkeley as a graduate student in the 1960's, majoring in 3 fields in the Zoology Department – Ecology, Aquatic Biology, and Instrumentation in Biology. He was a teacher at Berkeley and also at Marquette University in Wisconsin. The author left the world of Academia in 1967.

After that, he "experimented" briefly with hallucinogenic drugs for several months. The author then followed the New Age Movement for 10 years. Eventually he became assistant director of a yoga society in the Milwaukee area. He got saved out of that in July of 1977 (7/77). As of July 2020 he's been saved for 43 years.

The author has read hundreds of books on Bible prophecy and teachings on the Last Days, including those that deal with drawing close to the Lord and how to have an intimate rela-tionship with Him. He has always been interested in how one goes beyond the point of being a good, solid Christian to actually becoming the bride of Jesus Christ – a topic that very few Christian authors, pastors, and leaders teach about because most of them don't care about that particular topic in the first place. So, they don't teach it at all – except for a few – and the overwhelming majority of those few, teach it incorrectly.

It is the mission of the author to see Christians become the Bride of Christ and not miss the Rapture.

You can order this book online at
www.CreateSpace/5176390
or at
www.Amazon.com/dp/1505575826

or through
The Clarion Call
PO Box 14
Decatur, Arkansas 72722
1-479-212-2691

CPSIA information can be obtained
at www.ICGtesting.com
Printed in the USA
LVHW080430280321
682719LV00015B/517